UNACCOMPANIED YOUNG MIGRANTS
Identity, care and justice

Edited by
Sue Clayton, Anna Gupta and Katie Willis

First published in Great Britain in 2019 by

Policy Press
University of Bristol
1-9 Old Park Hill
Bristol
BS2 8BB
UK
t: +44 (0)117 954 5940
pp-info@bristol.ac.uk
www.policypress.co.uk

North America office:
Policy Press
c/o The University of Chicago Press
1427 East 60th Street
Chicago, IL 60637, USA
t: +1 773 702 7700
f: +1 773-702-9756
sales@press.uchicago.edu
www.press.uchicago.edu

© Policy Press 2019

British Library Cataloguing in Publication Data
A catalogue record for this book is available from the British Library

Library of Congress Cataloging-in-Publication Data
A catalog record for this book has been requested

978-1-4473-3186-5 hardback
978-1-4473-3188-9 paperback
978-1-4473-3187-2 ePdf
978-1-4473-3189-6 ePub
978-1-4473-3190-2 Mobi

The rights of Sue Clayton, Anna Gupta and Katie Willis to be identified as editors of this work has been asserted by them in accordance with the Copyright, Designs and Patents Act 1988.

All rights reserved: no part of this publication may be reproduced, stored in a retrieval system, or transmitted in any form or by any means, electronic, mechanical, photocopying, recording, or otherwise without the prior permission of Policy Press.

The statements and opinions contained within this publication are solely those of the editors and contributors and not of the University of Bristol or Policy Press. The University of Bristol and Policy Press disclaim responsibility for any injury to persons or property resulting from any material published in this publication.

Policy Press works to counter discrimination on grounds of gender, race, disability, age and sexuality.

Cover design by Qube Design Associates, Bristol
Front cover image: Eastwest Pictures (UK)

Contents

List of figures and tables   v
List of acronyms   vii
Notes on contributors   ix
Acknowledgements   xiii

Foreword   xv
Alf Dubs, House of Lords

Introduction   1
Sue Clayton, Anna Gupta and Katie Willis

Section 1: Framing the youth migration debate

one	Migration regimes and border controls: the crisis in Europe *Sue Clayton and Katie Willis*	15
two	Dilemmas and conflicts in the legal system *Sheona York and Richard Warren*	39
three	Caring for and about unaccompanied migrant youth *Anna Gupta*	77

Section 2: Exploring migrant youth identities

Preface: Voices of separated migrant youth   105
Sue Clayton

four	Narrating the young migrant journey: themes of self-representation *Sue Clayton*	115
five	From individual vulnerability to collective resistance: responding to the emotional impact of trauma on unaccompanied children seeking asylum *Gillian Hughes*	135
six	Spaces of belonging and social care *Louise Drammeh*	159
seven	'Durable solutions' when turning 18 *Lucy Williams*	187

Section 3: International perspectives

eight	A relational approach to unaccompanied minor migration, detention and legal protection in Mexico and the US *Mario Bruzzone and Luis Enrique González-Araiza*	211
nine	Unaccompanied migrant youth in the Nordic countries *Hilde Lidén*	235
ten	Life (forever) on hold: unaccompanied asylum-seeking minors in Australia *Kim Robinson and Sandra M. Gifford*	257

Conclusion — 279
Sue Clayton, Anna Gupta and Katie Willis

Index — 289

List of figures and tables

Figures
1	Unaccompanied minors claiming asylum in the EU, 2008–17	3
2	UASC protection rate trends, 2006–17 (% of asylum seekers aged under 18)	44
3	Asylum grant and appeal success rates for Eritrean unaccompanied minors, 2010–17	63
4	Narrative Liberation framework for responding to trauma	141
5	Structural relationships of unaccompanied young people	164
6	Hierarchy of Mexican law	214
7	Laws governing Mexican institutions involved in migrant protection	217
8	US migration enforcement and unaccompanied minor migrant protection agencies	222

Tables
1	Asylum applicants considered as unaccompanied minors in the EU, by country of citizenship, 2016–17	4
2	Initial grant rates for top eight nationalities (all applicants), year ending June 2015	44
3	Appeal success rate for top eight countries of origin, 2017	55
4	Applications from unaccompanied minors and outcome of applications, Sweden, Norway and Denmark, 2013–17	246

List of acronyms

AHRC	Australian Human Rights Commission
ARE	appeal rights exhausted
BASW	British Association of Social Workers
BIA	best interest assessment
BICA	Borders, Citizenship and Immigration Act
BID	best interest determination
BV	Bridging Visa
CAO	*Centres d'Accueil et d'Orientation* (reception and orientation centre)
CBP	Customs and Border Protection
CBT	cognitive behavioural therapy
CMM	coordinated management of meaning
COMAR	*Comisión Mexicana de Ayuda a Refugiados* (Mexican Commission for Refugee Aid)
CRS	*Compagnies Republicaines de Securité* (Republican security companies/French riot police)'
DHS	Department of Homeland Security
DIBP	Department of Immigration and Border Protection
DIF	*Sistema Nacional Para el Desarrollo Integral de la Familia* (National System for the Integrated Development of the Family)
ECHR	European Convention on Human Rights
ECPAT	End Child Prostitution and Trafficking
EMDR	eye movement desensitisation and reprocessing
EMN	European Migration Network
ERPUM	European Return Platform for Unaccompanied Minors
EU	European Union
FGM	female genital mutilation
HREOC	Human Rights and Equal Opportunity Commission
IFA	internal flight alternative
ILR	indefinite leave to remain
INM	*Instituto Nacional de Migración* (National Institute of Migration)
INS	Immigration and Naturalization Service
IOM	International Organization for Migration
IRO	Independent Reviewing Officer
LASPO	Legal Aid, Sentencing and Punishment of Offenders Act

LGDNNA	*Ley General de los Derechos de Niñas, Niños y Adolescentes* (General Law of the Rights of Girls, Boys, and Adolescents)
MSF	*Médecins Sans Frontières* (Doctors without Borders)
NGO	non-governmental organisation
NRM	National Referral Mechanism
ORR	Office of Refugee Resettlement
PPV	Permanent Protection Visa
PSG	particular social group
PTSD	post-traumatic stress disorder
RRC	Refugee Resilience Collective
SHEV	Safe Haven Enterprise Visa
TPV	Temporary Protection Visa
TVPRA	Trafficking Victims Protection Reauthorization Act
UAM	unaccompanied asylum-seeking minor (Australia) or unaccompanied alien minor (US)
UASC	unaccompanied asylum-seeking child/children
UDI	Norwegian Directorate of Immigration
UHM	unaccompanied humanitarian minor
UNCRC	United Nations Convention on the Rights of the Child
UNHCR	United Nations High Commission for Refugees

Notes on contributors

Mario Bruzzone holds a PhD from the Department of Geography at the University of Wisconsin–Madison, USA. His dissertation research examined the punitive politics surrounding Central American transit migration through Mexico. His scholarship has appeared in *Antipode*, *Cultural Geographies*, *Political Geography*, and *Urban Geography*.

Sue Clayton has directed two films on child asylum: *Hamedullah: The Road Home* (2013) and *Calais Children: A Case to Answer* (2017); both have been submitted in asylum and High Court appeal cases. She is Professor of Film at Goldsmiths University of London and consultant producer for ITV and Channel 4 News.

Louise Drammeh did her first degree in anthropology, after which she spent approximately two years in West Africa. Back in the UK, she followed a second degree in social work and then a masters in migration. She has been working with unaccompanied minors for over 15 years and she is currently combining this with a PhD around their experiences of the UK asylum system.

Sandra M. Gifford is Professor of Anthropology at the Centre for Urban Transitions at Swinburne University of Technology in Melbourne, Australia. Her research focuses on refugee settlement and wellbeing. Her key research focus is on what best predicts and supports good settlement among refugee background migrants with a focus on youth. She has published widely on Australian policy and practice relating to refugee settlement and how the Australian experience compares to other UNHCR settlement countries.

Luis Enrique González-Araiza is legal coordinator and in-house counsel for Dignidad y Justicia en el Camino A.C., the parent organisation of Guadalajara's FM4 Paso Libre migrant shelter. A sessional lecturer at the University of Guadalajara, Mexico, he also serves as Civil Society Representative to the Mexico's human-rights body CEAV (Comisión Ejecutiva de Atención a Víctimas).

Anna Gupta is Professor of Social Work in the Centre for Social Work, School of Law at Royal Holloway, University of London. Her research interests include families living in poverty and child protection services, work in the family courts, and with unaccompanied asylum-seeking children. She completed a study on the role of the social worker in adoption, with a focus on ethics and human rights with Professor Brid Featherstone, and is a co-author of a book: *Protecting Children: A Social Model*.

Gillian Hughes is a Consultant Clinical Psychologist and Systemic Psychotherapist who led the Child and Family Refugee Service at the Tavistock and Portman NHS Foundation Trust for seven years, and is now clinical services lead (London and SE) for the human rights charity, Freedom from Torture. She has brought narrative, liberation and community psychology approaches into her work throughout her career in the NHS. Gillian offers training and consultation in these approaches, particularly in relation to refugee and BME communities, and is a member of the Institute of Narrative Therapy teaching staff. She recently co-edited (with Taiwo Afuape) *Liberation Practices. Towards Emotional Wellbeing Through Dialogue* (2016).

Hilde Lidén is a Research Professor at the Institute for Social Research (ISF), Oslo. Her research interests are transnational migration, childhood and integration. Her research includes rights dilemmas in national and international policies and regulations on immigration, transnational families and citizenship, from a child's point of view.

Kim Robinson is lecturer in Social Work and Course Director for the Master's in Social Work, at Deakin University in Australia. She has worked as social work practitioner and manager in community health and refugee services, and educator for nearly 30 years in Australia and in the UK. Her research interests are human rights in health and social work settings, the provision of services to disadvantaged communities, and strategies for participation. She has published in the areas of asylum and refugee social work, mental health, family violence, and young unaccompanied minors.

Richard Warren is a caseworker and associate researcher/lecturer at Kent Law Clinic, University of Kent. He has a BA (Hons) in Social Anthropology, and MSc in Cross Cultural Research Methods (Migration Studies) and is currently studying for a PhD at the University of Kent. He is an accredited Senior Caseworker with the Law Society's Immigration and Asylum Accreditation Scheme with more than ten years' experience representing asylum seekers, refugees and migrants at all stages of the asylum/immigration process.

Notes on contributors

Lucy Williams is a freelance researcher and Senior Visiting Research Fellow at the University of Kent. She is involved in teaching, community work, activism and research with migrants, especially young people, facing detention, destitution and forced return to countries of origin.

Katie Willis is Professor of Human Geography at Royal Holloway, University of London. Her research focuses on migration, gender and families including the role of state policies and economic development strategies in shaping migrants' experiences. She is a member of the Editorial Collective of the Geographical Association journal *Geography*, and her publications include *Theories and Practices of Development* (Routledge).

Sheona York is a qualified solicitor with over 35 years' experience in immigration, asylum and public law. At the University of Kent Law Clinic since 2012, she combines supervising students working on cases with academic speaking and writing on immigration law issues of interest to practitioners, including deportation, statelessness, removability and Article 8 rights.

Acknowledgements

This book comes out of a seminar series entitled 'Unaccompanied children seeking asylum: Investigating professional practice, policy responses and research priorities' funded by the Economic and Social Research Council (ESRC). Between 2013 and 2016 we ran nine events bringing together academic researchers, lawyers, social workers, psychotherapists, foster parents, activists and young people who had arrived in the UK as unaccompanied migrants to explore the challenges that these young people face and the obstacles encountered by those seeking to support them. Many of the authors in this book were involved in the events, and we would like to thank them and all the other participants for their contributions. Rohma Ullah was the administrator for the series and was vital to its success, ensuring the events ran smoothly and making important suggestions when we were planning the next event. To encourage practitioner involvement we held two joint events in the series; one with Garden Court Chambers and one with the Child and Family Refugee Service at the Tavistock and Portman NHS Foundation Trust. We are very grateful to both these organisations for their involvement. Finally, we would like to thank Royal Holloway and Goldsmiths for all their help in running the series. Further information about the seminar series can be found at www.uncertainjourneys.org.uk.

We would also like to thank Isobel Bainton and Shannon Kneis at Policy Press for supporting us during the production of this book, and their understanding when there were delays. The comments provided on the book proposal, and the draft manuscript were very helpful in shaping the book and we are very grateful to the referees for their suggestions. As usual, Jen Thornton in the Geography Department at RHUL provided invaluable help with the diagrams, often at very short notice.

Finally, we would particularly like to thank Lord Alf Dubs for contributing the foreword to the book, and to acknowledge the significant advocacy work that he and his parliamentary colleagues undertake to improve the situation for unaccompanied young migrants.

Sue Clayton, Anna Gupta and Katie Willis
London, July 2018

Foreword

Alf Dubs, House of Lords

I am delighted to give my support to this collection, *Unaccompanied young migrants: identity, care and justice*, written and edited by leading advocates and experts on this topic in law, social sciences and social work, social geography, media and psychotherapy. I would like to share some thoughts on the current climate in Europe and beyond, to underline why this new, and holistic, analysis is so important at the current time.

From 1938 and 1940 Britain accepted almost 10,000 children from Germany, Austria, Poland and Czechoslovakia in the *Kindertransport* mobilisation. I know – I was one of them. This operation almost certainly saved our lives, as we would not have survived the Nazi regime otherwise. Prior to this, in 1937 Britain rescued almost 4,000 Basque children from the Spanish civil war, most of them orphaned after the bombing of Guernica. Local people built a tent settlement on Eastleigh Common in Hampshire, and the children were enthusiastically looked after there by local people of every age, class and political persuasion. The children went on to be fostered all over the UK. Many were later repatriated, while those with no-one to go back to made their lives here.

This offering of sanctuary to vulnerable children and young people, victims of war or persecution, is part of Britain's great humanitarian tradition of which we should be very proud. It was in this same humanitarian spirit that I responded to the recent refugee crisis in Europe by proposing in 2016 an Amendment to the UK Immigration Bill, committing the UK to admit vulnerable migrant children from the tens of thousands stranded in Europe – especially those in France, Greece and Italy. Fortunately the Amendment was passed despite initial resistance from the government. However the government subsequently and arbitrarily capped the numbers at 480 – and there have been, and still are, lengthy delays in the children coming here to the UK.

What has changed, and why the lack of welcome? We in Britain currently live under a government with a declared policy to create a 'hostile environment' for those seeking asylum. And all of us are subject to the negative stereotyping of refugees as criminal and aliens, from politicians and sections of the press.

This hostility is a relatively recent thing, and worryingly it seems to be mirrored across many of the world's wealthier nations. As the global south suffers crises of war and hardship, we see borders closing and walls being built across America, Australia and all over Europe. We see children in cages at the Mexican border. We see children living rough on the Greek islands, their futures uncertain, many in desperate conditions. We see children living in containers, and children living in the open, their tents slashed nightly by police, just across the Channel in Calais, France.

Fortunately there are many of us in Britain and around the world who care enough to put this right, and who, either through our professional work or as volunteers, academics or advisers, are working to protect the safety of these young people's journeys, and to secure good outcomes for them after arrival. This edited collection, written by people working on child refugee issues and directly with the young people themselves, is of immense value as it provides a nuanced and interdisciplinary view of the many challenges these young people face, and identifies best practices in working with them – as well as offering a much-needed current overview of the political, legal and other factors that frame their place in society.

From a UK perspective, there is critical discussion here around the Children Act of 1989, which ensures Local Authority care for any minor arriving in the UK from accepted crisis regions. However, as lawyers, social workers and others writing in this book draw out, the terms of the Children Act are often in conflict with immigration law, so that the rights and needs of young people as minors are subsumed by the demands and penalties of border control.

The collection also explores what a 'border' can be – is it determined by geographical features, the practices of state officials or international treaties – or all three? With comparisons to the US, the Nordic countries and Australia, the authors here look at how nation states in retreat from international cooperation present their own rules and defences, which in many cases breach international protocols. How to navigate such a minefield of conflicting rules and regulations is one of the greatest challenges for unaccompanied young people and their supporters.

The book goes on to look at issues of ongoing support for young people, particularly in the UK. We know that local authorities are their first port of call, but the authors caution that that provision of care can vary considerably. We also see discussed here, the tensions caused within foster families, school and the child's personal life, by the lack of certainty about their future status – as often their refugee case is not officially resolved so that a heavy cloud, of potential removal at age 18, hangs over them.

The chapters here that also should concern us all are those on the media, showing how the press often paints the picture of refugees as a swarm, a plague – something not even human, people who will threaten 'our' way of life. This ignores how many Britons came from elsewhere, and what a great contribution they have made to British life. Countering this, the writers here take care to present children's own stories, in their own words, and look at what psychological issues they may face, in their difficult transition to our culture and our asylum system. In this way, the writers always see them as human beings with dignity, and hopes for the future, unlike the press stereotypes.

Finally, I note that the authors have included the word 'Justice' in the title of their collection. This chimes very much with my own work and campaigns. For unaccompanied minors, their social care, education, future prospects – all these things – must be founded on good laws and good application of these laws, so that we do not confuse the care of refugee children, and our humanitarian tradition of welcoming refugees, with the exigencies of border policing, immigration targets and quotas.

I hope this book will offer some inspiration to the thousands of professionals and volunteers who have supported these young people both on their journeys and here at home – and to the young people themselves, who only ask for a chance to build themselves a future, whether uniting with family, or turning to us to be that family. The humanitarian will is there, and our laws and institutional practices need to support it.

Alf Dubs, House of Lords
July 2018

Introduction

Sue Clayton, Anna Gupta and Katie Willis

'You have got a swarm of people coming across the Mediterranean seeking a better life. I promise that everything that can be done will be done to make sure our borders are secure.'
   David Cameron, UK Prime Minister, 29 July 2015

'Accepting refugee children into the UK is a dangerous strategy – Cameron shouldn't be seduced'
   IndyVoices, *Independent*, 28 January 2016

'Outrage over 'child' migrants who will now sit with children in school classrooms'
   Daily Express, 20 October 2016

'When people come into our Country illegally, we must IMMEDIATELY escort them back out without going through years of legal manoeuvring. Our laws are the dumbest anywhere in the world. Republicans want Strong Borders and no Crime. Dems want Open Borders and are weak on Crime!'
   Donald Trump, US President, 30 June 2018

The issue of nationalism has dominated the political agenda of the UK, other European countries, the US and Australia in recent years, with increasingly draconian border controls regarded as the guarantee of a 'strong nation'. Within this rhetoric, distinctions between regional citizens, economic migrants, refugees and others are frequently obscured as governments and media cast the stranger, the outsider, as a threat and a disruption to perceived national values (Crawley and Skleparis, 2018). What has become known in Europe as the 'refugee crisis' of 2015 onwards has further intensified resistance to the 'swarm' or 'stream' of newcomers, the threat of whose presence was used to justify the aggressive Frontex (European Border and Coast Guard Agency) maritime security operation and the closure of several EU borders to undocumented migrants, as well as to shore up political movements such as Marine le Pen's Front National Party and the UK

Brexit 'Leave' campaign. Donald Trump's election success can also partly be attributed to his campaign promises to control immigration, especially across the US–Mexican border.

Where does this leave unaccompanied young migrants? In 2015 there were over 90,000 (Eurostat, 2017) such children in Europe, many of whom ought to qualify for protection under international conventions and law, but who are by no means all offered care and protection. While the numbers have declined since the 2015 high point, there are still thousands of young people who are travelling to Europe alone, seeking safety and security.

The contributors to this book passionately believe that the hurdles these children face, which begin with their leaving homes and families, and are intensified by the often dangerous and traumatic journeys to the west, do not become less as they reach our shores (see also Menjívar and Perreira, 2017). Rather they are then subject to national governmental regimes that, in many cases, including that of the UK, can involve years of state violence, non-acceptance, disbelief and compromised decisions which leave the young people exposed to highly precarious futures. These issues raise significant questions about social justice and the promotion of human rights in our society; questions for wider debate as well as urgent attention from professionals and other adults working with and caring for these young people.

The contradiction between their status as migrants and their status as children deserving of state care and protection is at the heart of many of the chapters of this book.

Who are the unaccompanied young migrants?

These unaccompanied children are part of the movements of hundreds of thousands of migrants fleeing violence, war, persecution and extreme poverty. In many cases, such as Eritrean young men fleeing to escape conditions similar to slavery associated with compulsory military service, the push factors are particularly pertinent to young people. However, in other cases, children are moving for the same reasons as adults: seeking safety and some form of security. Given these push factors, it is unsurprising that there was a massive increase in the number of unaccompanied children seeking asylum in Europe in 2015, with the growing instability and insecurity in countries of the Middle East and North Africa (see Figure 1). While the numbers declined in 2016 and 2017, they are still over 30,000.

The vast majority (89%) were male (Eurostat, 2018). This reflects both the reasons behind the flight from their country of origin, and

Figure 1: Unaccompanied minors claiming asylum in the EU, 2008–17

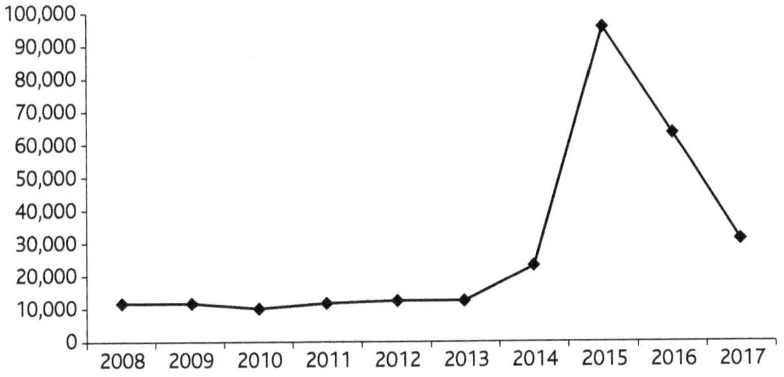

[Line chart showing values near 10,000 from 2008 through 2013, rising slightly in 2014, jumping to roughly 25,000 in 2014/2015 area, peaking near 95,000 in 2015, dropping to about 65,000 in 2016, and declining to about 32,000 in 2017.]

Source: Adapted from Eurostat (2018)

social norms regarding the roles and capabilities of young men and women. Young men, rather than women, are usually targeted for conscription into militia units, or forced military service, factors that would cause them to seek escape. Young men are also often seen as more capable and able to survive perilous journeys, while young women's perceived greater vulnerability means that they may be protected at home.

In 2017, the most important source country for unaccompanied asylum-seeking children (UASC) was Afghanistan, as it had been in 2016, but the second most important source country was Eritrea, a shift from the large number of Syrian minors who claimed asylum in 2016. Seven other countries were also classified as the countries of citizenship of over 1,000 unaccompanied young migrants seeking asylum in 2017 (see Table 1).

The classification of certain groups of migrants as 'unaccompanied asylum-seeking children' implies a fixity of identity and categorisation that hides a multiplicity of definitions and sources of information. It also presents an externally-derived and imposed legal definition on the young people involved. Categorisations matter as we will outline later in this introduction, and through the remaining chapters in the book.

While the idea of an unaccompanied migrant child sounds very straightforward, the reality is much more complex. Definitions of 'childhood' vary across time and space (Ansell, 2016). While in some contexts childhood may be a time of education and play, in others, childhood is associated with domestic labour and income generation. It is unsurprising, therefore, that the age at which childhood ends and adulthood begins also differs widely. However, the 1989 UN

Table 1: Asylum applicants considered as unaccompanied minors in the EU, by country of citizenship, 2016–17

Country of citizenship	Number		% of total	
	2016	2017	2016	2017
Afghanistan	23,990	5,340	37.9	17.0
Eritrea	3,335	3,110	5.3	9.9
Gambia	2,330	2,580	3.7	8.2
Guinea	1,165	2,165	1.8	6.9
Pakistan	1,945	1,845	3.1	5.9
Syria	11,990	1,765	18.9	5.6
Somalia	2,775	1,765	4.4	5.6
Nigeria	1,085	1,390	1.7	4.4
Bangladesh	740	1,320	1.2	4.2
Iraq	4,155	1,240	6.6	3.9
Other	9,770	8,885	16.6	28.3
TOTAL	63,290	31,405	100	99.9

Source: Calculated from data in Eurostat (2017, 2018)

Convention on the Rights of the Child (UNCRC) defines a child as anyone under 18 years of age. In implementing legislation based on this definition, being able to confirm a young person's age is clearly of great importance, so leading to ethical questions about how age is to be determined (see below).

As 'child' is often used in general speech in Europe and North America to refer to someone who is much younger than 18, terms such as 'youth' or 'young people' may be used. This is the term we have used in the title of the book, but throughout the book 'child' and 'children' may be used, particularly when discussing legally-ascribed identities where the UNCRC or similar conventions or legislation are being referred to. Migrants under 18 may also refer to themselves as 'children'.

Being an unaccompanied child migrant does not mean travelling alone; instead, the term is used to recognise the mobility of people under 18 who are migrating without an adult family member or carer. Sometimes the term 'separated' is used instead of 'unaccompanied' to reinforce the idea of family dispersal. In the UK, the term 'unaccompanied asylum-seeking child' or UASC, is a legal term meaning, 'a person under 18, or in the absence of documentary evidence establishing age, appears to be under 18, who is applying for asylum in his or her own right and has no relative or guardian in the United Kingdom' (Home Office, 2017). In some countries, such as Australia (see Chapter Ten), the term 'unaccompanied asylum-seeking minor' (UAM) may be used in legal definitions and government policy, while in US migration policy, such young people are referred to as 'unaccompanied alien children' (see Chapter Eight). Children who are trafficked may also arrive unaccompanied by a legal caregiver, but are also categorised differently in the law as victims of modern slavery (see Department for Education, 2017).

Fleeing persecution across international borders places these young people in the category of 'refugee' and therefore in a position to claim asylum. However, as later chapters (particularly Chapter Two) will elucidate, Article 1 A(2) of the 1951 Refugee Convention defines a refugee as a person who has 'a well-founded fear of being persecuted for reasons of race, religion, nationality, membership of a particular social group or political opinion'. To gain legal refugee status requires young people to prove that 'there is a genuine risk of the applicant 'being persecuted' that is causally connected to one of the five enumerated forms of civil or political status' (Pobjoy, 2017: 3). The provision of this evidence is often very difficult given the young people's lack of documentation, the conditions under which they fled their home, the trauma of the journey and their status as children. These factors, combined with a culture of disbelief, often exacerbated by political contexts where immigration is seen as a challenge to national security and identity, mean that children's narratives are frequently not believed.

Regional increases in migrant flows, definitional complexities and the way in which young people's information is evaluated all mean that collecting accurate data about unaccompanied asylum-seeking children is a significant challenge. However, data is important in identifying spatial and temporal patterns and examining the implications of classifications on young people's experiences. Additionally, listening to individuals is key in recognising the human agency behind the numbers, and also in acknowledging the potential forms of support that individuals may require. The focus on identity as one of the themes of the book encompasses both the externally-imposed identity categories that unaccompanied children are assigned, alongside the forms of identity that they claim as individuals.

Identity, care and justice

"I am just a Brummie lad" said 'Khalid' when filmed in Birmingham by Sue as part of a series on UASC.[1] Khalid had come to the UK from Afghanistan as an unaccompanied minor five years earlier, yet his identity and future as a 'Brummie' was precarious and contingent, as he approached 18 with his discretionary leave to remain in the UK having ended.

How Khalid and other unaccompanied migrant youth are constructed by others, and how they construct their own identities are complex, fluid and contextual, being significantly affected by the immigration policies and the nature of welfare systems in the countries in which they find themselves. Young people are so often defined by the labels placed by others on them, such as 'trafficked child'; categories that can determine provision (or not) of services, and categories that imply 'deserving' or 'undeserving' of recognition and rights. For example in Chase's (2012) study, unaccompanied migrant youth in their mid to late teens described the hostility and suspicion they encountered from immigration officials on arrival in the UK; however, the younger children described being met with sympathy and kindness.

In addition, the age assessment process conducted by immigration officials or local authority social workers is a highly-contested area of practice that determines whether a young person is treated as a child with access to support and protection under the UNCRC. As discussed in Chapter Three, local authorities in England and Wales have responsibility under the Children Act 1989 for unaccompanied young migrants deemed under the age of 18, with most coming into the care system. While there are real practical and material consequences for young people following an age determination decision, there are also significant emotional effects, as one young person explains in Dorling (2013: 37): "For my peace of mind I need to be my age. Two ages are not acceptable for my heart and mind".

Unaccompanied migrant young people must deal with the complexities of identity development, not only within an unfamiliar environment as a migrant, but also as they move from childhood to adulthood. Being branded 'asylum seekers' fundamentally determines how they are treated within the immigration and welfare system, but it can also differentiate them from citizens and lead to discrimination and stigma, so pervasive in the media and wider society (Chase, 2012). Many young people do not feel able to open about who they are; their own identities being subsumed by the institutional labels given to them, and society's responses to them as the stigmatised 'other' (Chase, 2012). For example, Khalid, mentioned earlier, never felt safe enough to let his peers know that he was an asylum-seeking young person.

As discussed in later chapters, particularly Chapter Seven, for any young person leaving care at 18, the transition to becoming an adult, often having to move from foster or residential care, can be fraught with difficulties and fear for the future (Allsopp and Chase, 2017). However, for unaccompanied migrant youth their temporary leave to remain in the UK is withdrawn and they face an uncertain future while they await a Home Office decision without the protection they received under the UNCRC. Their real anxieties and fears as a consequence of the uncertainty of their immigration status, the prospect of forced return to a country where they face dangers and have limited or no links and connections, and rejection by the society that had offered variable, but some degree of, care, can have a profound and detrimental impact on young people's mental and physical health. Chase and Allsop (2013) argue that young people's subjective wellbeing is linked to their notions of future, and being able to imagine and work towards future goals. However within the immigration systems, young people lack autonomy, identity and choice, but their need for a future often leads them to exercise what agency they have by making decisions against or regardless of policy intentions, such as going 'underground' and living undocumented with all the risks that this entails (see Chapters One, Eight and Nine).

There is much variation in the care and protection offered to unaccompanied migrant youth in the UK and internationally. Age, race, religion and gender can be important factors in determining young people's differential experiences of first entry into the UK (Chase 2012). However, factors beyond the individual young person have considerable impact as well. The policies across countries within the UK vary, as do practices across local authorities. The extent to which a 'culture of disbelief' permeates institutional contexts will impact on the responses to unaccompanied young migrants, as will resource constraints, and the values and beliefs of the individual professionals. As a profession, social work has a key role to play in promoting the rights and welfare of unaccompanied migrant children. However, the dominance of immigration control challenges the professional values promoting social justice and human rights for all. The challenging and often contradictory legal and organisational contexts in which professionals practise is discussed further in Chapter Three and various chapters in Section 2.

Unaccompanied migrant young people's capability to be heard and have their views taken seriously is very dependent on the adults in their lives. Social workers play an important role, but so do independent advocates from non-governmental organisations (NGOs), activist organisations and, in Scotland, the Scottish Guardianship Service (Crawley and Kohli, 2013). Lawyers also play a key role in ensuring young people's voices are heard and rights upheld in legal forums, although, as with other professional responses, legal representation for young people varies considerably. Campaigning lawyers, however, have played a crucial role in advocating for, and in many cases securing the rights of, unaccompanied migrant youth.

Nancy Fraser's (2008: 16) work on social justice and 'parity of participation' can be useful in conceptualising and challenging injustice. She discusses distributive injustice linked to material resources; misrecognition or 'cultural or symbolic injustice' linked to status and identity (such as race and immigration status); and misrepresentation that denies people participation on par with others, including in political arenas. This third dimension was added to highlight the structural exclusion of the 'global poor' to highlight transborder injustice, as Fraser (2007: 313, emphasis in the original) explains: 'disputes about *what* is owed as a matter of justice to community members now turn quickly into disputes about *who* should count as a member and *which* is the relevant community'. Unaccompanied young migrants are precariously positioned in relation to citizenship rights in a policy climate that is increasingly marked by conditionality and authoritarianism.

When exploring the promotion of social justice within her three-dimensional framework, Fraser identifies two ways of dealing with injustices: affirmative and transformative. On the one hand, affirmative strategies deal with the implications of injustices without challenging unequal social relations, with reference to 'remedies aimed at correcting inequitable outcomes of social arrangements without disturbing the underlying framework that generates them' (Fraser, 1995: 82). On the other hand, transformative strategies are about changing the way society is organised and aim at restructuring the underlying framework (Fraser, 2005: 73). Transformative strategies are therefore 'remedies aimed at correcting inequitable outcomes precisely by restructuring the underlying generative framework' (Fraser, 1995: 82). We would argue that both these strategies play a crucial role when working with unaccompanied young migrants. Social work and other professionals need to work with an individual young person to promote his or her rights and aspirations, and challenge the injustices she or he experience in affirmative ways. In addition, transformative strategies such as collective responses and social activism, which highlight the structural inequalities and injustices faced by unaccompanied migrant youth *as well as* adults experiencing forced migration, are necessary.

Introduction

Overview of the chapters

The book is divided into three sections, with chapters written by authors from a range of disciplines and professional practice including law, social work, media and communications, sociology, psychology and geography. Many of the book's authors participated in the Uncertain Journeys seminar series that the editors organised (2013–16).[2] By approaching this issue in an interdisciplinary way, we hope to provide a more nuanced and empathic understanding of the experiences of unaccompanied migrant youth, and build more strategic alliances for change between all those involved.

Section 1 frames the youth migrant debate through an examination of the migration regimes, legal frameworks and care systems that unaccompanied asylum-seeking children have to navigate. The chapters in this section consider the ways in which young migrants are categorised through externally-imposed identities as they are processed through legal and care systems. The focus in all three chapters is on the situation in the UK, particularly in England and Wales, but, where appropriate, there are links to other jurisdictions. In Chapter One, Sue Clayton and Katie Willis explore the disparities between the assumed international protection for unaccompanied child migrants, and how national migration regimes and border policies result in very different experiences of protection and mobility. They do this through an examination of the case of the unaccompanied children who were left abandoned in Calais when the Jungle camp was demolished in 2016. Sheona York and Richard Warren in Chapter Two continue the theme of how practice on the ground differs from what is supposed to happen in theory, in their discussion of dilemmas and conflicts in the legal system. In Chapter Three, Anna Gupta highlights the challenges within the care system in supporting unaccompanied asylum-seeking children whose identities are shifting as they grow older, and for whom getting older means growing insecurity as they may not be entitled to the protection of the state once they reach 18. The threat of forced removal if their asylum claims are not successful affects wellbeing and planning for the future.

Section 2 of the book explores migrant youth identities and draws more explicitly on the voices and experiences of individual unaccompanied asylum-seeking young people, so countering the official, institutional categorisations outlined in Section 1. In a preface to this section, Sue Clayton introduces the narratives of young people, recounting their experiences of journeys from their home countries to Europe and their lives in the UK, including the effects of uncertainty regarding turning 18. In Chapter Four, Sue discusses aspects of self-representation among the young people she has worked with, and how they both engage with and challenge external representations of unaccompanied minors. Gillian Hughes focuses on responses and therapeutic support in relation to wellbeing and mental health (Chapter Five). In particular, she stresses the need to move beyond ideas of individual vulnerability to understandings of collective resistance. In Chapter Six, Louise Drammeh continues this theme of collective support and the role of social relationships in ideas of belonging, drawing on her experiences as a social worker supporting young people who arrived in the UK as unaccompanied minors. Lucy Williams focuses, in Chapter Seven, on turning 18 and the debates around durable solutions for unaccompanied asylum-seeking children when they are no longer legally children.

Section 3 of the book moves beyond the focus on the UK to explore how unaccompanied minors are classified and supported (or not) in other countries. Mario Bruzzone and Enrique González-Araiza (Chapter Eight) examine the situation in the United States, where tensions around immigration, particularly across the southern border, have been increasing. They stress the importance of examining US policy towards unaccompanied minors in the context of the international migration circuits of Mexico and the Central American nations. In Chapter Nine, Hilde Lidén outlines the responses to UASC in the Nordic countries. While these nations have, for the most part, had a reputation for welcoming and supporting refugees, Hilde discusses changes in policies and the differences between countries. Finally, in Chapter Ten, Kim Robinson and Sandra M Gifford discuss the Australian case, focusing on how the experiences and treatment of unaccompanied minors has varied depending on the routes taken to Australia, and the increasing use of offshore processing in migration policy.

The book ends with a short conclusion where we outline some policy recommendations drawn from across the book. We also consider some of the future challenges and possible areas of optimism in the support for unaccompanied migrant youth.

Notes

[1] There is an archive of some of these films at www.bigjourneys.org

[2] For further information about the Uncertain Journeys series, see www.uncertainjourneys.org.uk

References

Allsopp, J. and Chase, E. (2017) 'Best interests, durable solutions and belonging: policy discourses shaping the futures of unaccompanied migrant and refugee minors coming of age in Europe', *Journal of Ethnic and Migration Studies*, DOI: 10.1080/1369183X.2017.1404265

Ansell, N. (2016) *Children, youth and development* (2nd edn), London: Routledge.

Chase, E. (2012) 'Security and subjective wellbeing: the experiences of unaccompanied young people seeking asylum in the UK', *Sociology of Health & Illness*, 35(6): 858–72.

Chase, E and Allsop, J. (2013) *Future citizens of the world? The contested futures of independent young migrants in Europe*, RSC Working Paper Series 97, Oxford: Refugee Studies Centre, www.rsc.ox.ac.uk/files/files-1/wp97-future-citizens-of-the-world-2013.pdf

Crawley, H. and Kohli, R.K.S. (2013) *'She endures with me': An evaluation of the Scottish Guardianship Service pilot*, London: Diana Princess of Wales Memorial Trust/Paul Hamlyn Foundation, www.scottishrefugeecouncil.org.uk/assets/0000/6798/Final_Report_2108.pdf

Crawley, H. and Skleparis, D. (2018) Refugees, migrants, neither, both: categorical fetishism and the politics of bounding in Europe's 'migration crisis', *Journal of Ethnic and Migration Studies*, 44(1): 48–64.

Department for Education (2017) *Care of unaccompanied migrant children and child victims of modern slavery: Statutory guidance for local authorities*, https://consult.education.gov.uk/children-in-care/care-of-unaccompanied-and-trafficked-children/supporting_documents/Revised%20UASC%20Stat%20guidance_final.pdf

Dorling, K. (2013) *Happy Birthday? Disputing the age of children in the immigration system*, London: Coram Children's Legal Centre, www.childrenslegalcentre.com/wp-content/uploads/2017/04/HappyBirthday_Final.pdf

Eurostat (2017) 'Asylum applications considered to be unaccompanied minors', Eurostat news release 80/2017, 11 May, http://ec.europa.eu/eurostat/documents/2995521/8016696/3-11052017-AP-EN.pdf/30ca2206-0db9-4076-a681-e069a4bc5290

Eurostat (2018) 'Asylum applications considered to be unaccompanied minors', Eurostat news release 84/2018, 16 May, http://ec.europa.eu/eurostat/documents/2995521/8895109/3-16052018-BP-EN.pdf/ec4cc3d7-c177-4944-964f-d85401e55ad9

Fraser, N. (1995) 'From redistribution to recognition. Dilemmas of justice in a post-socialist age', *New Left Review*, 212: 68–93.

Fraser, N. (2005) 'Reframing justice in a globalizing world', *New Left Review*, 36: 69–88

Fraser, N. (2007) 'Identity, exclusion, and critique: a response to four critics', *European Journal of Political Theory*, 6(3): 305–38.

Fraser, N. (2008) *Scales of justice: Reimagining political space in a globalizing world*, New York: Columbia University Press and Polity Press.

Home Office (2017) 'How many people do we grant asylum or protection to?', National Statistics, 25 May, www.gov.uk/government/publications/immigration-statistics-january-to-march-2017/how-many-people-do-we-grant-asylum-or-protection-to

Menjívar, C. and Perreira, K.M. (2017) 'Undocumented and unaccompanied: children of migration in the European Union and the United States', *Journal of Ethnic and Migration Studies*, DOI: 10.1080/1369183X.2017.1404255

Pobjoy, J.M. (2017) *The child in international refugee law*, Cambridge: Cambridge University Press.

SECTION 1

Framing the youth migration debate

ONE

Migration regimes and border controls: the crisis in Europe

Sue Clayton and Katie Willis

Introduction

The protection of unaccompanied young migrants seeking asylum, some of the most vulnerable people within the estimated 244 million people who are currently living outside their country of birth (International Organization for Migration, 2016), is encompassed in a number of key international agreements. According to Article 14 of The Universal Declaration of Human Rights, 'Everyone has the right to seek and to enjoy in other countries asylum from persecution.' This right is also embedded in the 1951 UN Refugee Convention (see Chapter Two). Additionally, the 1989 United Nations Convention of the Rights of the Child (UNCRC) provides an important framework for recognising children as independent social actors, but requiring child-sensitive approaches and protection. However, 'there is no single instrument in international law that sets out the full range of obligations that a state owes in respect of a refugee child' (Pobjoy, 2017: 22). Thus, despite these global level agreements, and perhaps also reflecting the lack of a single coherent regulation, how such instruments are implemented and experienced by migrants varies greatly, reflecting significant differences in the migration regimes adopted by individual states and groups of states.

This lack of coherence – for our concerns here, both within Europe, and beyond European borders – makes it extremely difficult for non-governmental organisations (NGOs) and other actors to assess and secure what provision can be made available to unaccompanied young migrants seeking asylum, and we would argue causes a great deal of unnecessary suffering as they either do not access their rights or are considerably delayed in doing so. Recent changes in Europe, including the 2016 EU/Turkey and the 2017 Italy/Libya agreements have further complicated the situation on the ground for the thousands of unaccompanied minors in Europe (see Amnesty International,

2017: 25–6, for discussion of implications of the EU/Turkey deal for unaccompanied children in Greece).

Such difficulties are predicated on contradictions inherent in the evolution of the state itself. Reece Jones, in his 2016 book *Violent Borders*, highlights the constructed nature of states: 'States have not always existed. Along with nations, borders and territories, they were created to address problems of control that emerged over the past 5,000 years' (Jones, 2016: 4). The socially-constructed nature of borders and the way in which borders are constantly being recreated through the actions of individual border guards, immigration officials and migrants have also come to the fore in recent work (see, for example, Mountz, 2010; Gill, 2016). Borders are now understood not only as lines on a map, or the hard materiality of wire fences, or brick walls, but through the discourses and practices that are used to exclude certain individuals or groups from a particular territory.

This chapter explores the diversity of migration regimes with reference to unaccompanied young people to reveal how they are forced to navigate complex legal systems, and the regulatory frameworks that are supposed to provide them with support and protection, but which all too often fail to deliver. We first examine the role of scale (global, regional, national, provincial, municipal) in the development and implementation of migration regulations for unaccompanied youth. There is a particular focus on the EU and its member states, as this exemplifies how regulations can be differently interpreted and implemented at different scales.

The chapter then considers border practices and the effects of offshoring to process migrants applying for asylum, or as an attempt to reduce immigration. The formal processing of migrants outside national territories demonstrates how migration regimes are not necessarily neatly mapped according to state boundaries. The porosity of borders is then considered. Following international agreements, it may be assumed that national borders would be relatively porous for unaccompanied young people seeking asylum, but practices on the ground, as well as within legislation, reveal, as we discuss later in this chapter, that there is significant diversity based on factors such as gender, age and perceived nationality.

After an overview of these broad themes, the chapter focuses on the case of unaccompanied minors who came to Calais as part of their intended journey to the UK. Drawing on Sue Clayton's work with young people in Calais, elsewhere in France, Belgium and the UK, we argue that laws which are supposed to protect unaccompanied young people are not implemented in full, and that young people are not able to access the support which would enable them to benefit from these laws.

Migration regimes and international law

Supporting refugees fleeing persecution, recognising the particular vulnerabilities of children, and protecting children migrating without adult family members are all incorporated into key international conventions and regulations (see Chapter Two for more detail). However, operationalising these through national laws and policies on the ground results in significant diversity as international consensus comes up against national politics and variations in willingness and ability to implement policies that fulfil the spirit of the international agreements. Laws and policies are also implemented at scales other than the national, most notably regional levels, such as the EU, and sub-national levels, including provincial or municipal level.

Within the EU, while there is freedom of movement between EU member states for EU nationals (following a transition period following accession for some countries), the nature of the Schengen Agreement means that there nonetheless remain some forms of border control within the EU. For example, the UK is only a partial signatory to Schengen, meaning that there are border controls to enter the UK from the states of Europe.[1] As will be discussed later in the context of Calais, this means that while refugees can in theory travel across Europe without having their documentation checked (King, 2016), the border between the UK and France is an external border of the Schengen zone. Post-Brexit arrangements are likely to complicate this further.

In relation to support for refugees, EU regulations relate to the EU as a whole, treating EU territory as one geographical space, but recognising individual national sovereignty within it. In 2013 the EU Dublin III regulation came into force. It specifies that though, generally speaking, a refugee should be processed in the EU country where they are first registered (fingerprinted), unaccompanied minors with close family in another European state are an exception, and should be allowed to proceed to the state where they have family to have their claim processed there. This is a very clear recognition in European regulations that age and migrant status are factors that justify differential treatment: borders operate differently according to legally-identified characteristics. A significant issue in relation to the operation of Dublin III is, however, the evidence required to support claims about family links, alongside the ongoing debates around age assessment (see Chapters Two and Three). In 2016, over 700 unaccompanied children came to the UK to join family members under the auspices of the Dublin III agreement (Unicef and Save the Children, 2017). Though, as discussed later in this chapter, Sue Clayton observed that, during the Home Office's response to the demolition of the Calais 'Jungle' camp, many with strong Dublin lll claims were missed.

The complex interactions of UK, EU and international law regarding unaccompanied asylum-seeking children (UASC) will be examined in more detail later in this chapter with reference to Calais, but will also be developed in later chapters. There will also be more detail on the different legal frameworks and policies adopted in Scandinavian countries in Chapter Nine. Kanics and Senovilla Hernández (2010) draw out good and bad practice from across the EU with regard to data collection, models of reception and the development of durable solutions. They demonstrate very clearly how, despite signing up to common EU regulations, EU member states interpret and operationalise the regulations in contrasting ways (see also Allsopp and Chase, 2017). The diverse nature of unaccompanied minors, for example in age, nationality, gender and religion, can also be reflected in differential application of legal protection. For example, de Graeve and Bex (2017) highlight the importance of an intersectional approach that acknowledges how different dimensions of identity interact in care relationships of unaccompanied minors in Belgium.

The focus of European attention on the plight of unaccompanied minors within the continent, or approaching its borders, is understandable, but it is vital to acknowledge the young people migrating elsewhere in the world. Unicef (2017: 6) estimated that in 2015–16 at least 300,000 UASC were registered in 80 countries, but the figure is likely to have been much higher because of the difficulties of collecting data. In Section 3 of this book, Robinson and Gifford discuss the situation in Australia (Chapter Ten), while in Chapter Eight, Mario Bruzzone and Enrique González-Araiza discuss the operation of controls on UASC at the US–Mexican border, a border where about 100,000 unaccompanied minors were apprehended in 2015 and 2016 (Unicef, 2017: 12).

Both Lebanon and Jordan have received significant numbers of refugees in recent years, most notably from Syria, but also from other countries in the region. UASC are part of these refugee flows, but their treatment as particularly vulnerable individuals has not always been recognised. Lebanon and Jordan have both ratified the UNCRC, but neither country is signatory to the UN 1951 Refugee Convention.

In the case of Lebanon, 2016 changes in documentation requirements for border entry and residency renewal have left UASC between the ages of 15 and 17 with no legal options. This is because people aged 15 and over must have their own documentation, but 15–17 year olds need to have a signature from a parent or guardian. As a study by Intersos and MMP (2017: 22) concluded, 'Unaccompanied minors, therefore, do not have any legal pathway to residency, despite being legally required to regularise their stay.' For UASC in Jordan, a 2014 law requiring refugees to live in formal camps, rather than within the wider Jordanian society, has failed to work in the 'best interests of the child' with regard to living conditions and access to services (Intersos and MMP, 2017).

Thus, the experiences of UASC in being able to claim their rights to protection under international agreements, are filtered through different scales of law and policy making.

Borders, territoriality and sovereignty

The complexity of migration regimes in dealing with international law reflects the widespread acceptance that nation states have sovereignty over their territory, including decisions about who should cross their borders. Here, however, we challenge assumptions about where borders are and their fixity, through examining processes of extra-territorial border policing, focusing on the Le Touquet Agreement, the work of Frontex in patrolling EU waters and Australia's formal offshoring arrangements with neighbouring islands. Extra-territorial border policing has taken on increasing importance in certain parts of the world as refugee flows have increased. While this form of border control may be a pragmatic decision for national governments, for unaccompanied minors, it can have very negative impacts on their wellbeing and ability to get to a place of safety.

To help in the management of the France–UK border, in 2003 UK and France signed the Le Touquet Agreement, which instituted UK border checks at all ferry ports along the northern French and Belgian coasts for border control and the policing of migrants (King, 2016). This was updated in January 2018 in the 'Sandhurst Treaty' (UK Government and Government of France, 2018). But the UK does not provide any processing of claims at Calais, making the 'queue' and its security the liability of the French. This was done in exchange for substantive payments to the French government, estimated to be £100 million with an additional £45 million committed for 2018 as part of the Sandhurst negotiations. This money is used to fund physical infrastructure, most notably fencing around the port entrances, and increased policing, including riot police (Compagnies Republicaines de Securité, CRS). The presence of the UK border on French soil, as well as the particularly brutal forms of border policing adopted, have had very negative impacts on UASC seeking to come to the UK, as we illustrate later in this chapter.

The EU has been developing 'border externalisation policies' since the 1990s (Casas-Cortes et al, 2017). These policies have involved trying to reduce migration towards Europe through working with non-EU countries to share surveillance and directly intervene in migrant flows. The massive increase in the numbers of refugees seeking to access Europe via maritime routes across the Mediterranean since 2013 has led to other forms of border policing such as shared EU activities and attempts to discourage migration by interventions in North African waters. However, shifts between EU-wide and national strategies, as well as focus on different parts of the Mediterranean, have resulted in diverse policies, sometimes with tragic outcomes.

Reporting on their 'Forensic Oceanography' project, Heller and Pezzani (2016) detail the disastrous consequences of the surveillance-based form of border policing, rather than humanitarian intervention, that characterised EU maritime bordering practices in the early 2010s. Following the deaths of at least 366 people near the Italian island of Lampedusa in October 2013, the Italian government launched the Mare Nostrum project, which patrolled the waters just off Libya and helped migrant boats that were in difficulty. Pressure from many European governments because of the number of refugees who were arriving on European soil through Italy led to the replacement of Mare Nostrum by the Triton programme, headed by the European Border and Coast Guard Agency – Frontex. While Triton has returned to a surveillance role to try and deter migrants, cargo ships and NGO vessels have been taking on a more significant role in rescuing boats in difficulty (Heller and Pezzani, 2016). While this form of border policing is not specifically targeted at UASC, among the thousands seeking to cross the Mediterranean there are large numbers of unaccompanied minors. The danger of the journey, exacerbated by the Triton programme (Heller and Pezzani would argue) means that UASC will have been among the 4,579 people who died making the sea crossing to Italy in 2016. Unicef estimates that this number included at least 700 children, and concludes that, 'the Central Mediterranean route is one of the world's deadliest' and that there are 'high rates of trafficking and exploitation facing children on the Central Mediterranean route from North Africa to Italy' (2017: 15).

Offshoring of migration control has been a significant aspect of Australian immigration policy in recent decades, and as Robinson and Gifford highlight in their chapter (Chapter Ten): 'Australia is the only country to have a policy of mandatory detention for all asylum seekers arriving unauthorised in Australia by boat, including children.' Detention can be outside Australian territory on the islands of Nauru and Manus, Papua New Guinea. It is certainly questionable as to whether detention in these spaces and in the conditions that have been publicised through the Nauru files (*Guardian*, 2018a), for example, represents an outcome which is in the best interests of the child when dealing with UASC, but the Australian model has been seen as a possible solution to the perceived migration problems of some other states (including EU states).

The governance of borders, where they are located, how they are managed and policed, and who is allowed through them and on what grounds, is of paramount importance to governments throughout the world. However, as will be argued in the rest of the chapter, the often contradictory, opaque and ever-changing nature of border governance means that unaccompanied child migrants are often left unable to cross international borders to safety, even when they have the legal rights to.

Children of the Calais Jungle

Legislative context

'These refugees are children, cold, alone and at risk. That's why I voted to help them' (Phillips, 2016). This statement, written as part of a newspaper opinion piece by the Conservative Member of Parliament Stephen Phillips, was in response to the UK House of Commons vote against Section 67c of the Immigration Act, in May 2016, which has become known as the 'Dubs Amendment'; an amendment which provides for an unspecified number of unaccompanied minors to be brought to the UK from Europe. Despite being a member of the ruling Conservative Party, Phillips had defied his party and voted to support the amendment. As discussed later in this chapter, a version of the amendment was eventually passed, but its implementation has been criticised by those seeking to support unaccompanied young migrants wanting to come to the UK.

This was at a time when there was growing media coverage and public concern about the plight of unaccompanied children travelling to Europe during what became known in Europe as the 'refugee crisis'. In 2015, more than 1 million asylum seekers had entered Europe either by the Turkey–Greece route, or the Libya–Lampedusa/Sicily route. At least 3,700 died at sea, among them unaccompanied children (Anderson, 2017). Save the Children estimated that approximately 25,000 unaccompanied young people entered the EU during 2015, but final figures suggest that a total of 90,000 that year requested asylum in Europe, up from an average of around 11,000 in the years up to 2013 (see Figure 1 in the Introduction).

The remainder of this chapter examines the particular case of nearly 2,000 unaccompanied young migrants who were based in the Calais Jungle in its final months in 2016, to consider altercations within and between UK, French and EU migration regimes; how control practices and policing were implemented; and the overall catastrophic effects of these actions on the young people themselves.

For those refugees who wanted to travel to the UK, Calais had become an important destination due to its proximity to the short vehicular ferry crossing and the Eurotunnel entrance. While media attention in 2015 and 2016 focused on the Calais site widely known as the 'Jungle', there had been prior settlements in the Calais area from the late 1990s when UK border checks were introduced in France, leading to an increase in migrants refused entry into the UK while still in French territory. The Sangatte camp, sited near the Channel Tunnel entrance, opened in 1999 and was administered by the Red Cross. However, neither the French nor the British authorities conducted any form of immigration processing there; consequently the numbers went on rising beyond the camp's capacity and conditions rapidly deteriorated. After a breakdown of talks between Home Secretary David Blunkett and French Interior Minister Nicholas Sarkozy, United Nations High Commission for Refugees (UNHCR) representatives were invited to make assessments of the occupants, and found considerable numbers had a genuine asylum case: these people were apportioned 50/50 to either the UK or France, with the UK accepting 1,100. Those not eligible for asylum were offered small cash pay-offs, and the centre was closed in 2002 (*Guardian*, 2002). From then on, the UK Home Office policy with regard to France was to focus exclusively on border security, increasing defences around the tunnel entrance and extending existing border arrangements with the Le Touquet Treaty (see above). We would argue that the UK's preference for investing in policing and offshore security outside its own geographical territory, with no attention paid to processing claimants at these border points, was a short-term and unsatisfactory policy, as it left many migrants with no means of establishing claims which, had they been made at UK land-side borders such as Heathrow or Dover, would have undergone fair processing/been accepted. This situation made undocumented minors the most exposed – without accommodation, processing or even NGO advice or protection. Thus hundreds of unregistered, unnamed, vulnerable children with strong legal claims to UK protection were left to suffer indefinitely within sight of the British flag.

The above arrangements were still in operation with the advent of the much larger settlement in the Calais Industrial Zone which became known as the 'Jungle'. By 2016 the Jungle had nearly 10,000 inhabitants and, because the camp was unrecognised by both British and French authorities, there was no registering of its inhabitants or processing of asylum claims on-site by either the French or the British. There were tensions between both countries as the numbers rose and policing costs grew ever higher. The situation along the Northern coast of France also caused contretemps between local and national regimes in France, with centre-right Mayor of Calais Natacha Bouchart calling for the Le Touquet Treaty to be scrapped, and making successive appeals to the national courts to allow the City of Calais the right to demolish the entire camp (*Independent*, 2016a). By contrast, Damien Carême, the Green Party Mayor of Grande-Synthe, an industrial satellite town of Dunkerque, fought with the French national government to successfully open in 2016 a camp for 1,200 migrants, mainly Kurdish and Syrian families, which was operated by MSF (Médecins Sans Frontières/Doctors without Borders). Dubbed the 'first official refugee camp in France' (Al Jazeera, 2016; *Telegraph*, 2016a), the Grande-Synthe camp boasted wooden accommodation huts rather than the flimsy tents of the Jungle, documentation for the inhabitants, a rudimentary security system, and uniquely provided access to local schooling for the children. While it prioritised families, it provided, as detailed below, a last-resort home for the unaccompanied young people expelled from Calais who subsequently became homeless. These differences between local and national policy and its implementation once again demonstrate how governance scales are key to understanding the challenges faced by UASC in their journeys.

Rising concerns in the UK over the perceived plight of unaccompanied young migrants in Europe, particularly in Calais, prompted Lord Alf Dubs to propose his amendment to the Immigration Bill (the 'Dubs Amendment' as discussed earlier) that was passing through Parliament in April 2016. In 1938 Lords Dubs, then aged six, was rescued from Nazi-occupied Czechoslovakia by the *Kindertransport* operation that brought nearly 10,000 children to safety in the UK. This made him all too aware of the role that the UK could (and should) make in protecting vulnerable children (*Washington Post*, 2016). The original amendment he proposed was defeated because it included a specific number (albeit a relatively low one), based on what its proposers thought a reasonable proportion of the 26,000 lone migrant children that the charity Save The Children estimated had arrived in Europe in 2015. As it transpired that estimate was low: there were 90,000 children seeking asylum in Europe and the UK was at that time only accepting around 3% of these.

On a further reading in May 2016, Parliament finally passed the Dubs Amendment (Section 67c 'Unaccompanied refugee children: relocation and support' of the 2016 Immigration Act). It states: 'The Secretary of State must, as soon as possible after the passing of this Act, make arrangements to relocate to the United Kingdom and support a specified number of unaccompanied refugee children from other countries in Europe.' However, beyond the general statement in the Act that the number of children 'shall be determined by the Government in consultation with local authorities', the Home Office did not propose any mechanism by which it would specify the number.

Thus by the end of May 2016, there were two pieces of legislation, one UK – the Dubs Amendment – and one EU – the Dublin III regulation, discussed earlier in this chapter – that provided mechanisms by which unaccompanied young people could travel to the UK, but neither was implemented by the Home Office. There was also no UK office for the processing of asylum applications at Calais, the UK border. The absence of any such a processing point at the UK border at Calais or any official monitoring at all of the eligibility of its 'queue', the nearby Jungle, meant that very few young people were able access these safe options. From 2013 when the Dublin III regulation came into force until spring 2016, not a single Calais child was brought to the UK under Dublin III. From spring 2016 until to October 2016, the UK charity Safe Passage managed to negotiate with the Home Office admission for two or three minors a week to the UK from Calais under Dublin III. The fact that the process of locating and monitoring, and advocating for these children was left to ad hoc charities and volunteers, supported by occasional pro bono work of UK and French lawyers, was a major reason why progress was so slow.

> Four kids have [recently] died trying to make the crossing illegally. We knew that most of the children we wouldn't be able to help, because we didn't have enough lawyers, we didn't have enough money, so every month that went by, there'd be another death ... We can't get back to the

situation where there are thousands of children on Britain's doorstep, with dozens dying each year, trying to make a journey they have every legal and moral right to make safely. (George Gabriel, Safe Passage, in *Calais Children: A Case to Answer*, 2017)

The demolition of the Calais camp

On 23 June 2016 the UK EU Membership Referendum returned a 'Leave' vote, increasing existing tensions between the UK and France over the Le Touquet Treaty, and the responsibility for the escalating size of the Calais Jungle (*Guardian*, 2016a). On 2 September 2016, French Interior Minister Bernard Cazeneuve announced that the French government would take down the Calais Jungle 'by the end of the year' (Reuters, 2016). By early October there were rumours among camp volunteers that demolition was imminent because of the potential application of a French law, known as the *trêve hivernale* (winter truce) which prohibits landlords from making anyone homeless between 1 November and 1 April (*The Connexion*, 2014). As the Jungle was not officially recognised by either the French or British authorities, this effectively ruled out the presence of the larger international NGOs who could have otherwise facilitated registration and census facilities, family tracing and legal advice, as well as the more basic necessities of food, water, sanitation and shelter. As it was, the work was managed by an assortment of volunteer organisations – mainly UK groups such as Care4Calais, Calais Action, Help Refugees, and Calais Refugee Community Kitchen, plus those specifically supporting the unaccompanied children like Refugee Youth Service, Hummingbird Centre, Jungle Books, Kids Café, and several others which Sandri (2018) describes as a movement of 'volunteer humanitarianism'. These groups not only had to continue their daily work of providing essential services during late September and early October 2016, but also, deeply concerned that there were no plans for the young people in place, undertook the fraught work of conducting censuses of the camp's inhabitants, particularly those alone and under 18. Given this was a fairly peripatetic population of 10,000, in a vast and unregimented area of heaped tents and lean-tos, with dozens of languages spoken – plus a fairly constant turnover of volunteers (many coming at weekends, or for short periods only) – it was no easy task. Even those groups most familiar with the Jungle, including the co-author of this chapter Sue Clayton (ITV, 2017), were surprised to see the list of names of minors rise from the low hundreds, to over a thousand, to at the final count a figure of over 1,900 young people, about to be left in limbo without even the Jungle for support. This was clearly a humanitarian crisis, or what UNHCR's Vincent Cochetel had called a "civil emergency" a year earlier, when he had asked for an "urgent, comprehensive and sustainable response" to the desperate conditions in Calais (*The Local-Fr*, 2015).

President François Hollande also made repeated appeals to the UK to work with the French to process the refugees, particularly the minors, but the UK government refused. Because of this uncertainty, and increasing clashes with French police and the heavily-armed CRS, many refugees, including unaccompanied minors, started to leave. No one knew how many minors fled the Jungle during October; it was one thing to attempt a census, but quite another to keep track of every child over the following weeks of chaos.

Between 20 and 28 October 2016, the French drafted hundreds of extra CRS into the Jungle. First, they put up notices saying that all food stalls and cafes must close, then erected a temporary registration point at some distance from the camp. Meanwhile, Sue along with other volunteers tried to make rudimentary assessments of those minors that may have rights under Dublin III or Dubs legislation. Sue worked with UK-based law firms to get lawyers to the camp to assess young people's claims, but time was against them. On 25 October the CRS and police began the clearance operation. The registration process quickly became violent and chaotic (*Calais Children: A Case To Answer*, 2017) with many lone minors afraid to leave camp to battle the heavily-armed ranks of CRS to reach the registration tent, and then to face an unknown outcome. Adults and families were made to queue over several days, after which they were to be bussed to regions far from Calais where their claims would be processed under French immigration law. Two thousand adults had already absconded, so the population had fallen from 10,000 to over 7,000. The French removed 5,000 adults and families, leaving almost 2,000 minors alone as the Jungle camp was then set alight, and large-scale industrial demolition began. Most of the minors, though not all, were held in containers on the east side of the Jungle which had previously housed families (*Daily Record*, 2016). Over 100, however, were later discovered to have absconded or been trafficked when the adults left, and over 100 others were not admitted to the containers because they had not completed registration. As British and French politicians continued to argue about who should take the young people, those in the containers were effectively jailed in the container compound, in contravention of their human rights, and given little food and no care or support.

Some Eritrean children breached the compound fence, walked a mile across the empty and now rat-infested camp in the pitch dark, and huddled freezing in the ruins of their old makeshift Ethiopian church (*Independent*, 2016b). However, still no UK officials had arrived to take their names, let alone process their legal claims to protection.

On 29 October President Hollande made the first public acknowledgement that there were unaccompanied minors in the Jungle (*Guardian*, 2016b). One hundred French MPs signed a petition saying that the British should at least assess their potential claims under UK legislation (we have described these legal options earlier in the chapter – the Dubs Amendment and Dublin III). Hollande made a personal phone call to UK Prime Minister Theresa May asking her to comply, but she refused (*Telegraph*, 2016b). However, following significant public pressure and the ongoing lobbying of groups such as Help Refugees and Safe Passage, the Home Office agreed to transfer around 200 minors under the Dubs Amendment. Reflecting the constructions of deserving migrants and the differential porosity of borders, the first group of young people accepted under Dubs were mainly girls, mostly from Eritrea (Townend, 2016). The rest of the minors continued to wait alone in the deserted Jungle, surrounded by fire, toxic smoke, bulldozers and vermin – hardly the 'specialist care' that the then Home Secretary Amber Rudd assured Parliament they were receiving (*Calais Children: A Case To Answer*, 2017). Finally, as after Sangatte, a pragmatic compromise deal was thrashed out between the French and the British. France would place the minors in accommodation known as CAO – Centres d'Accueil et d'Orientation (reception and orientation centres) (PS Migrants, 2017) but only on the assurance that the British would with all speed now begin the long-awaited assessment process, to establish such essential facts as nationality, ethnicity, vulnerability, claims to Dublin III and so on. On 2 November, 1,500 young people were at last bussed by the French to 64 centres which varied considerably in quality. Many were remote 'outward bound' centres only built for occupancy in the summer months and were freezing, and little food was offered. No specialist staffing was provided, and there were documented cases of assaults on the children by temporary and untrained workers (*Independent*, 2017a). The promised Home Office assessments were carried out but many interviews lasted five minutes or less, and were conducted without interpreters, with no written judgements being given. Approximately 700 Dublin III minors were accepted and brought to the UK between November 2016 and March 2017, but very many eligible young people were missed and all those eligible had suffered months or years of unnecessary delay. There was no further movement on Dubs.

Border porosity: who counts as a 'Dubs Amendment' vulnerable child?

In mid-November 2016, the Home Office finally announced its new Dubs criteria. Instead of all under 18s – all people fulfilling the age limit of a child under international law – eligibility was limited to those aged 12 or under; those viewed by the French authorities as being at high risk of sexual exploitation; those aged 15 or under who are of Sudanese or Syrian nationality. Accompanying siblings of a child meeting one of these criteria were also eligible if they were under 18 (Home Office, 2016: 6).

As the volunteer groups had assessed more than 75% of the unaccompanied minors from Calais to be Afghan or Eritrean, this was widely regarded as a Home Office attempt to significantly limit the number of eligible young people. Unicef and Save the Children (2016) criticised the tightening of the criteria, stating that the use of age and nationality went against both the Convention on the Rights of the Child and the Refugee Convention. They conclude that,

> More broadly, the Dubs Amendment was accepted in the spirit of helping the most vulnerable children caught up in this crisis across Europe. Any criteria should be based on prioritisation, not exclusion, and vulnerability and best interests should be the key factors in determining eligibility, not age and nationality (2016: 3).

The limiting of the Dubs criteria represents a border policing practice that hardens the border for some, and makes it more porous for others.

On 18 December, the Home Office declared their assessments of the young people in the CAOs to be over. No solution was offered for the 1,000 minors still in them. More minors absconded at this point; although technically some could qualify to remain in France, their experience of France had been a negative one. The CAOs had in most cases kept them isolated from French society, not providing French language teaching or schooling, or other integration into local communities. In addition, most had suffered from unremitting police and CRS violence in the Calais Jungle.

In February 2017 the then UK Home Secretary Amber Rudd changed the Dubs criteria again, now saying that the nationality requirements outlined in November 2016 would no longer apply, but that Dubs would be limited to 350 children from the whole of Europe, to include the children already transferred under section 67c of the 2016 Immigration Act. She claimed that this number had been decided through consultation with local authorities as to how many they could accept, as laid out in the original Dubs Amendment (Home Office, 2017).

Help Refugees (through lawyers Leigh Day) began judicial review proceedings claiming that the way the Home Office conducted the consultation with local authorities to determine the number of 350 was unlawful, with many local authorities having offered places which the Home Office ignored. In response, the Home Office increased the limit on the number to be allowed into the UK under Dubs to 480 (in total) in April 2017. Another UK law firm, Duncan Lewis, began a related action on behalf of an unaccompanied migrant known as ZS, the most vulnerable of 37 minors whom the firm identified as meeting the original Dubs criteria.

In an apparent bid to shift the focus away from the Calais situation and away from national governmental responsibility, the Home Office now stated that, 'The Government has invited referrals of eligible children from France, Greece and Italy. It will be the responsibility of France, Greece and Italy to decide which children to refer' (Home Office, 2017). There were no mechanisms in place for overseas countries to make such applications, or liaise with UK lawyers and others already working with likely candidates on the ground. Concerns in Parliament about the closure of the Dubs scheme led to a non-binding vote in March 2017 to keep it open, but the numbers and terms (which the Home Office had imposed and changed twice) remained subject to the High Court cases to be heard later in 2017 and 2018.

On 19 February 2017, the French government announced that as the UK had finished its process, it would close the CAOs by the end of March. More children left the centres with no clear destination. Many started heading back to Calais and nearby Grande-Synthe near Dunkerque, which had the only official camp in France. In March 2017, the Mayor of Calais and the local Prefect of Police of Pas-de-Calais instituted a zero tolerance campaign against returning refugees. Refugees were not allowed to 'install themselves' (*s'installer*) and any who were caught were repeatedly arrested and held in detention for up to four days. It also became a criminal offence for Calais citizens to offer shelter or even food to refugees, forcing volunteers to feed minors covertly and risk arrests and fines themselves (*Guardian*, 2017).

There were reports of police tear-gassing minors as they slept in the woods. Refugees tried more risky and dangerous methods of illegal entry to UK; injuries and deaths continued to be reported (Calais Migrant Solidarity, 2017). On 11 April, the Dunkerque camp burnt to the ground, so ruling out the last place of shelter for refugee minors in France.

The election of Emmanuel Macron as French President in May 2017 was followed by a threat from the new president to tear up the Le Touquet Treaty (*Telegraph*, 2017a) because it was seen as creating the conditions that generate the camps in Calais and elsewhere in France through the offshoring of the UK border and border controls (see also King, 2016). In July 2017, the French court over-ruled the Mayor of Calais' policy and ruled that the city of Calais must provide drinking water and sanitation in the Calais industrial zone where increasing numbers of young refugees were arriving, but did not have to provide accommodation (*The Local-Fr*, 2017). Reports suggest that police and CRS violence increased, but what is less often reported is that it is the UK government that continues to pay for this form of policing (*Telegraph*, 2017b).

In September 2017, Safe Passage's parent organisation Citizens UK bought a legal challenge criticising the process used to assess the Calais children for Dublin III eligibility. Their case was rejected by the High Court in September 2017 (Focus on Refugees, 2017) but won in the Court of Appeal in July 2018 where the judge said that the process used had been 'unfair and unlawful' (*Guardian*, 2018c). Similarly, Help Refugees, who had made a legal challenge in November 2017 claiming that the process of local authority consultation, used to determine the number of young people who could be admitted under Dubs, was conducted unlawfully also lost initially (*Independent*, 2017b) then went on to appeal. In October 2018, although the local authority consultation was declared lawful, the judges made similar comments to the Citizens UK case saying that there had been a breach of the 'duty of fairness' in the process because those minors refused entry were not given reasons for being denied permission (*Guardian*, 2018d). These judgements give minors the right to appeal negative decisions, but the length of time it has taken for the cases to be heard and these judgments to be delivered, means that in the meantime many minors have suffered, and may also now be too old to claim as children. The ZS case noted earlier, was heard in the High Court in February–March 2018 and judgment is expected in October 2018.

Volunteer groups in Calais estimate there are over 1,000 refugees back in Calais, of whom around 600 are unaccompanied minors who were in the Jungle at the time of its clearance. Others are now subsisting homeless in the streets in Brussels, where an unofficial camp has grown up near the railway station, and in Paris, where refugees moved to the district of La Chapelle after being dispersed from the Stalingrad quarter. In both cities they are subject to extreme police brutality including threats made with guns, tear gas, pepper spray, and being hit (*Calais Children: A Case To Answer*, 2017). There is no governmental or NGO solution in sight.

Conclusion

It is clear from the detailed analysis above of the Calais situation that international protocols are not observed on the ground in situations where national and territorial disputes skew such conventions in favour of national political and security interests.

To paraphrase Sandri (2018: 69–70):

> The UNHCR repeatedly expressed concerns over the Jungle camp and its deteriorating conditions, urging the UK and France to find solutions for those in Calais and to implement the Common European Asylum System and the Dublin III Treaty (UNHCR 2015). Despite these pressing concerns, and despite the situation in the Jungle being a humanitarian emergency, the French government provided minimal assistance to the population of the camp … UNHCR and other international aid organisations globally face fundamental challenges in persuading local governments to meet their obligations towards refugees and international systems of refugee protection.

Sandri also notes that this puts the 'volunteer-humanitarian' in a particular bind, as they both step in to fill the gaps in state provision – gaps that the larger international NGOs are frequently not able to fill – and seek to provide constructive critique of state and international policy. (The fact that volunteers were being arrested in Calais for feeding homeless and destitute children provides an acute example of this.) Such dilemmas are of particular concern to several of the authors in this collection (see Drammeh, Hughes, Gupta, York and Warren), who have found that our professional roles in this field cross into aid and advocacy as national government increasingly fails to adhere to the spirit of basic international agreements. We also consider it important that national governments offer more transparency about the underlying political and financial policies and arrangements that inflect the 'refugee debate'. In the case of Calais, it is clear that ongoing border tensions between the UK and France, intensified by the Brexit vote, were the driver behind UK government policy. Tess Berry-Hart, Founder of Calais Action, interviewed in Sue Clayton's film *Calais Children: A Case to Answer*:

> 'Now, the government is using security measures at the border, and building a wall to try and eliminate any migration to the UK. The Dubs scheme could have been a life-saver for so many minors in the UK, and yet because of the colouring of the debate over immigration and migration, the very vulnerable (that is unaccompanied children) have been made to suffer.' (*Calais Children: A Case To Answer*, 2017)

The EU Summit in June 2018 underlined the contradictions expressed in the quote above. While leaders made a statement expressing their agreement on heavily controlling refugee arrivals and effectively punishing those already here without papers, the difficult practicalities and humanitarian issues were left unaddressed. It was clear that each country would go on exercising its own regimes, with all the contradictions described earlier in this chapter (*Guardian*, 2018b).

This crucial and painful tension between political exigency, nationalistic politics and increasing xenophobia on the part of governments, versus a rising public sense that human rights are being eroded for many groups, but for lone child migrants maybe more than any other, is one which haunts many of the further debates in the chapters in this collection.

For the UK, this tension has found further expression in the 'Windrush scandal' – where the Home Office began targeting for removal people from the Caribbean countries who had been invited to the UK in the 1960s (one iconic carrier-ship was called the HMT Empire Windrush) to ease a labour shortage. These people who had considered themselves British citizens, had raised families, worked and paid taxes for over 50 years, suddenly found themselves and their children prey to detention and removal, and the Home Office admitted to having destroyed the original records that would have proved their status. It triggered the resignation of Home Secretary Amber Rudd, and caused a number of other appraisals of the 'hostile environment' policy imposed by Rudd and Theresa May, who had been the previous Home Secretary. Unaccompanied migrant children today live in the same shadow as the Windrush generation. For the children and young people, without long-term and humane decisions being made in their cases, and without the rights to education, work and family life that go along with such decisions, they remain in a dreadful and frightening limbo, so generating a system of institutionalised exclusion in the UK and Europe that belies our democratic values and undermines the long-fought-for ideals of suffrage and citizenship.

Note

[1] A key element of the Schengen Agreement was freedom of movement. As of July 2018, only six of the 28 EU member states are not part of the Schengen Area, which provides border-free travel. These six are Bulgaria, Croatia, Cyprus, Republic of Ireland, Romania and UK. Border controls can be implemented in times of emergency – this was done by a number of EU states as a response to the increase in the number of migrants from 2015 onwards.

References

Al Jazeera (2016) 'Refugee crisis: Cautious welcome to Grande-Synthe camp', 9 March, www.aljazeera.com/news/2016/03/refugee-crisis-france-dunkirk-camp-160309032001035.html

Allsopp, J. and Chase, E. (2017) 'Best interests, durable solutions and belonging: policy discourses shaping the futures of unaccompanied migrant and refugee minors coming of age in Europe', *Journal of Ethnic and Migration Studies*, DOI: 10.1080/1369183X.2017.1404265

Amnesty International (2017) *A blueprint for despair: Human rights impact of the EU-Turkey deal*, London: Amnesty International, www.amnesty.eu/content/assets/Reports/EU-Turkey_Deal_Briefing_Formatted_Final_P4840-3.pdf

Anderson, B. (2017) 'Towards a new politics of migration?', *Ethnic and Migration Studies*, 40(9): 1527–37.

Calais Children: A Case To Answer (2017) film, directed by Sue Clayton, UK: Eastwest Pictures, www.calais.gebnet.co.uk and https://vimeo.com/230595898

Calais Migrant Solidarity (2017) 'Deaths at the Calais border', https://calaismigrantsolidarity.wordpress.com/deaths-at-the-calais-border/

Casas-Cortes, M., Covarrubias, S., Heller, C. and Pezzani, L. (2017) 'Clashing cartographies, migrating maps: mapping and the politics of mobility at the external borders of E.U.rope', *ACME*, 16(1): 1–33.

The Connexion (2014) 'Winter evictions ban until April 1', *The Connexion – French News and Views*, 1 November, www.connexionfrance.com/Archive/Winter-evictions-ban-until-April-1

Daily Record (2016) 'Children 'forced to sleep by roadside' after Calais Jungle clearance declared complete', *Daily Record* 27 October, www.dailyrecord.co.uk/news/uk-world-news/children-forced-sleep-roadside-after-9135097

De Graeve, K. and Bex, C. (2017) 'Caringscapes and belonging: an intersectional analysis of care relationships of unaccompanied minors in Belgium', *Children's Geographies*, 15(1): 80–92.

Focus on Refugees (2017) 'Home Office win appeal yet safe passage arrangements not in place', 24 August, http://focusonrefugees.org/uk-home-office-win-appeal-yet-safe-passage-arrangements-not-in-place/

Gill, N. (2016) *Nothing personal? Geographies of governing and activism in the British asylum system*, Oxford: Wiley-Blackwell.

Guardian (2002) 'Sangatte closure date agreed', *Guardian*, 27 September, www.theguardian.com/uk/2002/sep/27/immigration.immigrationandpublicservices

Guardian (2016a) 'Shock in Calais: 'Perhaps the French and English were not best of friends after all'', *Guardian*, 25 June, www.theguardian.com/politics/2016/jun/25/shock-calais-french-english-not-best-friends-jungle-refugees-brexit

Guardian (2016b) 'Do your moral duty over Calais children, Hollande tells UK', *Guardian*, 29 October, www.theguardian.com/world/2016/oct/29/hollande-britain-must-take-fair-share-of-calais-refugee-children

Guardian (2017) 'Calais Mayor bans distribution of food to migrants', *Guardian*, 2 March, www.theguardian.com/world/2017/mar/02/calais-mayor-bans-distribution-of-food-to-migrants

Guardian (2018a) 'The Nauru Files', www.theguardian.com/news/series/nauru-files

Guardian (2018b) 'EU leaders hail summit victory on migration but details scant', *Guardian*, 29 June, www.theguardian.com/world/2018/jun/29/eu-leaders-summit-migration-doubts

Guardian (2018c) 'Home Office misled court about treatment of child refugees from Calais, judges find', *Guardian*, 31 July, www.theguardian.com/uk-news/2018/jul/31/home-office-misled-court-about-treatment-of-child-refugees-from-calais-judges-find

Guardian (2018d) 'Court upholds UK cap on number of child refugees, *Guardian*, 3 October, www.theguardian.com/world/2018/oct/03/court-upholds-uk-cap-on-number-of-child-refugees

Heller, C. and Pezzani, L. (2016) 'Ebbing and flowing: The EU's shifting practices of (non-)assistance and bordering in a time of crisis', Near Futures Online, http://nearfuturesonline.org/ebbing-and-flowing-the-eus-shifting-practices-of-non-assistance-and-bordering-in-a-time-of-crisis/

Help Refugees (2017) 'High Court grants permission to challenge high secretary Amber Rudd over Dubs children', https://helprefugees.org/high-court-grants-permission-challenge-high-secretary-amber-rudd-dubs-children/

Home Office (2016) *Guidance: Implementation of section 67 of the Immigration Act 2016 in France*, Version 2.0 (Archived), www.gov.uk/government/uploads/system/uploads/attachment_data/file/598563/Archived_Implementation_of_section_67_of_the_Immigration_Act_2016_in_France_v2.0.pdf

Home Office (2017) *Policy Statement: Section 67 of the Immigration Act 2016*, www.gov.uk/government/uploads/system/uploads/attachment_data/file/632633/Dubs_policy_statement_-_update.pdf

Independent (2016a) 'Calais Jungle refugee camp will be completely demolished 'very soon', says Mayor', *Independent*, 13 July, www.independent.co.uk/news/world/europe/calais-jungle-refugee-camp-demolition-mayor-natacha-bouchart-a7134426.html

Independent (2016b) 'Refugee children sleeping rough on site of destroyed Calais Jungle – three days after camp was "cleared"', *Independent*, 29 October, www.independent.co.uk/news/world/europe/calais-jungle-latest-refugee children-unaccompanied-minors-camp-migrants-destroyed-relocated-moved-a7386551.html

Independent (2017a) 'Child refugees in France 'neglected' in accommodation centres after UK Home Office rejections', *Independent*, 29 January, www.independent.co.uk/news/world/europe/child-refugees-crisis-france-accomodation-centres-uk-home-office-rejections-middle-east-syria-iraq-a7517141.html

Independent (2017b) 'Dubs amendment: Child refugees 'put in more danger' as court backs Government's refusal to take in more unaccompanied minors', *Independent*, 2 November, www.independent.co.uk/news/uk/home-news/dubs-amendment-child-refugees-danger-help-government-refusal-take-more-home-office-court-ruling-a8032986.html

International Organization for Migration (2016) '2015 Global Migration Trends Factsheet', http://publications.iom.int/system/files/global_migration_trends_2015_factsheet.pdf

Intersos and MMP (2017) *On my own: Protection challenges for unaccompanied and separated children in Jordan, Lebanon and Greece*, Intersos and Migration Policy Centre.

ITV News (2017) 'Who are the Calais jungle children eligible for UK home?' ITV News, 14 October, www.itv.com/news/2016-10-14/calais-children-new-home-in-uk/

Jones, R. (2016) *Violent borders: Refugees and the right to move*, London: Verso.

Kanics, J. and Senovilla Hernández, D. (2010) 'Protected or merely tolerated? Models of reception and regularization of unaccompanied and separated children in Europe', in J. Kanics, D. Senovilla Hernández and K. Touzenis (eds) *Migrating alone: Unaccompanied and separated children's migration to Europe*, Paris: UNESCO Publishing, pp 3–20.

King, N. (2016) *No borders: The politics of immigration control and resistance*, London: Zed Books.

The Local-Fr (2015) 'Calais: UN urges France to draw up crisis plan', *The Local-Fr*, www.thelocal.fr/20150807/un-tells-france-to-draw-up-civil-crisis-plan

The Local-Fr (2017) 'French Court orders Calais to Provide drinking water for migrants but not shelter', *The Local-Fr*, www.thelocal.fr/20170627/french-court-orders-calais-to-provide-drinking-water-for-migrants-but-not-shelter

Mountz, A. (2010) *Seeking asylum: Human smuggling and bureaucracy at the border*, Minneapolis: University of Minnesota Press.

Phillips, S. (2016) 'These refugees are children, cold, alone and at risk. That's why I voted to help them', *Guardian*, 27 April, www.theguardian.com/commentisfree/2016/apr/27/refugees-children-at-risk-voted-tory-whip-stephen-phillips

Pobjoy, J.M. (2017) *The child in international refugee law*, Cambridge: Cambridge University Press.

PS Migrants (2017) 'Les centres d'accueil et d'orientation (CAO)', www.psmigrants.org/site/ressources-juridiques/cao/

Reuters (2016) 'Calais migrant 'Jungle' camp to be dismantled 'as soon as possible', says France', Reuters, 2 September, www.reuters.com/article/us-europe-migrants-calais/calais-migrant-jungle-camp-to-be-dismantled-as-soon-as-possible-says-france-idUSKCN1182DR

Safe Passage (2017) 'Hundreds of unaccompanied refugee children 'could have been unlawfully denied family reunion'', 22 May, http://safepassage.org.uk/press_posts/hundreds-of-unaccompanied-refugee-children-could-have-been-unlawfully-denied-family-reunion/

Sandri, E (2018) "'Volunteer Humanitarianism': volunteers and humanitarian aid in the Jungle refugee camp of Calais', *Journal of Ethnic and Migration Studies*, 44(1): 65–80.

Telegraph (2016a) 'France's first ever internationally recognised refugee camp opens near Dunkirk', *Telegraph*, 7 March, www.telegraph.co.uk/news/worldnews/europe/france/12186407/Frances-first-ever-internationally-recognised-refugee-camp-opens-near-Dunkirk.html

Telegraph (2016b) 'Theresa May refuses to bow down to Francoise Hollande after he rings up to demand Britain accepts nearly 1,500 migrant children', *Telegraph*, 30 October, www.telegraph.co.uk/news/2016/10/29/france-demands-that-britain-accept-nearly-1500-migrant-children/

Telegraph (2017a) 'What is the Le Touquet border control treaty and can Emmanuel Macron tear it up?', *Telegraph*, 9 May, www.telegraph.co.uk/news/2017/05/09/le-touquet-treaty/

Telegraph (2017b) 'France won't scrap UK border controls in Calais but Britain must pay more, says French interior minister', *Telegraph*, 21 June, www.telegraph.co.uk/news/2017/06/21/france-wont-scrap-uk-border-controls-calais-britain-must-pay/

Townend, M. (2016) 'More than 50 child refugees arrive in Britain as Calais camp faces destruction', *Observer*, 23 October, www.theguardian.com/world/2016/oct/22/lone-child-refugees-unaccompanied-dubs-amendment-arrive-uk-calais

UK Government and Government of France (2018) *Treaty between the Government of the United Kingdom of Great Britain and Northern Ireland and the Government of the French Republic concerning the reinforcement of co-operation for the co-ordinated management of their shared border*, https://assets.publishing.service.gov.uk/government/uploads/system/uploads/attachment_data/file/674885/Treaty_Concerning_the_Reinforcement_Of_Cooperation_For_The_Coordinated_Management_Of_Their_Shared_Border.pdf

Unicef (2017) *A child is a child: protecting children on the move from violence, abuse and exploitation*, New York: Unicef, www.unicef.org/publications/files/UNICEF_A_child_is_a_child_May_2017_EN.pdf

Unicef and Save the Children (2016) 'What next for child refugees in Europe?', https://downloads.unicef.org.uk/wp-content/uploads/2016/12/Unicef-UK-and-Save-the-Children-Briefing-on-the-Refugee-Crisis-in-Europe-15_12_2016.pdf

Unicef and Save the Children (2017) 'Keeping families together: retaining children's rights to family reunion through Brexit', https://downloads.unicef.org.uk/wp-content/uploads/2017/06/KeepingFamiliesTogether_FINAL.pdf?_ga=2.131085199.1256661414.1508954257-1805529564.1497980189

Washington Post (2016) 'They were rescued as kids in WWII. Now they want to help today's refugee children', *Washington Post*, 27 March, www.washingtonpost.com/world/europe/they-were-rescued-as-kids-in-wwii-now-they-want-to-help-todays-refugee-children/2016/03/27/6acf58a9-3044-4c59-b1a7-db155f059820_story.html?utm_term=.89ea8f3db01b

TWO

Dilemmas and conflicts in the legal system

Sheona York and Richard Warren

Introduction

The unaccompanied child seeking asylum occupies an ambiguous space in political and legal discourses. The discourse of childhood often presents them as vulnerable victims of circumstances beyond their control, devoid of agency. On the other hand, in discourses around asylum and migration, terms such as 'illegal migrant' construct them as manipulative, potentially dangerous – the unknown and threatening 'other'. As soon as they arrive in the UK, young asylum seekers find themselves caught between two domains of law that mirror those contrasting political discourses: the protective framework of care law provided by the Children Act 1989 and motivated by the principle of the child's welfare being paramount – 'Every Child Matters' – and the punitive framework of numerous Immigration Acts dominated by the call for 'Securing our Borders: Controlling Migration' (UK Border Agency, 2010). It is the latter that has shaped the legal framework governing determination of young people's asylum claims.

It has long been recognised that child asylum seekers are a particularly vulnerable sub-section of an already vulnerable population. Yet despite this recognition, child asylum seekers coming to the UK face particular obstacles in making their claims for asylum. This chapter will explore the recent developments in the UK's approach to children seeking asylum. This chapter will consider how the asylum system has in many cases failed to provide durable solutions for child refugees. It will question why, despite well-written guidelines and public awareness of the specific protection needs of children from conflict zones, the success rate for child asylum claims is often lower than for adults from the same country. It will then consider the legal obstacles that young asylum seekers face and the complexities of the system they are forced to navigate.

This chapter opens with a comparison between law in theory and law in practice as it applies to young asylum seekers. We highlight specific problematic issues: assessing credibility, the provision of legal aid, and delay in decision making. Two case studies then illustrate the uncertain journeys through the legal process faced by two of the largest groups of asylum-seeking young people: Afghans and Eritreans.

The law in theory

UK asylum law and guidance provide a number of protective measures for young asylum seekers. However, as we will consider in the subsequent section, in practice many of these do not survive implementation by a government department whose primary drive is to reduce migration numbers.

Until 2008 the UK government opted out of applying the United Nations Convention on the Rights of the Child (UNCRC) to immigration issues. Child asylum seekers were treated as migrants first and children second. In 2008 the government removed the opt-out, and from November 2009, Section 55 of the Borders, Citizenship and Immigration Act (BICA) 2009 required the Secretary of State to ensure that immigration, asylum and nationality functions are discharged 'having regard to the need to safeguard and promote the welfare of children'. The case of *ZH Tanzania* interpreted this as requiring immigration decision makers to treat the 'best interests' of a child as a 'primary consideration'.[1] Home Office guidance now refers to enabling children to have optimum life chances so as to enter adulthood successfully (Home Office, 2016a: 45).

Other child-specific legal protections include prohibitions on detention except in very exceptional circumstances, for the shortest possible time and with appropriate care (Home Office, 2016b). The Dublin III Regulation, intended to inhibit 'asylum-shopping' within the EU, prevents the host country from returning children to other safe EU countries they have passed through.[2] There is also a duty to facilitate family reunion, which may require the UK to assist an asylum-seeking child to enter the UK from another member state to join a family member resident in the UK.[3]

In order to obtain asylum, an applicant has to demonstrate that they meet the definition of a refugee set out in Article 1A of the 1951 Refugee Convention[4] or that they qualify for humanitarian protection under the EU Qualification Directive.[5] In the UK all asylum applicants over the age of 12 are usually interviewed in order to assess whether they meet these legal definitions. The EU Reception and Procedure

Directives require that children be provided with legal representation prior to their asylum interview[6] and children's cases must be allocated to trained caseowners.[7] The UK Immigration Rules recognise that because of potential vulnerability, children's cases must be given particular priority and care:

> ... account should be taken of the applicant's maturity and in assessing the claim of a child more weight should be given to objective indications of risk than to the child's state of mind and understanding of his situation. An asylum application made on behalf of a child should not be refused solely because the child is too young to understand his situation or to have formed a well founded fear of persecution. Close attention should be given to the welfare of the child at all times.[8]

Home Office guidance on interviewing children requires the presence of a parent, guardian, representative or another adult, and sensitivity to a child's potential inhibition or alarm. The child should be allowed to express themselves in their own way and at their own speed. Regular breaks must be offered. If the child appears tired or distressed, the interview should be stopped.[9] For less mature children, the benefit of the doubt should be applied more liberally (Home Office, 2016b).[10]

Guidance also addresses the particular problems of assessing the risk on return for a child. Historically, 'asylum' has been equated with the protection of political or religious dissidents, generally adult males, with children viewed as dependants whose own risk would arise, if at all, from an imputed political opinion or religious belief. However, refugee law requires that the assessment of risk is based on the individual characteristics of the applicant, so an assessment of a child's claim must consider their age, maturity and past experiences.

The UN Refugee Convention has increasingly been interpreted by European states in a way that recognises specific forms of persecution that disproportionately affect children.[11] Children may have faced significant abuses at home, at work, on the streets and in institutions ostensibly there to protect them. This may include harmful traditional practices such as female genital mutilation (FGM) and forced marriage as well as domestic violence, child labour, and recruitment by armed groups. States are often complicit, or unable to provide enforceable legal protection.

UNHCR guidelines[12] call for children to be recognised as 'active subjects of rights', rather than being viewed through the prism of adult experiences. The 'best interests' principle requires that harm is assessed from the child's perspective and that consideration is given to socioeconomic rights, which may be as relevant in a child's claim as civil and political rights. For children, discrimination or an accumulation of less serious violations of rights may amount to persecution.

For anyone, adult or child, to qualify as a refugee under the 1951 United Nations Refugee Convention it is necessary to show a well-founded fear of persecution for one of the five Convention reasons.[13] The principal 'Convention reason' applying to children is that of belonging to a 'particular social group' (PSG). Age has been accepted as constituting a PSG, in that although age changes with time, at any specific time it is an 'immutable characteristic'. Therefore, children from groups such as 'street children', 'orphans' or 'children with disabilities' may, depending on country conditions, qualify for refugee status. The Asylum and Immigration Tribunal judgement in the case of *LQ Afghanistan*[14] accepted that an Afghan child with no family would face a real risk of persecution if returned alone to Kabul, given the nature of Afghan society and the lack of protection available to children.

Adult asylum claims based on a fear of non-state actors are frequently refused on the grounds that the applicant could return to a different, safe, part of their country ('internal flight alternative', IFA). For example, Afghan asylum seekers are often expected to return to Kabul. The legal test is whether such relocation would be 'unduly harsh', considering the specific characteristics of the applicant.[15] For children, UNHCR guidelines require consideration of their best interests and their long-term life prospects. What might be 'reasonable' for an adult may not be reasonable for a child.[16] Conversely, what is merely inconvenient for an adult might be 'unduly harsh' for a child.

When assessing claims for humanitarian protection based on a fear of 'indiscriminate violence', decision makers must also consider the individual characteristics of the applicant. The more the applicant is able to show that he or she is specifically affected by reason of factors particular to his/her personal circumstances, the lower the level of indiscriminate violence required for him/her to be eligible for subsidiary protection.[17] Therefore, in conflict zones where children are particularly affected, it should be easier for them to make out a claim for humanitarian protection.

Judicial guidance on the conduct of children's asylum appeals recognises the child's potential vulnerability. Judges are directed to exclude the public when a child is giving evidence, and children must be protected from improper or aggressive cross-examination.[18]

A 2008 practice direction[19] confirms that a child will only be required to attend and give evidence at a hearing where necessary to enable the fair hearing of the case and where their welfare would not be prejudiced.[20]

The law in practice

Thus the UK asylum process contains important legal protections for children. However, despite the progressive guidance and positive legal developments, the legal outcomes for children seeking asylum in the UK have historically been poor.

The number of unaccompanied minors arriving in the UK rose significantly in the years 2015 and 2016, with over 3,000 new arrivals each year. Home Office statistics recorded that, of 2,084 children's applications decided in the year ending June 2016, which was at the height of the large number of arrivals, 74% resulted in grants of asylum or another form of protection (Home Office, 2016c). However, most of these were grants of UASC leave,[21] a temporary status granted only on the basis that they are still under 18, following a *refusal* of asylum or humanitarian protection. UASC leave is granted where there are 'no adequate reception arrangements' in the home country. This is not a recognition of a risk of serious harm because of the lack of reception facilities, only that the conditions on return cannot be established and therefore leave is granted as an 'additional precaution'.[22] The Home Office now considers UASC leave to be 'precarious'[23] and thus not providing any basis for a subsequent claim to remain based on the right to private life under Article 8 of the European Convention of Human Rights (ECHR).

If we look at the long-term trend we can see that historically most unaccompanied minors have been granted such a status rather than Asylum or Humanitarian Protection (See Figure 2).

The data does now show a welcome increase in protection status being granted at initial decision in 2016 and 2017. Whether this is a long-term improvement in response to criticism remains to be seen.

However, if we consider the year 2015, which saw a significant rise in the number of new arrivals of unaccompanied asylum-seeking children, only 22.7% were granted asylum (21.7%) or humanitarian protection (1%). The grant rate for adults and UASC together was 35.2% (34.8% asylum and 0.4% humanitarian protection). In particular, for several major refugee-producing countries known for significant human rights violations, the grant rate of refugee status was lower for unaccompanied children than it was for adults (see Table 2).

Figure 2: UASC protection rate trends, 2006–17 (% of asylum seekers aged under 18)

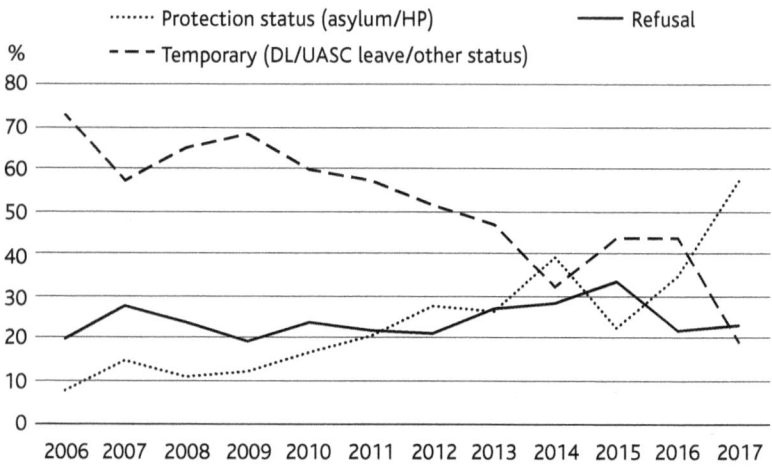

Source: Home Office immigration statistics year ending March 2018

Table 2: Initial grant rates for top eight nationalities (all applicants), year ending June 2015

	Grant rate for all initial decisions (%)		Grant rate for adults (calculated by subtracting UASC claims from total) (%)		Grant rate on initial decisions for applicants who arrived as UASC (%)	
	Refugee status	Humanitarian protection	Refugee status	Humanitarian protection	Refugee status	Humanitarian protection
Eritrea	41.3	1.3	41.9	1	37.8	3.2
Iran	53	0.3	53.7	0.3	34.6	0
Sudan	85	0.1	84.7	0.1	94.5	0
Syria	84.4	0.3	86.6	0.3	40.4[a]	0
Pakistan	19.5	0	19.5	0	23.1	0
Afghanistan	22.5	0	23.8	0.1	16.4	0.1
Iraq	13.7	1.2	13.9	0.8	8.9	11.1
Albania	0.5	0	0.7	0	0.2	0

Note: [a]The particularly low grant rate for young Syrians may be explained by the fact that the Home Office frequently dispute the nationality of young Syrians arriving without documentation.

Source: Data taken from Home Office: Immigration Statistics April–June 2016 for the year ending June 2015: https://www.gov.uk/government/publications/immigration-statistics-april-to-june-2016/asylum#data-tables. The Home Office records data for all initial asylum claims, and separate statistics for UASC asylum claims. The figure for adults has been calculated by subtracting the data for UASC from the data for all claims.

While there are many factors that may explain variations in grant rate, including changing countries of origin and changing Home Office policies, it is hard to understand why the grant rates should have been lower for minors given the additional legal protections accorded to children and the accepted child-specific persecution occurring in many of these countries.

For young asylum seekers the consequence of the difference in outcome is stark. Until recently, UK practice has been to facilitate the settlement of recognised refugees and those granted humanitarian protection, with a grant of five years leave to remain giving the right to work, access to welfare support and, importantly for young people, access to university education with home tuition fees and student loans; followed by indefinite leave to remain (ILR).[24]

In contrast, UASC leave lasts until the age of 17.5 years with no further leave except where the young person can qualify on another basis. Following intense litigation (see York, 2015, for a critical review) and new primary legislation directing judges on deciding Article 8 appeals,[25] it is now difficult for young people to qualify for further leave on the basis of their family or private life in the UK.[26] Many have formed strong attachments with foster carers and other significant adults during their stay in the UK, though these attachments are often treated as an aspect of their private life rather than family life. Since UASC leave is seen as 'precarious', judges are directed to attach little weight when balancing this against the state's right to enforce immigration control against a former child asylum seeker. The Upper Tribunal (Immigration and Asylum Chamber) case of Miah (section 117B NIAA 2002 – children) [2016] UKUT 00131(IAC) concerned a Bangladeshi trafficking victim who arrived aged 13. His parents hired him out to a master who enslaved him, beat him and abandoned him. The local authority placed him in foster care. He was granted discretionary leave. The tribunal accepted his account, including that he had no family, no social network or any source of income to return to and would face destitution on return. However, his appeal was not finally heard until he was 20, and was dismissed. Since his stay had been 'precarious', 'little weight' could be given to his Article 8 rights to respect for private and family life under the ECHR. The first tier judge[27] noted that applying the law in this way 'would appear to contradict numerous policy statements made by the Secretary of State about the importance of stability, roots and relationships for such children'.[28] Indeed, dismissing his onward appeal, the President of the Upper Tribunal stated that while the 'impact [of the law] on children will appear harsh and unfair to many, this is the unavoidable consequence of the legislative choice which Parliament has made'.[29] The Supreme Court is now due to consider whether this interpretation is compatible with Article 8 ECHR as understood in Strasbourg jurisprudence (see Warren, 2016, note 27).[30]

The UK's determination to cut off the rights and entitlements of young people from the age of 17.5 contrasts with some other European states' policies permitting young people in education or employment to renew their leave. Home Office guidance is clear that once a child reaches 17.5 they should be refused leave, and make use of the six months before becoming 18 to prepare for return. Once 18, no 'best interests' consideration applies to them (Home Office, 2016b: 68); they can be detained and removed, and not surprisingly many abscond from local authority care. The consequences of such policies are discussed further by Lucy Williams in Chapter Seven.

In 2013 Home Secretary (now, as at July 2018, Prime Minister) Theresa May promised to introduce a 'hostile environment' for irregular migrants (*Guardian*, 2013), a pledge made good by the passing of the Immigration Acts 2014 and 2016. Irregular migrants, including young people refused asylum, may not work, hold a bank account, drive a car, access anything but emergency health care, or live in private rented property; and the majority will have no access to any form of accommodation or subsistence.

Currently all UK 'looked after' children are entitled to 'leaving care' support until the age of 21, or 25 if they are in full-time education. However, when fully implemented, the Immigration Act 2016 will deny 'leaving care' support to those refused leave to remain. In contrast, provisions of the Children and Families Act 2014 extend the 'staying put' arrangements for UK and settled children in foster care until they are 21 years old – recognising that many young people need continuing support during a prolonged transition to adulthood (see also Chapter Three for discussion on leaving care support).

We would argue that the only secure legal status for a child asylum seeker is a grant of asylum or humanitarian protection.[31] The alternative is an increasingly abrupt transition at 18 to the 'hostile environment', as discussed in Chapters Three and Seven. This makes it essential that if a young person is a refugee that their asylum claim is processed promptly and correctly when they first arrive.

The next sections consider specific legal obstacles faced by young asylum seekers: credibility, legal advice and delay.

Credibility

The predominance of decisions based on credibility (whether the asylum seeker is to be believed) in immigration and asylum claims arises from the fact that, unlike in civil law matters, the burden of proof lies with the applicant (Home Office, 2015a: 8). Though the Immigration Rules place a duty on the Secretary of State in asylum cases to assess the information the applicant puts forward 'in co-operation with the person', in very few cases indeed is there any communication between the Home Office caseworker and an asylum applicant apart from formal interviews and refusals.[32] Home Office guidance hints at a cooperative procedure: 'Caseworkers must examine, investigate and research the available evidence and, if appropriate, invite submission of further evidence, although the caseworker may well be in a better position than the claimant to substantiate aspects of the account' (Home Office, 2015a: 8).

On credibility of children, Home Office guidance has this to say:

> For example, a 16 year old boy would not necessarily be able to provide details of his father's political activities and an illiterate farm worker would not necessarily be able to provide details of national political developments despite being a supporter of the political opposition. (Home Office, 2015a: 14)

However, Home Office asylum decision making in respect of children has always been bedevilled with the same overemphasis on credibility as in decision making on adult claims. A 2009 UNHCR report noted that while 1 in 10 of decisions examined did assess credibility in an age-sensitive manner,

> … in almost a half of the decisions assessed, there is no explicit consideration of age in the credibility assessment and no attempt to consider age-specific mitigating factors when considering the level of detail and consistency in the applicant's account … (UNHCR, 2009: 25).

The UNHCR report noted children being required to 'prove' aspects of their claim, and disbelieved if they could not provide enough evidence, and a failure of the Home Office to properly understand and apply the benefit of the doubt. National Audit Office reports have noted the ineffectiveness of the Home Office's own internal audits on decision making quality.[33]

There has been significant academic research concerning the assumptions made by decision makers assessing asylum-seeker's credibility, and the difficulties that especially young asylum seekers face in setting out a narrative history that conforms to certain expectations (Herlihy et al, 2002; Rouseea et al, 2002; Herlihy et al, 2010). The higher courts have cautioned decision makers against applying western conceptions of what is plausible behaviour in the context of claims from individuals from diverse backgrounds.[34]

However, the focus on credibility is built into primary legislation. Under Section 8 of the Asylum and Immigration (Treatment of Claimants) Act (AI(TC)A) 2004 certain behaviours have to be considered by decision makers as damaging to an applicant's credibility.[35] Home Office guidance cautions against applying this rigorously to children. Yet Section 8 is often referred to in refusal letters for young people who have passed through third countries such as Italy and Greece, where a failure to claim asylum there is said to damage their credibility despite evidence and case law pointing to the risk of harm for young asylum seekers in those countries.[36]

The difficulties of narrating a history of persecution are compounded for children and young people (Given-Wilson et al, 2017). Neurological and psychological evidence indicates that mental development continues into an individual's early twenties. Studies have shown that autobiographical memory develops through adolescence (Habermas and de Silveira, 2008). Furthermore, cultural factors can influence the ability to narrate a life history (Wang, 2004; Chen et al, 2013). Children from cultures where there is less emphasis placed on the individual may be less able to provide detailed memories focusing on their own feelings and motivations. Yet an inability to narrate details, provide a consistent account or provide an explanation for the actions of adults in the story are frequently used as justification for dismissing a claim.

Psychological issues can clearly have an impact on memory (Kuyken and Dalgleish, 2011) and it has been shown that mental illness among asylum-seeking children in western countries is a significant concern (Fazel et al, 2012). Brennen et al (2010) showed that adolescents exposed to war conditions had less specific autobiographical memories than those not exposed to war. Many young people who arrive in the UK report suffering from sleep disorders as a result of traumatic journeys, where vigilance at night is essential to their survival (Draper, 2016). Despite this, due to the difficulties faced by young asylum seekers in accessing mental health support (Mind, 2009), specific evidence of trauma may not be presented as evidence, and low level mental health issues may be overlooked when assessing a young person's credibility. Further discussion on the evaluation of young people's narratives and credibility is included in Chapter Three, and the implications for young people of the complications and stresses of asylum processes are discussed in Section 2 of this collection.

A number of more recent reports on children's asylum claims show that the failure to consider applications in an age-sensitive way and in accordance with guidance continues. Some specific issues are highlighted below.

Screening interviews; initial interviews

On arrival, children are generally first subjected to a screening interview to record basic personal details, a summary of their journey to the UK and information about the basis of the claim. A 2012 Children's Commissioner report revealed that children were being required to sign screening interview records in the absence of appropriate safeguards. That report concluded that newly-arrived children are generally not fit for interview. The Court of Appeal in the case of *AN (a child) & FA (a child)* v SSHD [2012] EWCA Civ 1636 held that a child should not be interviewed about the substance of their asylum claims without an appropriate adult. It was held inappropriate to interview a vulnerable child immediately following a long and tiring journey; and initial detention and interview should only be for the purposes of protecting their welfare. Where these principles have been breached '... it ought at the very least to be exceedingly difficult to persuade the court to admit material that has been thereby obtained'.[37]

However, all the cited reports give examples of children and young people being subjected to on-entry interviews carried out without a lawyer or responsible adult, and sometimes before being allowed to wash, eat or drink. In some cases that initial interview had a specific negative impact on the case (Warren and York, 2014). Clearly, so long as the Home Office asylum determination procedure *in practice* continues to be based on finding inconsistencies in a child's account, safeguards must be put in place. These include time to meet a legal adviser before any interview, adequate interpreting, a proper evidence trail and accurate recording of the interview.

At the time of writing in July 2018 this process had been recently amended to introduce a more limited on-entry welfare interview, in conjunction with the dispersal of newly-arrived child asylum seekers from Kent to other local authority areas. However, this interview still asks the young person on arrival to provide brief details of why they left their country.

Use of age assessments to dispute credibility

One of the first legal issues facing a young person seeking asylum is for children's services to decide if they are a child, and if so to establish their age and consequent entitlement to services under the Children Act 1989 if assessed as under 18. Statutory guidance issued by the Department for Education advises that age assessments should not be a routine part of a local authority's assessment of an unaccompanied child and should only be carried out where there is significant reason to doubt the claimant is a child (Department of Education, 2017). However, some local authorities appear not to follow this and carry out assessments on large numbers of those who have already been accepted as children. Thus the young person must relate their story to a second possibly sceptical government authority, again without any legal advice. The legal issues surrounding age assessments themselves are not discussed here (age assessments are discussed in Chapter Three), but the impact on credibility of having an assessed age different from the claimed age can be significant. The Home Office published policy on age assessments (Home Office, 2015b) acknowledges that an age assessment report is based on notes, rather than a verbatim record. Minor discrepancies between the age assessment and information given to the Home Office should, generally, not be investigated further, nor relied upon, and if they are the applicant '*must be given the opportunity to explain or clarify the discrepancy in question*' (Home Office, 2015b: 11, emphasis in the original). However, despite this impeccable guidance, discrepancies have been alleged and relied on in refusal letters without the age assessment information ever being made available to the applicant (Warren and York, 2014).

The satellite litigation on age disputes shows that the science does not support age assessments more accurate than plus or minus two years (Home Office, 2015b: 15–16). Despite this, some social workers make precise age assessments of only a few months difference from the claimed age. Such a decision in itself has sometimes provided the grounds for a negative credibility assessment of the whole of the applicant's evidence, both by the Home Office and in the tribunal.[38]

The next section considers a further cause for concern, which is the compromising of young people's access to legal advice and representation by the cuts to legal aid.

Changes to legal aid and the provision of advice and representation

The impact of good quality legal advice in securing favourable outcomes in asylum cases has been well documented. An empirical study published in 2011 of 182 appeals showed success rates of 31% for represented asylum appellants and 12% for those unrepresented (Thomas, 2011: 116–7). A 2012 Freedom of Information Act request to HM Courts and Tribunals Service revealed that, for the year April 2011 to March 2012, the success rate for unrepresented asylum appellants was 4.9%.[39]

Arguably legal aid[40] is even more important for young people, as they are likely to have even less understanding of the asylum process and be less able to prepare their own claim. Reports show the difficulties young people face in accessing good quality immigration advice (see, for example, Refugee Council, 2011), despite the availability of best practice guidance[41] and specific legal aid contract provisions for children's cases, such as legal representation at asylum interviews.

The introduction in 2013 of the Legal Aid, Sentencing and Punishment of Offenders Act (LASPO) 2012 led to a dramatic reduction in the availability of legal aid for immigration advice. However, we believe that changes in legal aid provision in immigration and asylum over the previous decade have had complex effects on the delivery of asylum legal aid, leading to a deteriorating service, especially for young people. Historically there had been concerns about the quality of legal work in this sector. To combat this, the Immigration and Asylum Act 1999 introduced a system of regulation for immigration and asylum advice, including a new regulatory body, the Office of the Immigration Supervision Commissioner (OISC) and the criminalisation of unregulated advisers. Then in 2004 the Legal Services Commission (LSC) introduced a separate accreditation scheme for those working under legal aid contracts, requiring a high level of expertise and knowledge. Both schemes were flawed from the beginning. Private solicitors not acting under legal aid were exempt altogether. Even those solicitors and advisers who passed the accreditation exams were often insufficiently experienced and insufficiently supervised to provide a good service, especially when faced with complex cases. The Legal Services Commission auditing concentrated on checking applicants' financial eligibility and the proper accounting for legal disbursements and this system did not include peer review of quality of casework. But the very structure of legal aid contracts, and the structure and level of payments for casework, were inimical to ensuring good quality work and, eventually, for many providers, led to poor work or insolvency or both.

In every contract round, numbers of experienced solicitors and reputable firms faced with new restrictive legal aid contracts limited themselves to private paying work or ceased legal work altogether (Singh and Webber, 2010). Providers found they could more easily make the contract pay by segmenting legal cases, assigning initial applications to the least-qualified staff, with the best-qualified and most experienced staff retained for the higher-paying onward appeals and judicial reviews. Thus each contract round saw more 'matter starts'[42] taken up by 'case segmentation' providers both large and small, private and not for profit.

However, this style of work was always singularly unsuited to a legal arena in which 'get it right first time' was fundamental to the success of a client's case. Crucially, in a world where the burden of proof falls upon the applicant, where the public body dealing with the case operates precisely on a consideration of small discrepancies, lack of detail, and where a first Home Office decision and the first tribunal determination act like an indelible mark on the applicant's entire future, case segmentation was for many an unmitigated disaster. Any solicitor dealing with onward appeals, or looking to assist 'failed asylum seekers', will see claims that have failed because of poor case preparation and wrong case strategies from the start.

In 2006 the LSC introduced the '40% success rate', penalising providers if they did not win over 40% of immigration and asylum appeals in the year. It did not matter if the client later won their case. Inevitably, to meet this target, providers refused funding even to meritorious cases. Research shows that 'if similar results were to be found across the country, it would suggest that legal representatives are wrongly refusing [funding] in almost four out of every five cases' (Devon Law Centre, 2010).

The case segmentation model became integral to the way legal aid casework was remunerated. It also underpinned the second catastrophic feature of pre-LASPO legal aid, namely the fixed fee, fixed for each segment or stage of a case. This militates against a professional approach to casework, and forces providers to choose quick cases that would 'cost' less than the fixed fee, and avoid complex cases unless they would cost three times the fixed fee (permitting a provider to bill for all the time spent). The value of the fixed fee was set so low that conscientious providers could not complete the work in the time.[43] All this was compounded in 2011 by the 10% reduction in all civil legal aid payments. The Legal Action Group

(2012) highlighted the insolvency of Refugee Migrant Justice (RMJ) in June 2010 and of the Immigration Advisory Service (IAS) in July 2011, which were responsible for around 35,000 immigration and asylum legal aid matter starts between them, and reported that 2011 saw a fall in around £20m spent on legal aid in immigration and asylum, of which £12m was in asylum, despite an 11% increase in the number of asylum claimants.

The effect of all this was that, even before LASPO became law, many applicants were unable to find representation even though asylum work would continue to be covered by legal aid. Following LASPO, two contract rounds have resulted in a significant consolidation of the asylum legal aid 'market' into a few large enterprises operating a case segmentation model, and a very few not-for-profit agencies relying on additional grants to support a holistic work model specialising in particular types of claims such as children, gender-based claims and trafficking. Advice and representation in asylum claims remained in scope. However, legal aid was removed for most non-asylum immigration matters including those based on family and private life, or the best interests of a child, even where a child or young person is the applicant.[44] The sections below examine the impact of these developments on unaccompanied asylum-seeking young people.

The impact of changes to legal aid and legal processes on young people

First, there are now so few asylum legal aid providers that many young people have had to travel long distances to find a solicitor. This has been particularly noticeable in Kent, which owing to its proximity to the continent has, until recently, been responsible for supporting a large number of new arrivals. Under the Immigration Act 2016[45] newly-arrived young people are now quickly transferred to other local authority areas, many with little experience of working with local asylum lawyers, and some areas with no lawyers at all (Refugee Children's Consortium, 2017).

Second, despite the fact a 'fresh claim' for asylum is eligible for legal aid, the work is subject to the fixed fee if the applicant is over 18. Because a prerequisite for most successful fresh claims is a meticulous, forensic consideration of all previous decisions and tribunal determinations, some providers refuse to take on such work. NGOs have proposed systems where volunteers might review a client's case to support a referral, or to apply for exceptional funding,[46] but no *pro bono* scheme could meet the demand.

Third, following the introduction of LASPO there has been no legal aid to support young people's wider arguments about their family and private life in the UK. Kent is host to many 'failed asylum seekers' who have formed families with local people. Some now have their own children who are British or who are European Economic Area (EEA) nationals. Some young people may well have an arguable claim based on both fear of return and Article 8 ECHR rights, yet only the protection claim will be funded by legal aid. Statistics show that until recently it has been hard to apply successfully for exceptional funding, but even since the case of *Gudanaviciene* (see note 46) few providers are willing to pursue such applications as they cannot rely on being paid for that work (Connolly et al, 2017).

Delayed decisions

A further concern is the delays in Home Office decisions. The immigration rules state that asylum claims from children should be handled with care and treated as a priority.[47] Former Home Office guidance set out a 'best practice' model in which a child's case would remain with a single Home Office case owner, who would conduct the interview. A decision would be made by Day 25 with an appeal being heard by Day 45.[48]

The reality is very different. Frequently the decision maker is not the same person who conducted the asylum interview. Because of the lack of legal aid solicitors, the large numbers of young people who arrived in Kent in 2015 had to wait for legal advice, and wait a further several months before interview. Decisions can then take many months. Statistics released following Freedom of Information requests show that for those arriving in 2015, a significant number were still awaiting an initial decision after 18 months with some waiting more than two years. For example, of the 1,130 young people who arrived in the fourth quarter of 2015, 438 (39%) had not received a decision within 18 months (FOI by Kent Law Clinic 45730). Following refusal an appeal must be lodged within 14 days, but statistics show that at periods it has taken an average of 40 weeks until the first tier tribunal hears and determines the appeal.[49] Cases appealed to the Upper Tribunal may take a further year. In a Kent Law Clinic research example (Warren and York, 2014), a child aged 15, refused after a lengthy delay, won his appeal only for it to be remitted back to the Home Office for another decision. After more delays and appeals he was finally refused when over 18.

Case law has established that an asylum claim must be assessed as at the date of the decision and on appeal, determined at the date of the appeal.[50] It is unlawful to refuse a child on the basis that they will be able to return in several years' time as an adult. The risk on return faced by a lone 13-year-old needs to be assessed on the hypothetical basis that they would be returned at that age, and if they are entitled to refugee status on arrival that should be recognised. Yet Kent Law Clinic have observed a refusal of a 14-year-old at risk of forcible recruitment on the basis that they 'would not be returned until over 18, when they will no longer belong to the particular social group at risk'. Other refusal letters failed to fully consider the best interests of the child, on the basis that when the young person is over 18 'the section 55 duty will no longer apply' (Warren and York, 2014).

Such refusals are being appealed. While the Home Office records data on unaccompanied children's asylum claims, HM Courts and Tribunals Service (HMCTS) does not keep separate data on the success rates for asylum-seeking children.[51] Therefore, there is no official record of how many children are forced to appeal in order to obtain a correct decision. However, legal firms specialising in children's cases report high success rates for claims decided while the child is still under 18.

Appeal success rates for all applicants are high (Table 3), indicating significant problems with initial decisions. A prompt decision on a child's asylum claim is particularly important, since delay may well lead to a child becoming an adult by the time of their appeal hearing. There is evidence that in the past some young people were not advised by their legal representatives to appeal their first refusal

Table 3: Appeal success rate for top eight countries of origin, 2017

Country of origin	Appeals determined	% Appeals allowed
All nationalities	9,224	35.5
Afghanistan	1,099	51.7
Albania	489	29.0
Eritrea	540	36.9
Ethiopia	177	42.9
Iran	2,172	46.1
Iraq	1,703	35.5
Sudan	143	50.3
Vietnam	242	40.9

Source: Home Office Immigration Statistics Year Ending March 2018: Table as_14: Asylum appeal applications and determinations, by country of nationality and sex: 2017, www.gov.uk/government/statistics/immigration-statistics-year-ending-march-2018

while a child, and accepted discretionary/UASC leave without fully comprehending its limited nature (Refugee Council, 2011; Warren and York, 2014). Further applications to remain were then refused, and appeals lost, with the Home Office arguing that the section 55 duty no longer applied, and as mature adults they would not be at risk. However, a number of factors may make it more difficult for a young person to succeed in a later appeal. They may be several more years away from the events that occurred and have greater difficulty recalling contested events; they may look visibly older and more confident, a factor relevant to whether a judge perceives they are able to survive on their own; and they will not have the formal protections afforded to children. While cases such as *KA (Afghanistan)* caution that there is 'no bright line' when assessing risk (as Kay LJ, the judge giving the lead judgement, stated 'persecution is not respectful of birthdays – apparent or assumed age is more important than chronological age'),[52] legal practitioners' experience shows that appeals are more difficult to argue once a young person is over 18. In practice, for asylum seekers the transition from childhood to adulthood is often abrupt, as is discussed further in subsequent chapters, including Chapter Seven.

It has been argued that where Home Office decision making leads to the 'conspicuous unfairness' of a young person being denied a grant of leave to which they were entitled to on arrival, the court should intervene and insist on a grant of leave as a 'corrective remedy'.[53] This line of argument was pursued most forcibly in the litigation surrounding family tracing, discussed in Case Study 1 below. However, the Supreme Court[54] dismissed the argument, reaffirming the Ravichandran principle (see note 50) that an asylum claim be assessed based on the facts at the date of decision. It stated further that it was not the court's role 'to require or encourage the Secretary of State to grant leave in such circumstances either in order to mark the court's displeasure at her conduct, or as a sanction for her misconduct'. After all, the court's proper sphere is illegality, not maladministration.[55] The Supreme Court further dismissed a claim that a delayed appeal for a young asylum seeker was not an effective remedy. Thus lengthy delays in the asylum process are continuing to disadvantage young asylum seekers.

Below we present two case studies showing how young asylum seekers from two of the main countries of origin have been treated in the UK asylum system to illustrate the issues presented above. In 2015, 21% of child asylum applications were from Afghans and 23% were from Eritreans.

Case study 1: Afghanistan and family tracing

Afghan young people represent a significant proportion of young asylum seekers. Research has drawn attention to the difficulties that they face in the UK and on return to Afghanistan (Gladwell et al, 2016). Between 2007 and 2015, 2,018 former asylum-seeking children were removed to Kabul after being refused asylum.[56]

The UNHCR identifies specific groups likely to be at risk.[57] Claims arise from the complexities of the ongoing conflict between the Afghan government with its allied militias, and a proliferating number of insurgent groups. Young people fear harm from or forcible recruitment to armed groups;[58] reprisals for the family support of one side of the conflict (or for refusal to take sides); conflicts arising from land disputes in the extended family; and the general insecurity and difficulty in sustaining a livelihood. Some young Afghans have been surviving as informal refugees in Iran or Pakistan and fled deteriorating conditions.[59]

Despite evidence showing the poor conditions faced by internally displaced persons (IDPs) (Amnesty International, 2012, 2016) the UK holds it reasonable for an adult male to relocate internally to Kabul to avoid problems in their home area.[60] But it is accepted that a minor returning to Afghanistan with no family to return to is likely to be at risk of serious harm or persecution because of their young age and vulnerability.[61]

In 2015 just 17% of Afghan minors were granted asylum by the Home Office. This falls to 9.5% for those who had turned 18 at the date of the decision.[62] Many were refused on credibility grounds, and in the alternative on the basis that they would not be removed before they were 18, at which point it would be safe for them to return to Kabul. Some refusal letters state that the Afghan government will provide them sufficient protection from non-state actors of persecution. Many of those not believed are told that their families 'will' care for them on return.

Given the accepted risks to unaccompanied young people, a key issue that has emerged in these cases is family tracing. The litigation on this issue provides a good example of the way in which a law established to protect a young person can easily become another legal obstacle.

Article 19(3) of the EU Reception Directive provides that member states shall 'endeavour to trace' the family of a young asylum seeker where it is in their best interests to do so, and where no danger would arise for the claimant or the family. The UK regulations[63] place that tracing duty on the Secretary of State; the same Secretary of State that is responsible for deciding their asylum claim. Litigation drawing attention to the Home Office's failure to fulfil that duty, in an attempt to assist unaccompanied children in their asylum claims, has led to a defensive response in which the duty to trace has become intertwined with the credibility assessment of the child's asylum claim.

In the Court of Appeal case *DS (Afghanistan) v Secretary of State for the Home Department* [2011] EWCA Civ 305,[64] it was accepted that between 2006 and 2010 the Home Office had been systematically failing in its duty to trace the families of young asylum seekers, and therefore had failed to have regard to the best interests of those applicants. The court rejected the Home Office argument that a referral to the Red Cross was sufficient to fulfil this duty. The court further decided that the Home Office's failure to seek the young person's family was relevant to his asylum claim, in that it potentially deprived him of corroboration of his claim that he would be returning as an unaccompanied child and therefore at risk, as accepted in the case of *LQ (Afghanistan)*.[65] These arguments were pursued further in the case of KA, a young Afghan who had been refused asylum and had since turned 18. It was argued that at the time he arrived he was entitled to refugee status as an unaccompanied child, and had the Secretary of State complied with the duty to trace his family and failed, then they must have accepted his asylum claim. Therefore, the court should now grant a 'corrective remedy' by granting leave, although the young person was not entitled to refugee status on the facts current at the time of his appeal.

The recognition that unaccompanied children may qualify for asylum on this basis alone raised the possibility that large numbers of separated Afghan children could qualify for refugee status. However, the courts have responded by reiterating that in any asylum claim the burden remains squarely on the applicant to establish any facts they are relying on, a principle that applies to children as much as it does to adults.[66] Here the burden of proof falls on the child to prove a negative – that they cannot contact their family. In the case of HK and others (minors – indiscriminate violence – forced recruitment by Taliban – contact with family members) Afghanistan CG [2010] UKUT 378 (IAC)[67] the court held:

> Where a child has close relatives in Afghanistan who have assisted him in leaving the country, any assertion that such family members are uncontactable or are unable to meet the child in Kabul and care for him on return, should be

supported by credible evidence of efforts to contact those family members and their inability to meet and care for the child in the event of return.

Court of Appeal judges have since commented that Afghan families who have sent their children out of the country at considerable cost are unlikely to want to cooperate with the Home Office for the return of their child. Therefore, even if it were possible to contact an Afghan minor's family, they would have a strong incentive to support the applicant's account of persecution, and so any corroboration from that source would be of doubtful value.[68]

Responding to the litigation, the Home Office issued family tracing questionnaires requiring accurate family contact details. The Home Office could then state in a subsequent refusal that it had fulfilled the tracing duty, but that the UK authorities actually had no ability to carry out family tracing and so the child should approach the Red Cross International Tracing Service. Yet a failure to return the form, or the provision of information lacking in detail, could then be used to suggest that the young person had failed to cooperate with the Home Office, undermining their credibility.

This effectively compels an applicant to approach the Red Cross to trace their family rather than risk a later accusation that they have failed to pro-actively seek their family, and even a late attempt at approaching the Red Cross before an appeal hearing could be viewed by an immigration judge with suspicion and questions asked about why this had not been attempted immediately on arrival. Yet a child may have quite valid concerns about relying on the Home Office or Red Cross to seek out their family. Based on our experience, individuals already in touch with their family have been accused of failing to submit their family phone number during their Home Office interview, without having being told why it is required and without any acknowledgement of the reasonableness of concerns they may have about a UK state official contacting a relative in Afghanistan or elsewhere.

This reliance on family tracing as a credibility test has drawn the Red Cross into the difficult position of being asked to provide supporting evidence in a young person's asylum claim. Determined to remain neutral, the Red Cross issue standard letters that state:

> In the view of the British Red Cross, the fact that a tracing request is or is not opened should not be considered as evidence that the sought person is/is not missing or indeed

that the person does/does not exist. Neither should the opening of a Tracing Request be considered as credible evidence of efforts to contact family members, nor should the decision not to open such a Tracing Request be seen as absence of such credible evidence.

Of course only those who open a tracing claim will have such a letter to submit as evidence of the Red Cross' position on this.

This saga shows how what should have been an aspect of supporting the welfare of a child has now entered the adversarial asylum process as another area in which an applicant's credibility can be doubted. The tracing episode illustrates the conflict between the Home Office's role in enforcing immigration law and acting in the best interests of a child. The tracing duty could have been placed on the local authority or on an independent guardian. Making one party to an adversarial legal dispute about a child also responsible for an essential welfare issue was always likely to be problematic.

Postscript: As of July 2018 evidence shows that the security situation in many parts of Afghanistan is continuing to deteriorate, with specific provinces now controlled by the Taliban, which is itself increasingly in conflict with Daesh (ISIS). Recent Home Office statistics demonstrate that there has been an increase in grants of asylum to unaccompanied Afghan children, with 43% of those under 18 at the date of asylum granted refugee status or humanitarian protection in 2017. However, that falls to 26% for those who arrived as children but are over 18 at the time of the decision. Current country guidance cases maintain that in no province is the level of general violence sufficiently severe for an adult male to be at risk on account of this alone, and that relocation to Kabul is generally available. In March 2015 the Afghan Minister for Refugees warned European governments against the forced return of 'vulnerable' groups such as women and children and those from insecure provinces (all but three in his view). This led to legal challenges to charter flights carrying 'failed asylum seekers', in which it was argued that young adults who had arrived as children and had spent a significant period of time outside Afghanistan should be considered 'vulnerable' since they would be ill equipped to return to an insecure environment. At present such attempts have met with limited success,[69] and as the security situation continues to deteriorate further challenges are being pursued.

Case study 2: Eritrea

Throughout 2015 the largest number of young asylum seekers to the UK were from Eritrea. The numbers rose from 80 in 2012 to 736 in 2015.[70] Although less reported in the media than the conflicts in Afghanistan, Iraq and Syria, Eritrea is sometimes referred to as the 'North Korea of Africa', and the human rights situation for young people in Eritrea has been widely documented in a series of reports by human rights organisations (Human Rights Watch, 2009; Amnesty International, 2015). In June 2015 the UN Commission of Inquiry on Human Rights in Eritrea produced its detailed findings. This reported that

> systematic, widespread and gross human rights violations have been and are being committed by the Government of Eritrea and that there is no accountability for them. The enjoyment of rights and freedoms are severely curtailed in an overall context of a total lack of rule of law (OHCHR, 2015, p.449).

This report fully documented the practice of forced recruitment to indefinite national service, where young recruits, both male and female, suffer severe deprivations and are subject to forced labour that effectively abuses, exploits and enslaves them for years. A large number of young Eritreans flee to pre-empt the inevitable recruitment to national service.

Until March 2015 the UK Home Office policy, following established case law,[71] was to grant refugee status to young Eritrean asylum seekers approaching military draft age, where it was accepted that they had fled Eritrea illegally in order to avoid national service. It had been recognised that most Eritreans are unable to leave their country legally; that the government operates a shoot to kill policy at its borders; and those who returned after an illegal exit would be viewed as betraying the country: and so such applicants should qualify for refugee status on political grounds.

However, as the numbers of young Eritrean arrivals increased in 2014 and 2015 this policy changed. The Home Office suggested that since the most recent country guidance case in 2011 there had been a significant change in the country conditions. It proposed that those leaving Eritrea illegally now would not be viewed as traitors by the Eritrean government provided that returnees pay a 2% 'diaspora tax' on any earnings and sign a letter of apology to the government. The

UK government considered this to be 'not unreasonable', despite the diaspora tax having been condemned by the United Nations Security Council.[72] The Home Office further argued that while returnees may be required to complete national service, this would not be indefinite, or in itself amount to a breach of human rights.

The basis of this change of policy was a fact finding mission report by the Danish Immigration Services, which was based primarily on interviews conducted with anonymous sources and foreign nationals living in Eritrea. The report has since been subjected to significant criticism.[73] The UK's own Independent Advisory Group on Country Information have criticised the Danish report for being marred by serious methodological concerns.[74] Even members of the team that worked on the Danish report have criticised its conclusions, and subsequently the Danish Immigration Service reversed its own policy position (*The Local*, 2014). However, the Home Office continued to rely on it and indeed sought to commission its own factfinding report in which UK officials conducted interviews in Eritrea. Again the methodology has been questioned, with country experts suggesting that the UK is just searching for the evidence it would like to find to back up its policy (see Dr John Campbell's comments in *Guardian*, 2016).

That policy change led to refusal of asylum to large numbers of young Eritrean asylum seekers. The rate of grant of asylum fell from 91% in the 4th quarter of 2014 to 21% in the 3rd quarter of 2016 (Figure 3). Most of those young people have been granted UASC leave instead. However, appeal statistics show that the new Home Office policy position was not accepted by the courts. In the months April to June 2016, fully 88% of appeals by Eritreans were allowed.

What this meant in practice was that young Eritreans were having to attend a Home Office interview, receive a refusal based on discredited evidence, and wait for up to a year before their appeal was heard. They then faced the experience of giving evidence in court solely to respond to an official refusal letter that had sought to cast doubt on the truthfulness of their claim and suggested that they should apologise to the Eritrean government for leaving. There remains a real possibility that some young people who failed to appeal or missed the appeal deadline are left with an insecure status that will expire when they turn 17.5. They will have the difficulty of finding legal representation for a fresh claim, and the risk of losing their entitlements to work, housing and support. Once more, as in relation to Afghan young people, we see how the Home Office's defensive response to the arrival of large numbers with arguable asylum claims leads to hardship and injustice for young people.

Figure 3: Asylum grant and appeal success rates for Eritrean unaccompanied minors, 2010–17

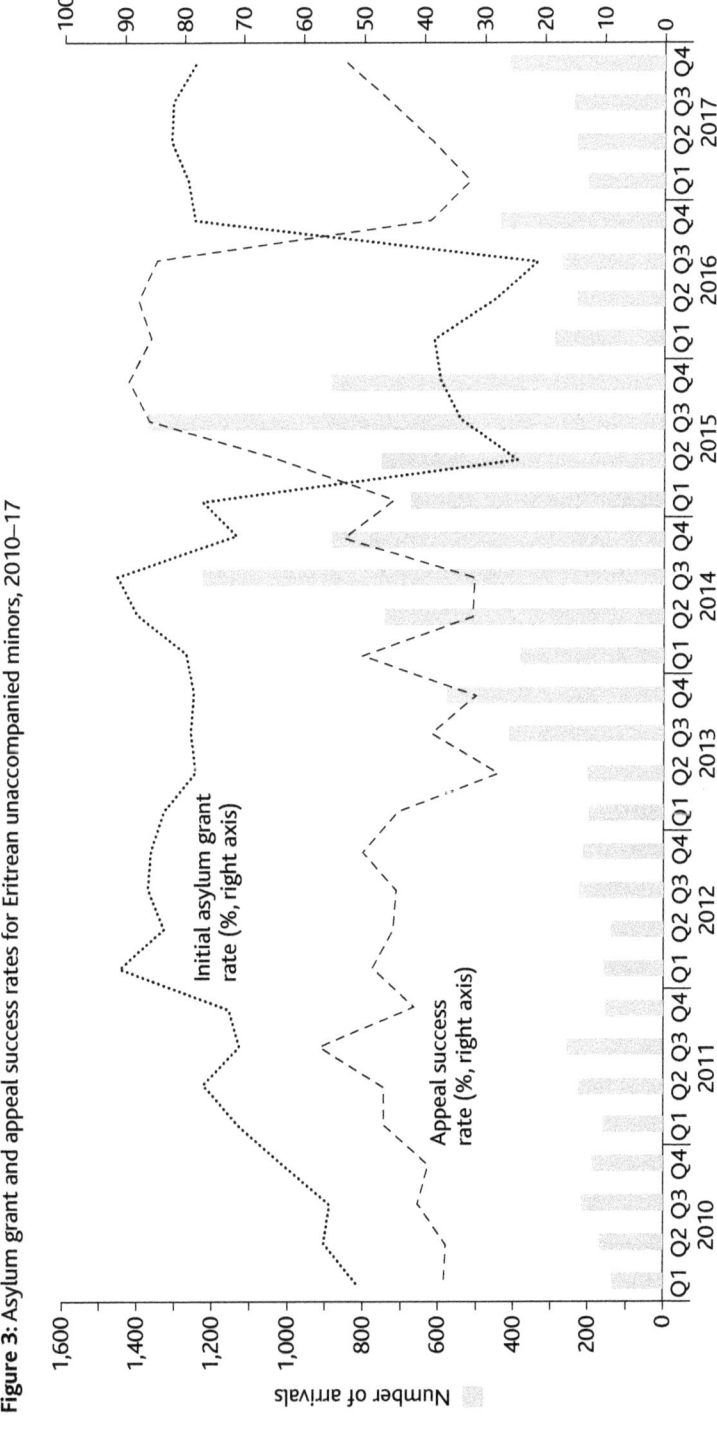

Source: Home Office immigration statistics year ending March 2018

In December 2016 the much awaited Upper Tribunal country guidance case of *MST and Others (national service – risk categories)*[75] confirmed what had been clear to the majority of those researching Eritrea: that there had been no significant improvement in the human rights situation and that the majority of those who have escaped national service face a risk of persecution if returned. While young Eritreans are now being granted refugee status again, it is likely that the UK government will continue searching for ways to deter them.

Conclusion

In this chapter we have observed how, despite the existence of sensitive child appropriate official guidance, the legal process is fraught with legal obstacles for young people claiming asylum. The above examples illustrate the conflicts between well-recognised legal duties to children and the seemingly unceasing desire to enforce restrictive immigration policies, regardless of human cost. It would therefore seem appropriate to reappraise the current approach to the asylum process for unaccompanied children.

To provide a proper evidence-based context for such a reappraisal there needs to be a greater recognition of what actually happens to teenagers with UASC leave when they reach 18, and a wider debate about the social costs of such policies. While some are removed, many are not,[76] and enter a period of legal limbo in the UK, surviving with no legal status, street homeless or sleeping on friends' floors, working illegally and running the risk of entering the criminal justice system, often making repeated attempts to regularise their status, sometimes at significant financial cost to themselves and those supporting them. Those who had been resident since 13 or 14 and had begun to integrate find themselves unable to complete courses of study, or continue with chosen career plans. We question whether it is a sensible use of resources to abandon young people with potentially promising futures, who have been supported throughout their adolescent years, as the clock strikes midnight on their 18th birthday.

The Home Office view is that such young people should seek voluntary return. This policy rests on a belief that to grant a more permanent form of leave to remain would act as a 'pull factor' that will induce more families in places like Afghanistan to pay for their children to make the dangerous journey to Europe to seek asylum (*Guardian*, 2015). However, having made the arduous journey to the UK, young 'failed asylum seekers' from war-torn states may well see even the UK's 'hostile environment' as more benign than the conditions from which they escaped, or the conditions they endured en route. Notably, a 2014 joint Home Office-Kent Social Services project aiming to encourage young Afghan 'failed asylum seekers' to return home voluntarily by promising them a short period of formal education failed to recruit a single applicant. At a workshop reviewing the outcome of the project, Home Office officials referred to countries such as Afghanistan as presenting 'challenges' to return, meaning too dangerous.[77]

A number of suggestions have been put forward for how the claims of asylum-seeking children could be handled in a way that more appropriately considers their best interests. One possibility is that the refugee status determination procedure should be fundamentally re-orientated for children, with a focus placed on their best interests and the search for a durable solution. It has been suggested that an independent party should be responsible for determining a young person's best interests rather than the Home Office, or that a division of the Family Court should take responsibility for handling protection claims by children, employing a more inquisitorial legal framework in place of the current adversarial asylum process.[78] However, there is a danger that applying a significantly different framework for children risks further strengthening the sharp boundary that exists when a child turns 18.

Another promising approach might be to recognise that the transition from child to adult is gradual, varies between different cultures and individuals and that protection needs do not immediately cease once a child turns 18. In the UK the reality of an extended period of adolescence is recognised through the extension of an obligation on local authorities to provide support for care leavers until the age of 25 in certain circumstances and a greater commitment to the staying-put principle where some young people over the age of 18 can remain in foster care until the age of 21. Arguably this should be mirrored in the immigration law treatment of such young people. At present though it is the UK government's intention to remove young people refused asylum altogether from the leaving care provisions of the Children Act 1989 and prevent those with UASC or discretionary leave from accessing support for higher education,[79] discriminating between UK and foreign children and making for an even more abrupt transition at 18.

Nevertheless, even within the current framework, there are some simple improvements that could be made. First, the Home Office needs to be better held to account for poor decision making based on a failure to apply its own guidance in relation to credibility. A starting point would be for the Home Office to publish separate statistics on children's appeal outcomes.

Second, legal aid should be made available for all aspects of a young person's immigration status. So long as the UK maintains a complex and adversarial system of immigration law where the burden of proof rests with the applicant, it is essential to provide qualified legal support so that unaccompanied young people are able to prepare and present their cases adequately.[80]

Finally, to cut down on delay; if the Home Office were to ensure that young people's asylum claims were dealt with within the timeframe set out in previous guidance, and if the Ministry of Justice were to ensure that children's appeals were listed and heard promptly, fewer young people would suffer the injustice of being entitled to refugee status on arrival, but reaching 18 before a determination is finally made. Regular statistics should be published on the timescale so that the Home Office can be held to account.

It will be argued that these suggestions require significant resources, but arguably less than the eventual total cost of dealing with the consequences of an increasing number of unsupported young people remaining in the UK with no rights. And while none of these suggestions would resolve some of the underlying dilemmas and conflicts in the legal system, they would mitigate some of the current injustices.

Notes

[1] *ZH Tanzania v SSHD* [2011] UKSC 4. Note however, that it is to be 'a primary consideration', but not 'the paramount consideration' and so the child's best interests can in some circumstances be outweighed by an accumulation of other considerations.

[2] Regulation (EU) 604/2013 Article 6

[3] There has been significant litigation in order to make the Home Office fulfil this obligation by taking children from the 'Jungle' camp in Calais. See *R (on the application of ZAT and Others) v Secretary of State for the Home Department (Article 8 ECHR – Dublin Regulation – interface – proportionality) IJR [2016] UKUT 00061 (IAC)*.

[4] Article 1A defines a refugee as a person who '… owing to well-founded fear of being persecuted for reasons of race, religion, nationality, membership of a particular social group or political opinion, is outside the country of his nationality and is unable or, owing to such fear, is unwilling to avail himself of the protection of that country'.

[5] EU Qualification Directive 2004/83/EC provides subsidiary protection to those who faces a real risk of suffering serious harm (as defined in the directive) in their home country.

[6] Directive 2005/85/EC (Asylum Procedures) Article 17

7   Directive 2003/9/EC (Reception of Asylum Seekers) Article 19
8   Immigration Rules paras 350–351
9   Immigration Rules para 352
10 Home Office (2016b). However, see *KS (benefit of the doubt) [2014] UKUT 00552 (IAC)* for a judicial consideration of what this means in practice.
11 The EU Qualification Directive 2004/83/EC includes 'Acts of a child specific nature' in its definition of acts of persecution at Article 9, although this term is not defined further.
12 UNHCR, Guidelines on International Protection: Child Asylum Claims under Articles 1(A)2 and 1(F) of the 1951 Convention and/or 1967 Protocol relating to the Status of Refugees, page 3 para 3. UNHCR guidelines are non-binding on the UK but can be persuasive in UK courts as an aide to interpreting the Convention.
13 UN Convention on Refugees 1951 article 1A(2). The convention reasons are: race, religion, nationality, political opinion and membership of a particular social group.
14 *LQ (age: immutable characteristics) Afghanistan* [2008] UKAIT 00005.
15 *Secretary of State for the Home Department (Appellant) v. AH (Sudan) and others* [2007] UKHL 49, confirming *Januzi v Secretary of State for the Home Department* [2006] UKHL 5.
16 UNHCR, Guidelines on International Protection: Child Asylum Claims under Articles 1(A)2 and 1(F) of the 1951 Convention and/or 1967 Protocol relating to the Status of Refugees page 21, para 55.
17 See case of *Elgafaji (Justice and Home Affairs)* [2009] EUECJ C-465/07.
18 Child, vulnerable adult and sensitive appellant guidance Joint Presidential Guidance Note No 2 of 2010.
19 *Child, Vulnerable Adult and Sensitive Witnesses*, Practice Direction First Tier and Upper Tribunal, Lord Justice Carnwath, Senior President of Tribunals, 30 October 2008.
20 In the case of *AM (Afghanistan) v Secretary of State for the Home Department, [2017] EWCA Civ 1123*, the Court of Appeal strongly reaffirmed how such guidance should be applied, where the tribunal had failed to protect the rights of a vulnerable child witness.
21 Unaccompanied Asylum-Seeking Child Leave, Immigration Rules Chapter 11 para 352ZC. Until 6 April 2013 Discretionary Leave (DL) was granted on the same basis, but 'outside the immigration rules'.
22 A position endorsed by the Court of Appeal in *DS (Afghanistan) v Secretary of State for the Home Department* [2011] EWCA Civ 305 & in *ZH (Afghanistan) v. Secretary of State for the Home Department,* [2009] EWCA Civ 470
23 Section 117B of the Nationality, Immigration and Asylum Act 2002 inserted by s19 of the Immigration Act 2014 stipulates that judges should accord 'little weight' to a private life developed while an individual has a 'precarious legal status'. The

Home Office has argued that anything short of indefinite leave to remain should be considered 'precarious' and the tribunal in a series of cases has so far accepted this position. For discussion, see Warren (2016).

24 Until recently, 'active review' has been applied to those who have committed criminal offences and may lead to a delay in settlement status or attempts at exclusion from refugee status depending on the severity of the offence committed. In March 2017 a new policy of actively reviewing refugee status after five years with a view to revoking it was introduced, increasing the insecurity of those granted asylum who would normally have qualified for settlement. (See Home Office Refugee Leave Version 4.0 March 2017.) However, revocation of status is a significant decision that attracts a right of appeal, and having granted refugee status, the burden is on the Home Office to show that any change is significant and non-temporary. Thus refugee status still provides more security than UASC leave.

25 s19 Immigration Act 2014, see n27.

26 9 July 2012 saw major changes to the Immigration Rules, aiming to determine how article 8 ECHR should be applied in future. Those granted discretionary leave before July 2012 could in some cases apply for ILR after six years. The new rules require an individual still under 18 to have resided continuously for seven years. Once over 18, but under 25 they require residence for more than half their life. Once over 25 they require at least 20 years continuous residence, or must show that there are very significant obstacles to their integration in their country of return (Immigration rule 276ADE).

27 Asylum appeals are heard by immigration judges of the First Tier Tribunal (Immigration and Asylum Chamber). Onward appeals can be made to the Upper Tribunal on a point of law. The Upper Tribunal is a court of record and selected judgments are published as guidance to the first tier judges.

28 *Miah (section 117B NIAA 2002 – children)* [2016] UKUT 00131(IAC) para 20.

29 *Miah (section 117B NIAA 2002 – children)* [2016] UKUT 00131(IAC) para 24.

30 There are indications that the Court of Appeal does not favour the Home Office's more expansive use of the term precarious (See *Rhuppiah v Secretary Of State for the Home Department [2016] EWCA Civ 803*, which was heard in the Supreme Court in July 2018. Judgement is awaited.)

31 However, note the new policy on active review of refugee leave. See note 24.

32 See immigration rule 339I. The Solihull Early Legal Advice Pilot, set up in 2007 and not finally evaluated until 2013, introduced a cooperative process into asylum claims, where the Home Office caseworker and the applicant's legal representatives worked together to produce the best case before a decision was made. Predictably, as expected, it increased grants of asylum, and appeared particularly helpful in complex cases, but other outcomes were more diffuse. It was not introduced more widely, as finally deemed not to be 'cost effective'; see *Evaluation of the Solihull Pilot for the UK Border Agency and the Legal Services Commission*, Independent Evaluator Jane Aspden, 2008, and *Evaluation of the Early Legal Advice Project Final Report*, Research Report 70, Home Office, May 2013.

33 NASF Quality Subcommittee meeting at Asylum Aid, April 2012.

34 'In many asylum cases, some, even most, of the appellant's story may seem inherently unlikely but that does not mean that it is untrue ... Inherent probability, which may be helpful in many domestic cases, can be a dangerous, even a wholly inappropriate, factor to rely on in some asylum cases. Much of the evidence will be referable to societies with customs and circumstances which are very different from those of which the members of the fact-finding tribunal have any (even second-hand) experience.' Neuberger LJ in *HK v SSHD [2006] EWCA Civ 1037* [28–29]

35 This legislation has been read down to some extent by judges in the case of *JT (Cameroon) v SSHD [2008] EWCA Civ 878* which confirms that judges must still consider the evidence as a whole.

36 The cases of *M.S.S. v. Belgium and Greece*, ECtHR Application no. 30696/09 and *N.S v Secretary of State for the Home Department* (C-411/10) held respectively that there was a risk of breach of art 3 ECHR for asylum seekers in Greece, and that where Member States 'knew or ought to have known' that there is such a risk, it amounts to a breach of art 3 to purport to return an asylum seeker to that country. Several of our clients have had s8 AI(TC)A 2004 findings made against them in relation to Greece despite these judgments.

37 *AN (A child) & FA (A child) v SSHD [2012] EWCA Civ 1636.*

38 We have seen examples of tribunal determinations where the immigration judge, having noted such a Social Services age assessment, determines that the applicant 'has lied about their age'. In law, and especially in immigration law, there is a big difference between being determined 'not to have satisfied the relevant standard of proof' on an issue, and being determined a liar.

39 HM Courts and Tribunals Service First Tier Tribunal (Immigration and Asylum Chamber) FOI [Freedom of Information] Request Reference 77257. It needs to be recognised though that many of those who are unrepresented may have been refused legal aid as a result of their cases being assessed as weak, and so not satisfying the merits test for legal aid.

40 In the UK legal aid is administered by the Legal Aid Agency (LAA). Asylum seekers are entitled to Legal Help (LH), which covers advice and representation prior to an asylum interview, subject to a means test. Only those under 18 are entitled to publicly funded representation at an asylum interview. At the appeal stage, asylum seekers can obtain Controlled Legal Representation (CLR) in order to help them prepare and present the appeal. At this point, legal aid is conditional on satisfying both a means and a merits test.

41 ILPA has published a number of best practice guides for working with children: www.ilpa.org.uk/pages/publications.html

42 'Matter starts' are units of work remunerated under legal aid, limited numbers of which are doled out to contracted providers. They are not equivalent to the whole of a client's case.

43 The fixed fee does not apply in children's asylum claims, but our research showed that some solicitors acting for children were unwilling to complete the extension form required to obtain an increase in the upper spending limit on their case, and instead restricted their case preparation to that which could be fitted into the nine hours' work.

44 Following a judicial review by the Children's Society in which significant evidence was provided documenting the impact of a lack of immigration legal aid on children, on 12 July 2018 the Government announced that legal aid for children's immigration matters would be brought back into scope. Reference to written ministerial statement of Lucy Frazer, 12/07/18. HCWS853.

45 Sections 69–73 introduce a scheme to transfer responsibility for an asylum-seeking child between local authorities.

46 s10 LASPO 2012 provided for legal aid to be provided exceptionally in cases where a failure to do so would lead to a breach of fundamental rights. This scheme was initially held not to apply to immigration, but this was found to be unlawful – see *R (on the application of Gudanaviciene and others) v Director of Legal Aid Casework and another (British Red Cross Society intervening)* [2014] EWCA Civ 1622.

47 Immigration Rules para 350.

48 Home Office, *Processing children's asylum claims*, April 2013 version: the timetable is omitted from the 2016 version (Home Office, 2016b).

49 *Tribunals and Gender Recognition Certificate Statistics*, Quarterly July to September 2016, Ministry of Justice Statistics, Main Tables, T3, 8 December 2016. This statistic is for Asylum/Protection appeals. Other types of appeal have delays far in excess of this. At the time of writing the average time for an asylum/protection appeal to be heard had fallen to 26 weeks for protection claims.

50 *Senathirajah Ravichandran v. Secretary of State for the Home Department*, United Kingdom: Court of Appeal (England and Wales), 11 October 1995.

51 A number of Freedom of Information requests made by these authors for appeal success rates for UASC were refused on the basis that the data was not easily accessible within the £600 financial limit.

52 *KA (Afghanistan) & Ors v Secretary of State for the Home Department* [2012] EWCA Civ 1014 para 18

53 *R (Rashid) v Secretary of State for the Home Department* [2005] EWCA considered a case in which the Home Office, in a series of 'startling and prolonged' failures, failed to apply an appropriate policy and then delayed consideration until the policy had changed. The court ruled that the applicant should be entitled to ILR as a remedy. Prominent cases involving young people include *AA (Afghanistan) v Secretary of State for the Home Department* [2007] EWCA Civ 12, *R (S) v Secretary of State for the Home Department* [2007] EWCA Civ 546 and *SL (Vietnam) v Secretary of State for the Home Department* [2010] EWCA Civ 225.

54 *TN & MA (Afghanistan) v SSHD* [2015] UKSC 40 para 51 referring to Sir Stanley Burnton LJ's judgment in *EU (Afghanistan) v Secretary of State for the Home Department* [2013] EWCA Civ 32, [2013] Imm AR 496. Ravichandran n90.

55 *R (S) v Secretary of State for the Home Department* [2007] EWCA Civ 54 [41], Carnwath LJ, cited with approval by the Supreme Court.

56 Children: Deportation: Written question 13206. Asked on 23 October 2015 by Louise Haigh MP. Corrected on 9 February 2016 by James Brokenshire MP.

57 UNHCR Eligibility Guidelines for Assessing the International Protection Needs of Asylum-Seekers from Afghanistan, 19 April 2016.

58 It should be noted that what has been termed 'forcible recruitment' may involve broader coercive strategies, including fear, intimidation and the use of tribal mechanisms to pressurise individuals into joining armed groups. See UNHCR (2012).

59 The vast majority of Afghan refugees reside in Pakistan (1.3 million) and Iran (approx 980,000) (UNHCR, 2016). Recent reports have documented the plight of young Afghans without status in Iran who face forcible removal to Afghanistan or recruitment by the Iranian regime to fight in Syria (Human Rights Watch, 2017). There have also been increasing reports on the plight of Hazara refugees facing increasing persecution in Pakistan (Human Rights Watch, 2018).

60 *AK (Article 15(c)) Afghanistan CG* [2012] UKUT 00163 (IAC); AS (Safety of Kabul) CG [2018] UKUT 118

61 *AA (unattended children) Afghanistan CG* [2012] UKUT 00016 (IAC)

62 Home Office (2016c), Table as09.

63 The Asylum Seekers (Reception Conditions) Regulations 2005, reg 6.

64 *DS (Afghanistan) v Secretary of State for the Home Department* [2011] EWCA Civ 305.

65 *LQ (age: immutable characteristics) Afghanistan.*

66 Para 34 HK (Afghanistan) [2012] EWCA Civ 315.

67 HK and others (minors – indiscriminate violence – forced recruitment by Taliban – contact with family members) Afghanistan CG [2010] UKUT 378 (IAC), headnote 3.

68 *AA (Afghanistan) v The Secretary of State for the Home Department* [2013] EWCA Civ 1625, Underhill LJ, [52].

69 *HN & SA vs Secretary of State for the Home Department [2016] EWCA Civ 123. Appealed from Naziri & Ors, R (on the application of) v Secretary of State for the Home Department (judicial review – scope – evidence (IJR) [2015] UKUT 437 (IAC).*

70 Home Office (2016c), as08.

71 *MO (illegal exit – risk on return) Eritrea* CG [2011] UKUT 00190 (IAC).

72 See reference to it being in violation of Security Council Resolutions 1844 (2008), 1862 (2009) and 1907 (2009).

73 Human Rights Watch (July 2015, Letter to the UK Independent Chief Inspectorate of Borders and Immigration on Flawed UK Country Information and Guidance Reports on Eritrea); UNHCR (Dec 2014) Fact Finding Mission Report of the Danish Immigration Service, *"Eritrea – Drivers and Root Causes of Emigration, National Service and the Possibility of Return. Country of Origin Information for Use in the Asylum Determination Process"*, UNHCR's perspective.

74 Report by the Independent Advisory Group on Country Information on Eritrea Country Information and Guidance Reports produced by the UK Home Office, 13 May 2015.

75 *MST and Others* (national service – risk categories) *Eritrea CG [2016] UKUT 00443 (IAC)*.

76 It should be noted that the Home Office has difficulty enforcing removal to a number of countries, such as Eritrea. Eritreans refused asylum may find there are real practical obstacles to them being accepted for return even if they desired to. Statistics show that overall, enforced removals have decreased year on year since 2004 (Home Office, 2018). In recent years the UK has relied on promoting voluntary returns. However, those from conflict zones such as Iraq or Afghanistan who are found by the tribunal not to be objectively at risk of persecution may be very reluctant to take voluntary return, either due to a continuing subjective fear of return or for other reasons, such as the need to repay debts to family or agents for their journey.

77 Sheona York attended the Positive Futures: Roundtable Event on 17 July 2014.

78 See Refugee Children's Rights Project and Immigration Law Practitioner's Association (ILPA), *Minutes of the Expert Roundtable on the UNCRC 1989 and its application to child refugee status determination and asylum process*, 23 April 2012.

79 See Part 5 and Schedule 12 of the Immigration Act 2016 – not currently in force.

80 The Government has recently accepted the need to bring immigration legal scope for children. See note 44. However, immigration legal aid will still be out of scope for former asylum seeking children once they have turned 18.

References

Amnesty International (2012) *Afghanistan: Fleeing war, finding misery: The plight of the internally displaced in Afghanistan*, ASA 11/001/2012, London: Amnesty International.

Amnesty International (2015) *Eritrea: Just deserters: Why indefinite national service in Eritrea has created a generation of refugees*, AFR 64/2930/2015, London: Amnesty International.

Amnesty International (2016) *Afghanistan: My children will die this winter – Afghanistan's broken promise to the displaced*, ASA 11/4-17/2016, London: Amnesty International.

Brennen, T., Zotović, M., Solheim Skar, A.-M., Mehmedović, I., Popović, N., Hasanović, M., Blix, I., Kravić Prelić, N., Pajević, I. and Gavrilov-jerkovic, V. (2010) 'Trauma exposure in childhood impairs the ability to recall specific autobiographical memories in late adolescence' *Journal of Traumatic Stress*, 23(2): 240–7

Chen, Y., McAnally, H.M. and Reese, H. (2013) 'Development in the organisation of episodic memories in middle childhood', *Frontiers in Behavioural Neuroscience*, 7: 84

Connolly, H., Crellin, R. and Parhar, R. (2017) *An Update to: Cut off from Justice: The impact of excluding separated and migrant children from legal aid*, University of Bedfordshire/The Children's Society.

Department for Education (2017) *Statutory Guidance for local authorities on the care of unaccompanied asylum seeking and trafficked children*, https://assets.publishing.service.gov.uk/government/uploads/system/uploads/attachment_data/file/656429/UASC_Statutory_Guidance_2017.pdf

Devon Law Centre (2010) *Final report of the Asylum Appellate Project*, Devon: Devon Law Centre.

Draper, A. (2016) *Report: An emotional health and wellbeing specialist early intervention framework*, www.uaschealth.org/category/general/

Fazel, M., Reed, R.V., Panter-Brick, C. and Stein, A. (2012) 'Mental health of displaced and refugee children resettled in high-income countries: risk and protective factors', *Lancet*, 379: 266–82.

Given-Wilson, Z., Hodes, M. and Herlihy, J. (2017) 'A review of adolescent autobiographical memory and the implications for assessment of unaccompanied minors' refugee determinations', *Clinical Child Psychology and Psychiatry*, 23(2): 209–22.

Gladwell, C., Bowerman, E., Norman, B., Dickson, S. with Ghafoor, A. (2016) *After return: documenting the experiences of young people forcibly returned to Afghanistan*, London: RSN.

Habermas, T. and de Silveira, C. (2008) 'The development of global coherence in life narratives across, adolescence: temporal, causal, and thematic aspects', *Development Psychology*, 44(3): 707–21.

Herlihy, J., Scragg, P. and Turner, S. (2002) 'Discrepancies in autobiographical memories – Implications for the assessment of asylum seekers: repeated interview study', *British Medical Journal*, 324: 324–7

Herlihy, J., Gleeson, K. and Turner, S. (2010) 'What assumptions about human behaviour underlie asylum judgements', *International Journal of Refugee Law*, 22(3):351–66.

Home Office (2015a) *Asylum Policy Instruction: Assessing credibility and refugee status*, Version 9.0, 6 January.

Home Office (2015b) *Assessing age for asylum applicants*, June 2015 (Asylum policy collection).

Home Office (2016a) *Families and Children Section A General Guidance*, Chapter 45 Enforcement Instructions and Guidance, January.

Home Office (2016b) *Processing children's asylum claims*, Home Office Asylum Policy Instructions, 12 July.

Home Office (2016c) *National Statistics: Asylum*, April to June 2016, 25 August, www.gov.uk/government/publications/immigration-statistics-april-to-june-2016/asylum#unaccompanied-asylum-seeking-children

Home Office (2018) 'Immigration statistics, year ending March 2018', www.gov.uk/government/statistics/immigration-statistics-year-ending-march-2018

Human Rights Watch (2009) *Service for life: state repression and indefinite conscription in Eritrea*, www.hrw.org/report/2009/04/16/service-life/state-repression-and-indefinite-conscription-eritrea

Human Rights Watch (2015) *Letter to the UK Independent Chief Inspector of Borders and Immigration on flawed UK country information and guidance reports on Eritrea*, www.hrw.org/news/2015/07/01/letter-uk-independent-chief-inspector-borders-and-immigration-flawed-uk-country

Human Rights Watch (2017) 'Iran: Afghan children recruited to fight in Syria protection gaps increase children's vulnerability', 1 October, www.hrw.org/news/2017/10/01/iran-afghan-children-recruited-fight-syria

Human Rights Watch (2018) *Pakistan's Hazara community under attack*, 30 April, www.hrw.org/news/2018/04/30/pakistans-hazara-community-under-attack

Independent Advisory Group on Country Information (2015) *Report by the Independent Advisory Group on Country Information on Eritrea Country Information and Guidance Reports produced by the UK Home Office*, https://assets.publishing.service.gov.uk/government/uploads/system/uploads/attachment_data/file/559475/Eritrea-report-IAGCI-19-May-2015.pdf

Kuyken, W. and Dalgleish, T. (2011) 'Overgeneral autobiographical memory in adolescents at risk for depression', *Memory*, 19(3): 241–50.

Legal Action Group (2012) 'Reductions in Legal Aid', 5 July, http://legalactiongroupnews.blogspot.co.uk/2012/07/reductions-in-legal-aid-cases.html

Mind (2009) *A civilised society: Mental health provision for refugees and asylum seekers in England and Wales*, London: Mind, www.mind.org.uk/media/273472/a-civilised-society.pdf

Office of the Children's Commissioner (2012) *Landing in Dover: The immigration process undergone by unaccompanied children arriving in Kent*, http://dera.ioe.ac.uk/13638/1/force_download.php%3Ffp%3D%252Fclient_assets%252Fcp%252Fpublication%252F556%252FLanding_in_Dover_-_FINAL_NON_EMBARGOED_REPORT.pdf

OHCHR (2015) *Report of the detailed findings of the commission of inquiry on human rights in Eritrea*, A/HRC/29/CRP.1.

Refugee Children's Consortium (2017) *Briefing on the National Transfer Scheme, August 2017*, http://refugeechildrensconsortium.org.uk/wp-content/uploads/2017/08/RCC_National-Transfer-Scheme-Briefing_August2017.pdf

Refugee Council (2011) *Lives in the balance: the quality of immigration legal advice given to separated children seeking asylum.*

Rouseea, C., Crepeau, F., Foxen, P. and Houle, F. (2002), 'The complexity of determining refugeehood: A multidisciplinary analysis of the decision-making process of the Canadian Immigration and Refugee Board', *Journal of Refugee Studies*, 15(1): 43–70.

Singh, A. and Webber, F. (2010) *Excluding migrants from justice – the legal aid cuts*, IRR Briefing paper no. 7, London: IRR.

Guardian (2013) 'Immigration bill: Theresa May defends plans to create "hostile environment"', *Guardian*, 10 October, www.theguardian.com/politics/2013/oct/10/immigration-bill-theresa-may-hostile-environment

Guardian (2015) 'Migrant children leaving care to have support cut under new proposals', 30 December, www.theguardian.com/uk-news/2015/dec/30/uk-immigration-bill-proposals-cut-state-support-migrant-children-leaving-care

Guardian (2016) 'UK 'using misleading information' to return Eritrean asylum seekers', *Guardian*, 22 January, www.theguardian.com/uk-news/2016/jan/22/uk-using-misleading-information-return-eritrean-asylum-seekers-home-office-guidance

The Local (2014) 'Denmark admits 'doubts' about Eritrea report', *The Local*, 10 December.

Thomas, R. (2011) *Administrative justice and asylum appeals*, Oxford: Hart Publishing.

UK Border Agency (UKBA) (2010) *Protecting our border, protecting the public – 5 year strategy for enforcing our immigration rules*, London: UKBA, http://webarchive.nationalarchives.gov.uk/20100303205641/http://www.ukba.homeoffice.gov.uk/sitecontent/documents/managingourborders/crime-strategy/protecting-border.pdf?view=Binary

UNHCR (2009) *Quality Initiative Project Sixth Report to the Minister*, London: UNHCR Representation to the UK in London, www.refworld.org/docid/56a9c5434.html

UNHCR (2012) *Forced recruitment for the Taliban in Afghanistan: UNHCR's perspective*, www.ecoi.net/en/file/local/1113497/2016_1341992043_4ffc31a32.pdf

UNHCR (2014) *Fact finding Mission Report of the Danish Immigration Service, 'Eritrea – Drivers and Root Causes of Emigration, National Service and the Possibility of Return. Country of Origin Information for Use in the Asylum Determination Process', UNHCR's perspective*, www.ft.dk/samling/20141/almdel/uui/bilag/41/1435206.pdf

UNHCR (2016) *Global Report 2016*, Geneva: UNHCR.

Wang, Q. (2004) 'The emergence of cultural self-constructs: Autobiographical memory and self-description in European American and Chinese children', *Developmental Psychology*, 40: 3–15.

Warren, R. (2016) 'Private life in the balance: constructing the precarious migrant', *Journal of Immigration, Asylum and Nationality Law*, 30(2): 124–141.

Warren, R. and York, S. (2014) *How children become failed asylum-seekers*, University of Kent.

York, S. (2015) 'Immigration control and the place of article 8 in the UK courts – an update', *Journal of Immigration, Asylum and Nationality Law*, 29(3): 289–307.

THREE

Caring for and about unaccompanied migrant youth

Anna Gupta

Introduction

Unaccompanied young migrants face significant uncertainty and harm not just in and during their journeys from their countries of origin, but in their experiences within the care and immigration systems in the UK, and in their everyday lives, especially when making the transition to adulthood. Following on from the previous chapter, which looked at the legal complexities of their immigration status, this chapter discusses the provision of care and protection for unaccompanied young migrants within current legal and policy frameworks. The United Nations Convention on the Rights of the Child 1989 (UNCRC) and domestic child welfare legislation, such as the Children Act 1989, provide a framework for the provision of state services; however, children's experiences of care and support services vary greatly (Children's Commissioner for England, 2017).

This chapter will focus on practice within the context of the Children Act 1989 and other relevant legislation in England, but reference is made to other countries in the UK. A central issue is the tensions between immigration and care priorities, particularly in relation to social workers responsible for safeguarding and promoting the child's welfare within local authorities experiencing increasing financial cuts and influenced by wider political discourses and government policies. Consideration is given to how children are constructed as 'deserving' or 'undeserving', and how these constructs impact on the care and support services received. While the vulnerabilities of unaccompanied young migrants and their needs as individuals for tailored support services must be recognised, their agency in making decisions about their own lives must also be acknowledged. The challenges and opportunities for achieving this in the current political, policy and practice contexts will be critically examined in this chapter and many of the issues raised are discussed in more detail in subsequent chapters in Section 2.

Legal and policy frameworks for the provision of care and protection

Unaccompanied migrant children arrive in the UK and come to the attention of state services in various different ways. Some will come as part of government programmes. Many other young people will arrive via clandestine routes such as in the back of lorries, and are found by authorities where they are dropped off. Others who are trafficked in order to work in illegal enterprises may be discovered by police during raids – for example, the many Vietnamese boys working in cannabis factories. Wherever they come from and however they arrive in the UK, all children are entitled to the same rights enshrined in the UNCRC as children born here, and depending on the UK country in which they arrive, the domestic childcare legislation applies in terms of their status, entitlements and rights to protection and support. In England the Children Act 1989 is the key legislation, supported by regulations and guidance, such as the *Care of unaccompanied migrant children and child victims of modern slavery: Statutory guidance for local authorities* (DfE, 2017a).

According to the UNCRC all under the age of 18 years must enjoy all the rights and protections without discrimination. However, up until 2008 the UK government had maintained a reservation in relation to Article 22, which provides that states should ensure that children have the right to special protection and help if they are seeking asylum or are refugees, as well as all the other rights in the Convention. In 2008 the Labour government removed the UK's opt-out of Article 22, with the result that all children in the UK are entitled equally to the protections afforded by the UNCRC regardless of their immigration status.

Article 3 of the UNCRC is central to any decision making about separated young people: 'whether undertaken by public or private social welfare institutions, courts of law, administrative authorities or legislative bodies, the best interest of the child shall be a primary consideration'. The 'best interests' principle is described as 'a holistic concept, embracing the child's physical, mental, spiritual, moral, psychological and social development' (DfE, 2017a: 8). The removal of the reservation in relation to Article 22 led to Section 55 of the Borders, Citizens and Immigration Act 2009, which requires immigration officials when carrying out their functions to have regard to the need to safeguard and promote the welfare of children who are in the UK. However, as discussed in the previous and other chapters in this book, the experiences of many of the children are a far cry from the ideals of the UNCRC. A review of the literature on the subjective wellbeing of children subject to immigration control conducted by the Children's Commissioner for England (2017: 33) concluded that: 'Children consistently characterized their experiences within the UK immigration system as confusing, stressful and degrading: they perceived the system as adversarial and felt powerless, which was aggravated by the lack of adequate guidance and support throughout the process'.

Other key Articles enshrined in the UNCRC include Article 12, which concerns a child's right to express their views, feelings and wishes in all matters affecting them, and to have their views considered and taken seriously. Article 20 requires governments to give special protection and assistance to children who cannot be cared for by their immediate family, including alternative care that is continuous and respects the child's culture, language and religion. Article 22 also states that governments must help refugee children who are separated from their parents to be reunited with them.

The principles of the Children Act 1989 are generally compatible with the UNCRC. The child's welfare needs to be the paramount concern (s.1.1), and children's wishes and feelings need to be ascertained and given serious consideration (s.1.3). Section 17 of the Children Act 1989 places a general duty on every local authority to safeguard and promote the welfare of children in need within their area by providing services appropriate to those children's needs. Unaccompanied migrant minors are considered children in need, and there is a duty on the local authority to undertake an assessment of their needs and provide accommodation. Most separated children are given support under section 20 of the Children Act 1989 and will become 'looked after' by the local authority. These children and young people are entitled to the same local authority provision as any other looked after child (or more widely understood as being a 'child in care'), which includes placement in foster or residential care, education and therapeutic support. At 31 March 2017, unaccompanied asylum-seeking children represented 6% of the looked after children population (DfE, 2017b).

Under section 20 of the Children Act 1989 the local authority does not acquire parental responsibility for the child or young person and it does not involve the local authority applying for an order for the court. Children are accommodated under section 20 by virtue of there being 'no person who has parental responsibility for him' (section 20 (1) (a)). However, it is not usual but on occasion local authorities apply to the family court for a care order in relation to unaccompanied children.

Through a care order the local authority legally acquires parental responsibility for the child. Coram Children's Legal Centre (Dorling et al, 2017: 43) suggests that local authorities should consider applying for a care order (section 31 of the Children Act 1989), particularly for younger children and those with significant vulnerabilities, including victims of trafficking and children with capacity issues. During the care proceedings process in the family courts, a Children's Guardian and solicitor are appointed to represent the child or young person's views and interests, and there is judicial oversight of the local authority's care plan.

In a court judgement *Re J (Child Refugees)* [2017] EWFC 44, Mr Justice Jackson made care orders in relation to two children from Afghanistan aged nine and ten, but made it clear that whether it is appropriate to apply for a care order will depend on the facts of the individual case. He laid out the advantages and disadvantages of the two options, including that children accommodated under section 20 may have lower priority for therapeutic services; and there may be a lack of purpose and planning (for example, trying to regularise the child's immigration status), and looser responsibilities should the children, for example, go missing. However, he concluded that:

> It is neither in the interests of individual children, nor, I think, in the wider public interest for Local Authorities to feel that they have to bring care proceedings to no good purpose, as would be the case if every unaccompanied asylum-seeking child was to be brought within care proceedings (para. 25).

By contrast many older youth only receive services under section 17 of the Children Act 1989 and do not become looked after children, reducing their entitlement to a range of services, including access to education and therapeutic services. In 2003 a court judgement following a judicial review of the London Borough of Hillingdon, known commonly as the 'Hillingdon judgement' made explicit the level of support that was expected of local authorities for unaccompanied children and young people. This support includes the following:

- All unaccompanied children should, on arrival, be supported under section 20 of the Children Act 1989 until an assessment has been completed.

- Based on assessment of need, most unaccompanied children, including 16- and 17-year-olds, should be provided with section 20 support.
- The majority of unaccompanied young people will be entitled to leaving care services.
- Section 17 (which generally provides less care and support than Section 20) can be used to accommodate unaccompanied children in exceptional circumstances.

The section of the Children Act 1989 under which the child is supported not only determines the level of support with which they are provided as a child, but also affects whether they are entitled to leaving care services from the local authority once they reach 18. General legislation in relation to children leaving care, including the Care Leavers (England) Regulations 2010 amended in 2014, are relevant for unaccompanied migrant young people who are or were looked after by the local authority; however, there is often much confusion about the entitlement of unaccompanied migrant youth to leaving care support. Former unaccompanied children who have turned 18 and have been granted leave to remain, or who have an outstanding asylum or other human rights claim or appeal, are entitled to the same level of care and support from the local authority as any other care leaver. The majority of separated young people should be entitled to leaving care support when they turn 18. However, young people who arrive, or start receiving support, within 13 weeks of their 18th birthday will not qualify for full leaving care services even if they have been provided with support under section 20 of the Children Act 1989 for the weeks leading up to their 18th birthday. The problems for young people in this period leading up to and following their 18th birthday are exacerbated by this time also being a crisis point with their asylum applications, as discussed in Chapter Two, so it can mean that a young person goes from being a looked after child, with foster family and in education, to their case being in limbo, or worse settled against then, in a matter of days or weeks.

Prior to the Immigration Act 2016, local authority Children's Services could provide accommodation and financial support for a care leaver who is 'appeal rights exhausted' (ARE) following an unsuccessful asylum claim. Human rights assessments by social workers are also undertaken to determine whether support is necessary to prevent a breach of the care leaver's human rights. The aim of such an assessment is to consider whether withdrawing support from a young person would result in a breach of either Article 3 (inhuman/

degrading treatment) or Article 8 (right to family/private life) of the European Convention on Human Rights (ECHR). At the time of writing (July 2018), not all of the regulations of the Immigration Act 2016 have been confirmed, but access to local authority leaving care support once this part of the Act is implemented will only be available for young people who:

- have been granted leave to enter or remain in the UK; or
- are asylum seekers awaiting a decision on their claim or the result of an appeal; this includes young people who were refused first time around, but have made further submissions or a fresh claim based on their need for asylum or international protection; or
- have made another type of immigration application (for example Article 8 of the European Convention on Human Rights protecting the right to private and family life) and the application or an appeal against refusal has not been finally determined.

Initially the changes are only to apply to England, although the government may choose to extend them to Wales, Scotland and Northern Ireland (Dorling et al, 2017: 53).

The express purpose of these exclusions under Schedule 12 of the Immigration Act 2016 is, in the words of James Brokenshire the then Minister for Immigration, to:

> prevent adult migrant care leavers who have exhausted their appeal rights and have established no lawful basis to remain here from accessing local authority support under the 1989 Act. [...] The provisions in the 1989 Act are geared to support the needs and onward development of young adults leaving local authority care whose long-term future is in the UK. Those provisions are not appropriate to the support needs, pending their departure from the UK, of adult migrants who the courts have agreed have no right to remain here. (Hansard HC, 17.11.15 col 520, 521)

Kotilaine (2016) argues that in removing local authority leaving care support from young people who have no lawful basis to remain in the UK, the balance between competing priorities of welfare over border control shifts decisively in favour of the Home Office. The result of this exclusion from leaving care provisions is that unaccompanied migrant young people who were supported and protected (albeit to varying degrees) are suddenly abandoned by the local authority that has looked after them, with often an absence of clear plan for alternative support and protection, leaving them once again at risk of various forms of harm and exploitation.

Implementing policy and law in practice

The legal frameworks for the care and protection of children and young people summarised briefly in the section above convey entitlements on the basis that the person is under the age of 18 when they arrive in the UK. However in 2016 a House of Lords European Union Select Committee report, *Children in crisis: unaccompanied migrant children in the EU*, found that the needs of unaccompanied migrant children are systematically not being met, either in the UK or the rest of the EU. Legal recognition has not always guaranteed the protection of young people's rights, as the situation they encounter in countries where they seek refuge reflects fundamental tensions between immigration policy and child welfare (Aspinall and Walters, 2010).

This chapter critically examines how local authorities carry out some of these duties and obligations; the contextual influences on professional practice and service delivery; and how these impact on the experiences of unaccompanied migrant youth. Major determinants of young people's treatment are: the central tension between child welfare and immigration control; the influence of political and mainstream media discourses on social work and other professional practice, including the culture of disbelief, suspicion and racism towards unaccompanied migrant children; and the impact of stringent cuts to local authority budgets and services under 'austerity' policies.

Age assessments

Age assessments are the process by which many unaccompanied migrant youth are determined to be a child or not. In Chapter Two, York and Warren looked at the impact of age assessments on from the asylum and immigration law perspective; this section considers them from the care/legal perspective. Assessing the ages of unaccompanied migrant youth is a highly contested and controversial area of work in the UK and internationally (Hjern et al, 2012). For the individual young person the significance of the decision is enormous, as it will determine whether they receive support under the Children Act 1989 and protection under the UNCRC. If assessed as being under 18, the young person would normally be regarded as a child in the care of the state; however, if assessed as an adult the young person receives considerably less support, could be detained and possibly faces the prospect on imminent forced removal from the UK.

The age assessment process is exacerbated by the fact that many unaccompanied young people, including those who are trafficked, arrive in the UK without documentation or with documentation deemed to be forged or counterfeit. If an asylum seeker's claim to be a child is doubted by the Home Office, and there is little or no documentary evidence to prove their age, the Home Office will conduct an initial assessment of the individual based solely on appearance and demeanour. It is Home Office policy that unless the physical appearance/demeanour of the individual very strongly suggests that they are significantly over 18 years of age, they should be given the benefit of the doubt and treated as a child until a more holistic assessment can be made by a local authority (Dorling et al, 2017). Even if the Home Office treats an individual as an adult, if a referral is made to children's services, the local authority must make their own decision as to the young person's age, as a gateway decision for the purposes of deciding whether they are entitled to services under the Children Act 1989. There may be occasions where a local authority feels that an age assessment is not necessary but where the Home Office requests an assessment before it will treat the young person as a child for immigration purposes. In these circumstances the local authority will need to discuss with the Home Office the reasons as to why the young person should be treated as a child without further assessment (Dorling et al, 2017). Government guidance to local authorities states that:

> Where an age assessment is required, local authorities must adhere to standards established within case law. Age assessments should only be carried out where there is reason to doubt that the individual is the age they claim. Age assessments should not be a routine part of a local authority's assessment of unaccompanied or trafficked children. (DfE, 2017a: 13)

Before 2015, there was no official guidance provided to local authorities on how to conduct an age assessment. Instead the approach taken evolved through practice by local authorities and legal challenges to the processes used. The first significant case to deal with the issue of local authority duties and processes when undertaking age assessments was *B v London Borough of Merton [2003] EWHC 1689 (Admin.)* (known as the 'Merton judgement') in 2003. The judge in the Merton judgement detailed a number of basic principles to be considered in order to make assessments lawful. These included:

- Two qualified and properly trained social workers should conduct the age assessment.
- An appropriate adult should be present to ensure the child understands, to support assist and advise, to observe the process and to ensure rights are upheld.
- An assessment cannot be made solely on the basis of appearance, and should be a holistic one taking account of the young person's appearance, demeanour, background and credibility.
- The child should be informed of the purpose of the assessment.
- The child should be informed of the consequences of the assessment decision.
- There is a duty to give adequate, cogent and relevant reasons for decisions made at the end of assessments.
- A child-friendly approach must be taken and there should be procedural fairness throughout the assessment process.

The Merton judgement also included the guidance that '... an untrue history, while relevant, is not necessarily indicative of a lie as to the age of the applicant. Lies may be told for reasons unconnected with the applicant's case as to his age' (paragraph 8). Subsequent case law has elaborated on the requirements of social workers completing age assessments.

In October 2015, best practice guidance for social workers on conducting age assessments was published by the Association of Directors of Children's Services (ADCS, 2015) compliant with the Merton judgment and other relevant case law. The requirement that social workers undertake single agency age assessments has been criticised, including by the British Association of Social Workers:

> Given the combination of the inherent inaccuracy of determinations, the importance of the rights at stake, and the established principle that best results are achieved by holistic assessment, this ethical principle supports multi-disciplinary determinations. (BASW, 2015: 3)

Although the Home Office and other public bodies require that social workers determine the date when the young person was deemed to have been born, there is currently no available method that can accurately assess the age of young asylum seekers, if valid documents are missing. The Royal College of Paediatrics and Child Health (2007) recognises that age determination is an inexact science and the margin of error can sometimes be as much as five years either side, especially around the time of puberty. Ethical questions have been raised in relation to the use of skeletal and dental X-rays for legal purposes without therapeutic value, given the (albeit very small) exposure of the individual to ionising radiation (Hjern et al, 2012). A growing concern that age assessment by the use of radiography is imprecise, unethical and potentially unlawful has led every relevant statutory and professional body in the UK to argue against its use (Aynsley-Green et al, 2012).

The challenges inherent in undertaking more holistic social work age assessments have also been identified. Children and young people subject to immigration control come from cultures and contexts in which childhood is defined in different ways reflecting the social, economic and political circumstances of these societies. In many countries, birth dates are not registered, documented, celebrated or even necessarily known (Dorling et al, 2017); significant variations exist in the physical development of children and these may be exacerbated by experiences of children in their country of origin and the long and difficult journey to the UK (Crawley, 2007); and young people coming from countries of war and conflict may challenge Western conceptions of childhood as 'dependent' and 'powerless' (Legget, 2008). Young people may not understand the process, fear authority figures, or say what they think is the 'right answer' or what they have been told to say (Dorling et al, 2017). Rigby and Whyte (2015: 39) suggest that:

> 'Evidence' and 'truth' may become tenuous and fluid concepts as children's narratives fragment on constant retelling and reprocessing of their journeys and experiences. Children may also choose to tell some professionals one version of events and others a slightly different version, depending on the situation. These changes in children's stories are generally an indication of the complexities of lives and journeys, and their perceptions of events, and should not be used to challenge the credibility of children in either the asylum or child protection systems.

The age assessment decision-making process will also be impacted by the individual social workers conducting these assessments and the context in which they work. The report *Beyond Proof: Credibility assessment in EU asylum systems* (UNHCR, 2013) highlights the relevance of the psychology of the applicant, the interviewer and, if different, the decision maker, as well as the interactions between these people in relation to making judgements about credibility. Factors affecting the individual decision maker's practice include the individual circumstances and contextual factors; their state of mind, including the impact of case-hardening, credibility fatigue, emotional detachment, stress and vicarious trauma; as well as political, societal and institutional contexts. Studies looking at age determination practices highlight a strong culture of disbelief within the Home Office and local authorities with entrenched beliefs that the majority of age-disputed young people are adults posing as children (Crawley 2007; Cemlyn and Nye, 2012). This is fuelled by political and media discourses, as exemplified by some newspaper reports and politicians' comments when children were accepted into the UK following the closure of the camp in Calais in October 2016 (see for example the report by Weaver, 2016). Critical awareness of the political context of asylum is required by social workers and other professionals, in order to recognise and challenge the negative, racist and xenophobic political and media constructions of asylum seekers (Masocha and Simpson, 2011).

Cemlyn and Nye (2012: 685) argue that the age assessment process can be seen 'as paradigmatic for the tensions facing social work with asylum seekers between a focus on the rights of service users and the demands of conformity to the restrictions of immigration law'. Not only can social work practice be affected by anti-immigration discourses, but social workers undertaking age assessments work in large bureaucratic organisations that are under severe financial pressures. Cemlyn and Nye (2012) suggest there is some evidence of a potential conflict of interest where the outcome of the age assessment process has financial implications for the local authority if the individual is assessed to be a child. Age assessments are not used solely to determine whether a young person is under or over 18; being assessed as either under or over 16 will have considerable implications for young people in terms of the level of support and resources available to them (Wright, 2014). For the young person it can be very confusing as to the role of the social worker, as someone responsible for their care and protection, as well as determining their age and eligibility for services. A number of authors have highlighted the contradictions social workers face in relation to their professional values promoting social justice and human rights, alongside the social work task increasingly having become embedded in immigration control (Humphries, 2004; Kvittingen, 2010). Cemlyn and Nye (2012: 682) explain that:

> A situation therefore prevails in which the practice of individual social workers, who are caught between regulatory and financial pressures and their loyalty to professional values, is at the fulcrum of influence in terms of the experience of young separated asylum seekers.

The possibility of getting it wrong makes age assessment a highly risky endeavour as children may be denied the special protection of the UNCRC and domestic child care legislation. The *Young Lives in Limbo* research project conducted by the Welsh Refugee Council (Clarke, 2011) found very inconsistent practice across local authorities, young people experiencing considerable distress during the process, and some being wrongly assessed as adults. The study identified significant mental health implications for young people's sense of identity; sense of self and trust in others; education development and safety (especially the risk of absconding). Abdullah (aged 15) explains "I felt very scared. They asked me questions about my life, my family. I told them the truth. They told me they don't believe me, that I am a liar" (Clarke, 2011: 48).

While individual young people continue to require a date of birth in order to navigate the myriad of public services and there needs to be some form of determination where there is good reason to doubt a child's stated age, much can be done to improve current processes. The age assessment may take time, more than one or two interviews, while professionals get to know the young person. It should involve multi-agency perspectives (such as health and education) from others who are involved with the young person. Importantly practitioners need to be attentive to their power, be critically reflective and demonstrate an awareness that age assessments are affected by racially-biased and culturally-based preconceptions, including of age-related behaviour and appearances; subjective judgements; management pressures to reduce costs; and political and media constructions of asylum seekers (Kvittingen, 2010). Dorling (2013) also highlights the unsatisfactory nature of the current process whereby a young person can only use the lengthy and costly process of judicial review to challenge the legality, rationality and fairness of their assessment.

Care and protection

As discussed in earlier sections, unaccompanied migrant children (including young people going through the age determination process) are entitled to protection and assistance under the UNCRC and the legislative framework under which this is provided by local authorities in England and Wales is the Children Act 1989. Assessment and care provisions for the child should commence immediately as for any looked after child, irrespective of whether an application for an asylum claim has been submitted to the Home Office.

Generally, the local authority responsible for the child is the one in which they first present; however, some children are transferred to another local authority under voluntary transfer arrangements between local authorities in order to distribute the responsibility for unaccompanied minors more evenly (DfE, 2017a). Upon a child being referred to a children's services department, an assessment should be undertaken to determine their immediate needs and that should be followed with a more detailed assessment to develop a care plan to address the range of their developmental needs (DfE, 2017a).

Being assessed as either under or over 16 will have significant implications for a young person in terms of the level of support and resources available to them. Although the decision about the type of placement should depend on the child or young person's individual circumstances and needs, in practice determined age is often the deciding factor. An unaccompanied minor assessed to be under 16 years of age will be placed in a foster placement or residential children's home, where they will be cared for by foster parents or care workers, be supervised and have access to services and payments (such as a clothing allowance) that other looked after children receive. Children's experiences in these placements differ greatly. For example, some young people have described foster care positively when it was somewhere they felt valued and cared for (Wade et al, 2012). However, other young people have felt that they were treated differently, were uncared for and isolated (Chase et al, 2008).

Unaccompanied migrant youth who have been assessed as being 16 or 17 are likely to be placed into accommodation ranging from supported lodgings to independent living in shared accommodation with no adult supervision and where they receive less practical and emotional support, even when considered a child in care under section 20 (Crawley, 2007; Wright 2014). Wade et al (2012) found that a minority of young people (those aged below 16 at arrival) are afforded access to foster care and that among those aged 16 plus, the vast majority are placed in private sector shared housing with varying levels of support. Many young people are placed in accommodation outside the local authority with statutory responsibility to support them, further lessening the support networks available (Humphris and Sigona, 2016). Further discussion about the placements for unaccompanied migrant children and how they can create (or not) a sense of belonging is included in Chapter Six.

While social workers are the key professionals responsible for the care and protection of unaccompanied migrant youth, a multi-agency care plan should be developed that considers the child's wishes and feelings. Children need to be linked in with appropriate education provision. Unaccompanied migrant youth in Chase's (2013) study often identified 'college', 'school', and 'learning' as being among the most positive aspects of their current lives. Addressing young people's physical and mental health needs is also essential. This will include, for example, considering specialist mental health support and ensuring that appropriate and good-quality interpreters are used if required. Attention to the child's immigration status and access to good quality legal advice is essential, as is developing links with general youth services and specialist refugee support organisations. Feelings of connectedness and positive relationships with peers and caring adults are important to young people's positive mental health (Meloni and Chase, 2017), as is discussed further in later chapters.

Young people experience the negative effects of forced migration on their physical and emotional wellbeing prior to and on their journeys to Europe. However, these difficulties can be compounded by their experiences once in the UK, in an environment in which they often experience discrimination on the basis of their race or religion and stigmatisation in an often 'hostile environment', as well as the uncertainties of not knowing what their final immigration status (or lack of it) will be (Children's Commissioner for England, 2017). Despite constantly facing stigma and prejudice, and feeling their identities were defined and agency constrained by their immigration status, many unaccompanied migrant young people in the studies reviewed by the Children's Commissioner for England (2017: 33) maintained 'surprising levels of self-esteem, motivation and belief in their capacity to overcome adversity'. The promotion of unaccompanied young people's strength and positive mental health is discussed further in Chapter Five.

Chase (2013) highlights the importance of devising care and support packages that are individualised, involve young people, and are able to nurture consistency, predictability and a secure sense of the projected self for young people surviving trauma and loss. However, this can be difficult to achieve in current organisational and policy contexts. The care offered to unaccompanied asylum-seeking children varies considerably across local authorities as they interpret their responsibilities to unaccompanied and former unaccompanied migrant youth differently, with stringent cuts to budgets further polarising such experiences (Connolly and Pinter, 2015). The *Becoming Adult* research project noted that financial constraints are affecting the care local authorities are able to provide to young people seeking asylum, with services for older children particularly affected. The authors also identified that a loss of specialist teams has led to a loss of critical expertise and 'a risk that the best interests of "foreign" children in care become deprioritised and that they experience a decline, qualitatively and quantitatively, in services and support' (Sigona et al, 2017: 3).

Local authorities have a duty to protect these highly vulnerable children from abuse and exploitation. When a young person first presents to a local authority, professionals need to be alert to the possibility that the child may have been trafficked to the UK for the purposes of exploitation. If this is identified or suspected, there needs to be multi-agency child protection investigation involving the police, in line with statutory guidance, and the young person will be referred to the National Referral Mechanism (NRM) and assessed as a possible victim of human trafficking/modern slavery (DfE, 2017a).

Many unaccompanied children are at risk of going missing from care, often within the first 72 hours, while others may be at risk of repeated missing episodes due to ongoing exploitation. Research by ECPAT UK and Missing People (2016) found that, from September 2014 to September 2015, 28% of trafficked children (167 children) in care and 13% of unaccompanied asylum-seeking children (593 children) in care went missing at least once. Of the 760 trafficked or unaccompanied children who went missing from care, 207 had not been found at the end of the project. This research and the work of Humphris and Sigona (2016) have identified a worrying lack of consistency in the way in which local authorities identify risk of trafficking, exploitation and going missing, with many children becoming 'invisible'. Children trafficked into the UK for the purpose of criminal activities are vulnerable to being dealt with by the criminal justice rather than care systems and also to going missing. Vietnamese boys trafficked for cannabis cultivation are at particular risk (ECPAT UK and Missing People, 2016). Reasons for going missing include: control/influence of traffickers; lack of trust in adults who are there to keep them safe; feeling isolated; lack of engagement with school and social networks; uncertain immigration status; and stressful procedures (ECPAT UK and Missing People, 2016).

While trafficked children and victims of modern slavery are often demarcated from other unaccompanied migrant children, the definitions are often blurred, and exploitation needs to be viewed as a continuum. Creating binaries can construct some children as 'deserving' victims of abuse and others as 'undeserving' migrants (O'Connell Davidson, 2011). The *Trees only move in the wind* (UNHCR, 2010) report highlights the large sums of money often involved in the journey of separated children to Europe. Many families will have entered into significant debt to pay for the journey. These payment arrangements and debt bondage can have serious implications for the safety of the children once they have started their journey and after they have arrived in Europe. Studies in Afghanistan indicate that the consequences of indebtedness will also impact on the lives of separated young people who are forcibly removed to their country of origin (Gladwell and Elwyn, 2012; Schuster and Majidi, 2013).

As indicated above, the majority of unaccompanied migrant youth should become children looked after by the local authority and be subject to the review processes for all children in care. Regular child in care reviews are forums to bring the young person and key professionals together, and must take place chaired by an Independent Reviewing Officer (IRO) (Department for Education, 2015). The primary task of the IRO is to ensure that the care plan for the child fully reflects the child's current needs, takes account of their wishes and that the actions set out in the plan are consistent with the local authority's legal responsibilities towards the child.

Children's descriptions of experiences of social workers in the studies reviewed by the Children's Commissioner for England (2017) were varied, with some speaking about the positive difference social workers made in their lives, and others feeling that social workers were not interested in their wellbeing. Support for unaccompanied migrant youth is most effective where this is provided through a stable, continuous relationship with the child, with trust being a key factor. However, the adverse impact of austerity measures has led leaders and managers of children's services in England to express concerns about their ability to undertake their statutory duties to vulnerable children and recruit and retain high quality social workers (ADCS, 2017).

Independent guardianship has been considered as a way forward in supporting unaccompanied migrant youth to manage their way through the complex immigration and welfare systems (Save the Children, 2008; UNHCR, 2009). England has no independent guardian service, with local authority social workers fulfilling the guardianship role. However, in Scotland a pilot guardianship service for unaccompanied migrant children was established, funded by the Scottish Government and charitable foundations. The service was developed following recommendations of a report by Hopkins and Hill

(2006) that separated children require an independent adult who is not their social worker to ensure their needs and interests are met, as social workers can be constrained in advocating for the young people by the organisational contexts in which they work. A positive evaluation of the Scottish Guardianship Service was conducted by Crawley and Kohli (2013). The study concluded that:

> Overall, we consider that the Scottish Guardianship Service contained a wealth of evidence about the benefits of Guardianship for young people who are seeking asylum or have been trafficked. The voices of young people were strong and clear. They believed that the Service put them – rather than the processes to which they were subjected – at the centre and that the Guardians provided them with a level of acceptance and support which, for complex reasons, they were unable to secure from other adults in their lives (pp 89–90).

Making transitions to adulthood

Leaving care at 18 and making the transition to adulthood without a supportive family can be a frightening prospect for many young people. However, unaccompanied migrant youth face an even more uncertain future as their temporary leave to remain in the UK is withdrawn and they await a Home Office decision that could lead to forced removal from their established networks in the UK to countries where they face dangers and may have few or no connections. In Chase's (2013) study young people talked of experiencing a range of emotional health problems, including chronic depression, suicide attempts and, in some cases, periodic mental illness requiring them to spend time in hospital psychiatric units. Problems were particularly acute as they made the transition from child to adult within the immigration system. Nadine, aged 18, who had left Rwanda at the age of six and spent many years in refugee camps outside Rwanda talks about what she said to her solicitor about the prospect of being forcibly return to Rwanda:

> 'I said to him [solicitor], "if they tell that to me, I will just tell them, I will just hold a gun and I will say, 'you know what, you can either shoot me right now or, I don't know, go and put me somewhere in a hole rather than take me to Rwanda. OK?' Because I have got nothing to go there for". If they tell me, "we have found your parents living safely

there, they have gone back to their normal way" ... oh my God, I will say, "please take me tomorrow morning". But telling me they are going to give me money to start a new life ... I don't know ... do anything you want but taking me there, no chance' (Chase, 2013: 865–6).

For any young person in care, a local authority should, prior to them turning 16, develop a 'Pathway Plan' based on an assessment of their needs as they make the transition to adulthood. A local authority has continuing obligations to support any child over the age of 16 who is, or has been, in care for at least 13 weeks since the age of 14 and been looked after at some time after their 16th birthday, until they are 21 (or 25 if pursuing a programme of education or training). These obligations include providing a personal advisor, conducting a needs assessment, and developing a Pathway Plan in collaboration with the young person. The Pathway Plan should be based on an assessment of their needs and cover areas such as: accommodation, practical life skills, education and training, employment, financial support, specific support needs, and contingency plans (Department for Education, 2015).

Pathway planning to support an unaccompanied child's transition to adulthood needs to cover the areas that would be addressed within any care leaver's plan as well as any additional needs arising from their immigration status and the action required to resolve this. However, as discussed in Chapter Two, there will be much uncertainty and may be considerable delays before Home Office decisions are made and legal processes exhausted. As a result, social workers need to plan for various possible outcomes for those turning 18. This is often known as 'triple planning' requiring consideration of three possible outcomes, as Dorling et al (2017: 52) explain:

- equipping the young person to have a future in the UK if they receive some form of leave to remain in the UK past their 18th birthday.
- preparing a young person to be returned to their country of origin either if they are refused an extension to remain in the UK and are being returned, or if they decide to return of their own accord.
- supporting young people who have been refused leave to remain in the UK and who have exhausted all appeals but are not removed. This may be for a number of reasons, such as difficulties in getting permission for

them to return to their country of origin or place from which they fled (because for example nationality is being disputed).

Pathway planning for unaccompanied migrant youth can be a difficult and emotionally demanding process for the young person and professionals working with them. For example, how do professionals begin, emotionally and practically, to plan for Nadine's forced removal back to Rwanda? For other young people it may be easier to promote connections to possibilities in countries of origin when their return seems inevitable.

Chase and Allsop (2013) argue that young people's subjective wellbeing is linked their notions of future and being able to imagine and work towards future goals. Many young people denied leave to remain exercise what agency they have by making decisions, such as going 'underground' and living as an undocumented migrant with all the risks that this entails. A crucial ethical question that rarely gets asked is whether social workers and other professionals should enter into discussion about this option with young people, especially when the only other option of forced return appears as, if not more, dangerous. It is however vital that social workers link unaccompanied young people to refugee and community groups to give them the tools and abilities they require to make informed decisions regarding voluntary return, forced removal and the consequences of living in the UK illegally (Wright, 2014). Further discussion on planning for durable solutions for unaccompanied migrant youth is included in Chapter Seven.

There has been some confusion over whether local authorities are required to provide support to young people who have not received, or no longer have, leave to remain, often 'appeal rights exhausted' (ARE) cases, and who are still in the UK. Most young people aged 18 or over who are ARE and have no further lawful basis of stay in the UK will become 'unlawfully in the UK' and be subject to restrictions in their ability to access leaving care support under the Immigration Act 2016 (Dorling et al, 2017). Young people who are not able to receive leaving care support may still be entitled to continue to receive some help from children's services if it would breach their rights under the European Convention on Human Rights (ECHR) not to provide this support. There is very little guidance on how a local authority should conduct a Human Rights Assessment, although a useful framework is provided on the No Recourse to Public Funds website.[1] As with other social work assessments, the process and decision will be affected by the individual professional's values and assumptions, organisational cultures and resources, and policy frameworks.

Very limited information is available about the outcomes for young people who have been returned voluntarily or forcibly, or indeed those that go 'underground'. Gladwell and Elwyn (2012) undertook a study of young people returned to Afghanistan and found that:

> ... for a proportion of the young people the UK government deemed it safe to return, it has been anything but safe ... For others, although they have not faced specific threats on return to Afghanistan, they have suffered with cultural reintegration, lack of employment and mental health issues. Some have reintegrated successfully and built a life for themselves, but many have tried to leave Afghanistan once again (p 52).

The authors conclude that local authorities have a moral if not legal duty to unaccompanied migrant youth as former children in care to monitor young people who are returned and provide support, both pre- and post-return, to give them the best possible chances of success (Gladwell and Elwyn, 2012).

Conclusions

In this chapter the provision of care and protection for unaccompanied young migrants within current legal and policy frameworks in England has been discussed. Although there are differences in the legislative frameworks of the other countries of the UK, all reflect the principles of the UNCRC. Despite these unifying principles, children's experiences of care and support services vary greatly, depending on individual characteristics, such as age and race, as well as professional practices, organisational and wider policy contexts. The *Becoming Adult* project concluded that:

> the principle of the 'best interests of the child' that underpins the child protection regime is being transformed by the concomitant pressures from budget cuts, expanding market logics in the asylum system and widespread anti-immigration attitudes that find expression in the policy goal of producing a 'hostile environment' for foreigners (Sigona et al, 2017: 2).

Social workers and other professionals have to grapple with these fundamental tensions between immigration policy and child welfare, and between professional values and managerial demands. Despite the inevitable constraints imposed on practitioners and managers, it is important to recognise the agency of workers and unaccompanied migrant youth. Much can be done to ensure that care and support services help young people to promote their voices, rights and welfare within a social justice framework.

For individual practitioners developing supportive relationships with young people, getting to know the individual and their story, and critically reflecting on their own personal values and assumptions is crucial. A range of intersecting power relationships, including discrimination on the basis of their race and/or religion, frame the lives of unaccompanied migrant youth. Workers must be attuned to a young person's experiences of discrimination and 'othering' processes in order to address these. This includes attention to overt practices and less overt micro-aggressions that may be perpetuated by themselves or other professionals. Recognising and challenging institutional harm caused by immigration and asylum processes and deficient care services for unaccompanied migrant youth can be difficult for social workers and other professionals, but an important element of anti-oppressive and critical social work practice.

On an organisational level, providing time for workers to develop relationships with young people and creating a culture and space for practitioners and managers to critically reflect and engage in ethical debates (in groups or via supervision) about the provision of services for unaccompanied migrant youth and how all young people can be treated with respect, humanity and with their human rights upheld is vital.

An effective multi-professional/agency response to the needs of unaccompanied migrant children and young people that acknowledges the importance of relationships and the promotion of a sense of belonging and future through all practices is crucial. Developing young people's links with voluntary, NGO refugee and anti-deportation organisations is also important to ensure information is provided for them to make informed decisions, sound legal advice is obtained, and contact maintained if in detention or forcibly returned.

Williams and Briskman (2015) draw on the concept of 'moral outrage' and argue that the translation of personal distress into public issues is at the heart of the political project of social work. In this context it is also important to use our professional voices and experience to act in solidarity with unaccompanied migrant youth and those affected by forced migration and controlled borders through dialogue and social activism.[2]

Notes

[1] www.nrpfnetwork.org.uk

[2] See, for example, www.socialworkerswithoutborders.org

References

Aspinall, P. and Walters, C. (2010) *Refugees and asylum seekers. A review from an equality and human rights perspective*, London: Equality and Human Rights Commission.

Association of Directors of Children's Services (ADCS) (2015) *Age assessment guidance: Guidance to assist social workers and their managers in undertaking age assessments in England*, October, http://adcs.org.uk/assets/documentation/Age_Assessment_Guidance_2015_Final.pdf

ADCS (2017) *A country that works for all children*, ADCS position paper, October, http://adcs.org.uk/assets/documentation/ADCS_A_country_that_works_for_all_children_FINAL.pdf

Aynsley-Green, A., Cole, T.J., Crawley, H., Lessof, N., Boag, L.R. and Wallace, R.M.M. (2012) 'Medical, statistical, ethical and human rights considerations in the assessment of age in children and young people subject to immigration control', *British Medical Bulletin*, 102(1): 17–42.

British Association of Social Workers (BASW) (2015) *BASW response to the age assessment guidance document*, July, http://cdn.basw.co.uk/upload/basw_115208-6.pdf

Cemlyn, S.J. and Nye, M. (2012) 'Asylum seeker young people: social work value conflicts in negotiating age assessment in the UK', *International Social Work*, 55(5): 675–88.

Chase, E. (2013) 'Security and subjective wellbeing: the experiences of unaccompanied young people seeking asylum in the UK', *Sociology of Health & Illness*, 35(6): 858–72.

Chase, E and Allsop, J. (2013) '*Future citizens of the world'? The contested futures of independent young migrants in Europe*, RSC Working Paper Series 97, Barnett Papers in Social Research, Working Paper 13-05, Oxford: Refugee Studies Centre, www.rsc.ox.ac.uk/files/files-1/wp97-future-citizens-of-the-world-2013.pdf

Chase, E., Knight, A. and Statham, J. (2008) *The emotional wellbeing of unaccompanied young people seeking asylum in the UK*, London: British Association for Adoption and Fostering.

Children's Commissioner for England (2017) *Children's voices: A review of evidence on the subjective wellbeing of children subject to immigration control*, Office of the Children's Commissioner, www.childrenscommissioner.gov.uk/wp-content/uploads/2017/11/Voices-Immigration-Control-1.pdf

Clarke, S. (2011) *Young lives in limbo: The protection of age-disputed young people in Wales*, Cardiff: Welsh Refugee Council.

Connolly, H. and Pinter, I. (2015) *'Cut off from justice: The impact of excluding separated migrant children from legal aid'*, Children's Society, June, www.childrenssociety.org.uk/sites/default/files/LegalAid_Full_0.pdf

Crawley, H. (2007) *When is a child not a child? Asylum, age disputes and the process of age assessment*, London: ILPA

Crawley, H. and Kohli, R.K.S. (2013) *'She endures with me': An evaluation of the Scottish Guardianship Service pilot*, London: Diana Princess of Wales Memorial Trust/Paul Hamlyn Foundation, www.scottishrefugeecouncil.org.uk/assets/0000/6798/Final_Report_2108.pdf

Department for Education (DfE) (2015) *The Children Act 1989 guidance and regulations. Volume 2: care planning, placement and case review*, London: DfE, www.gov.uk/government/uploads/system/uploads/attachment_data/file/441643/Children_Act_Guidance_2015.pdf

DfE (2017a) *Care of unaccompanied migrant children and child victims of modern slavery: Statutory guidance for local authorities*, https://consult.education.gov.uk/children-in-care/care-of-unaccompanied-and-trafficked-children/supporting_documents/Revised%20UASC%20Stat%20guidance_final.pdf

DfE (2017b) *Children looked after in England (including adoption), year ending 31 March 2017*, SFR 50/2017, 28 September, https://assets.publishing.service.gov.uk/government/uploads/system/uploads/attachment_data/file/664995/SFR50_2017-Children_looked_after_in_England.pdf

Dorling, K. (2013) *Happy birthday? Disputing the age of children in the immigration system*, London: Coram Children's Legal Centre, www.childrenslegalcentre.com/wp-content/uploads/2017/04/HappyBirthday_Final.pdf

Dorling, K., MacLachlan, S. and Trevena, F. (2017) *Seeking support: a guide to the rights and entitlements of separated children*, London: Coram Children's Legal Centre, www.childrenslegalcentre.com/wp-content/uploads/2017/05/Seeking-Support-2017.pdf

ECPAT UK and Missing People (2016) *Heading back to harm: A study on trafficked and unaccompanied children going missing from care in the UK*, www.ecpat.org.uk/Handlers/Download.ashx?IDMF=875b65b5-08d4-4e9f-a28c-331d1421519f

Gladwell, C. and Elwyn, H. (2012) *Broken futures: young Afghan asylum seekers in the UK and in their country of origin*, New Issues in Refugee Research, Research Paper No. 244, August, Geneva: UNHCR, https://hubble-live-assets.s3.amazonaws.com/rsn/attachment/file/9/Broken_Futures_RSN_2012.pdf

Hjern, A., Brendler-Lindqvist, M., and Norredam, M. (2012) 'Age assessment of young asylum seekers'. *Acta Paediatrica*, 101(1): 4–7.

Hopkins P.E. and Hill, M. (2006) *'This is a good place to live and think about the future': The needs and experiences of unaccompanied asylum seeking children and young people in Scotland*, Glasgow: Scottish Refugee Council.

Humphries, B. (2004) 'An unacceptable role for social work: Implementing immigration policy', *British Journal of Social Work*, 34: 93–107

Humphris, R. and Sigona, N. (2016) 'Mapping unaccompanied asylum seeking children in England', Becoming Adult Research Brief Series, no. 1, London: UCL, https://becomingadultproject.files.wordpress.com/2016/07/research-brief-series-01_2016.pdf

Kotilaine, J. (2016) 'Duties of local authorities to unaccompanied migrant children', *Family Law Week*, 1 September.

Kvittingen, A. (2010) *Negotiating childhood: Age assessment in the UK asylum system*, Oxford: Refugee Studies Centre.

Legget, S. (2008) *Enhancing social work practice with refugee children in exile*, Social Work Monographs, Norwich: University of East Anglia.

Masocha, S. and Simpson, M. (2011) 'Xenoracism: Towards a critical understanding of the construction of asylum seekers and its implications for social work practice', *Practice*, 23(1): 5–18.

Meloni, F. and Chase, E. (2017) 'Transitions into institutional adulthood', Becoming Adult Research Brief no. 4, London: UCL, https://becomingadultproject.files.wordpress.com/2017/12/ba-brief-4-low-res.pdf

O'Connell Davidson, J. (2011) 'Moving children? Child trafficking, child migration, and child rights', *Critical Social Policy*, 31(3): 454–77.

Rigby, P. and Whyte, B. (2015) 'Children's narrative within a multi-centred, dynamic ecological framework of assessment and planning for child trafficking', *British Journal of Social Work*, 45(1): 34–51.

Royal College of Paediatricians and Child Health (RCPCH) (2007) *X-Rays and asylum seeking children: Policy statement*, RCPCH.

Save the Children (2008) *Guardianship for separated children in the UK: Stakeholder views*, London: SCUK.

Schuster, L. and Majidi, N. (2013) 'What happens post-deportation? The experience of deported Afghans'. *Migration Studies*, 1(2): 221–40.

Sigona, N., Chase, E. and Humphris, R. (2017) 'Protecting the 'best interests' of the child in transition to adulthood', Becoming Adult Research Brief no. 3, London: UCL, https://becomingadultproject.files.wordpress.com/2017/12/ba-brief-3-low-res.pdf

UNHCR (2009) *Proposals on a guardianship role within UK Border Agency asylum decision-making procedures*, Geneva: UNHCR.

Wade, J., Sirriyeh, A., Kohli, R. and Simmonds, J. (2012) *Fostering unaccompanied asylum-seeking young people: A research project*, London: BAAF, www.york.ac.uk/inst/spru/research/pdf/FosterUAS.pdf

UNHCR (2010) *Trees only move in the wind: A study of unaccompanied Afghani children in Europe,* Geneva: UNHCR.

UNHCR (2013) *Beyond proof: Credibility assessments in EU asylum systems*, Brussels: UNHCR.

Weaver, M. (2016) 'Give child refugees dental tests to verify age, says David Davies', *Guardian*, 19 October.

Williams, C. and Briskman, L. (2015) 'Reviving social work through moral outrage', *Critical and Radical Social Work*, 3(1): 3–17

Wright, F. (2014) 'Social work practice with unaccompanied asylum-seeking young people facing removal' *British Journal of Social Work*, 44(4): 1027–44.

SECTION 2

Exploring migrant youth identities

Preface to Section 2:
Voices of separated migrant youth

Sue Clayton

Sue Clayton worked with separated refugee youths between 2006 and 2017 as a filmmaker and academic, and more recently as a consultant for the BBC, ITV News and Channel 4 News. She has interviewed over 200 young refugees and is developing a website (www.bigjourneys.org) to archive them. These stories are told in the way the young people wished to tell them. Her subjects have been anonymised for reasons of privacy. Together they present a collective picture of typical life journeys – hopes, fears and aspirations – which can be read to inform and inflect the chapters that follow. Our thanks to the young people for sharing their testimony.

Life back home

Y, 15, from Eritrea, talks about his family

'My father died when I was small and so it was just me, my mother and my older brother. Then my brother was conscripted to the army, and in my country that means you belong for life and you must never say anything bad about the government. And we did not know where he is because everything is secret. It was just me and my mum.

'When I was 12 my mum got the money to send me to Asmara, the capital, to go to school there. I was sad not to see her but I tried to focus on my studies. Then when I was 14 she said: "Soon it will be time when they will make you join the army, and you will have to prove you are loyal like your brother did, by killing people from round here, from the place that you know. They keep asking me where are you? And I am afraid."

'My mum was able to get the money from my uncle, and the uncle said "You have to start your journey, and there is another boy going, you go with him." I cried and said no. My uncle said, "You must do this, it is what your mother wants." I thought "I am too young to be doing this on my own. And I will not see my mother again."'

A, from Afghanistan, describes his family being broken up when he was 14

'The Taliban was after my family because my father had a connection to the British Army. He had been a driver. He would sometimes go off for long periods of time and we did not know where he was, or what he was doing.

'I was visiting relatives for the evening, and when I came back near our house I was told not to go in. The neighbours stopped me from going in. I could hear some women screaming and crying. The Taliban, or someone, some group, some people I don't know, they had come and attacked my father and my mother. I was not allowed to see their bodies. I wish I had seen them, so that I could have said goodbye to them. All I remember is the screaming and someone putting (their) hands over my eyes and I think they brought the bodies out.

'Then my uncle said, you will have to go away.'

Crossing continents

D, from Eritrea, 17, describes the journey to Libya

'I was just 14 when I left Eritrea. Me and some other boys, we got across the border into Sudan and we went across Sudan, we got into trucks and sometimes the men in the trucks were very hard to us, they beat us and they did bad things to us. But in Libya we had a worse time because in Libya there are people that kidnap you. I was held twice. The first time it was a prison, the second time is just bad people. They hold you in [a] special place, like an old shed, there was no roof on the shed so it was freezing at night, and burning hot in the day. We were chained to these big oil drums and we had to stay like that until they called our families and made them pay to let us go. I was beaten very badly and I have the scars on my arms and my back.'

A, from Somalia, recalls the friends he lost on the way

'There are many people I met on the way, who become like friends, some of them made it but many of them didn't make it. Some died in the desert, some are still in prison in Libya or in Sudan, some died in the sea while we were coming to Italy. So not all of us made it. Some have survived, but still they are like in a coma. They still remember what they passed through so they are still suffering.'

The sea crossing

B, from Somalia, describes the crossing from Libya to Sicily, which he made at age 17

'We were like a hundred and fifteen, something like that, women, children and men. So one by one they started packing us in the boat. There was no space even for sitting. I remember the guy who was steering the boat, he was just an immigrant like us – he just didn't have to pay because he drives the boat. We kept going, going, going the whole day without seeing nothing. I was sitting at the back of the boat. The guy, the driver who had the GPS, we got to know one another because we kept chatting. At some point I realised he didn't know how to use the GPS as he'd said – he'd just wanted to get on the boat. So I was really scared because I didn't know how to swim, and I knew that if the boat capsized I'd be the first person to die there. I remember all the women started crying when they heard that we were lost in the ocean, we didn't know where we were going. We had the satellite phone that they had given us, but the problem was, when we switched on the satellite phone, it was speaking a language that we didn't understand. They gave me the phone, I was trying to play with the phone, trying to understand the system. Finally just like a miracle I saw "English" written! The language became English suddenly! We were so happy. Next we had to figure out how to put credit on the phone, and then we tried to call one Somali guy who works in Rome. He is a very famous journalist – almost all the immigrants know him. But his phone was switched off. So we said to everyone on the boat, "Does anyone have any friend or family In Europe, their phone number?" And there was only one, an Eritrean girl, she said she had a cousin in Italy. So she called him on the satellite phone and she explained our situation – that we were lost in the ocean, and the ocean was getting too risky as water was now coming inside the boat. The cousin said he would see what he could do. So we had to just hope and just go ahead. Finally someone calls back and asks who are we. I don't know who it is, someone the cousin had called. She asked us if we can still see the moon or the sun, and we say "Yes, we can see where the sun is setting!" So she told us go directly towards where the sun is setting, and she would try and trace our satellite and see who she could help us. She said she would call back. We kept going for hours, and it got dark again. Then we realised our satellite phone battery was dying, was dead. So all the people started losing hope. All the ladies were crying. And I was thinking to myself, "This is going to be my last time on earth, my last day."

'At the night-time we saw a ship, a boat, so we kept following it. We thought, let's see where it would go. But we were worried because we thought it might be a Libyan boat, and if it was Libyan and they catch us then they will torture us or they will kill us. But we take the risk. And we start to wave our clothes and shout for help. But it went away in the dark and did not see us. And again we give up hope.

'Then almost at dawn, we see a light on the horizon. At first we think it is the sun starting to come up, but then we see that, no, it's a ship's light, and the ship is coming towards us. Everyone starts to cry and to pray and again, praying thank you for sending us this ship. But then everyone because they are excited, moves from side to side on the boat and we start to capsize and I think, "What if we die now when help is so near." Some people fall into the water, but we hold on to them, and the ship comes nearer and I see a name of the side – it is like an Italian name, it is like a football team, I think a name like Juventus. Sounds like Juventus. So I think this is it, we are safe, we will get to Italy.

'First they take out the women and children, and they are crying again, we're all crying. I will never forget the man who lifted me out of the boat. His eyes were blue, as blue as the ocean. I had never seen blue eyes like that before. I started to realise that after all the time I had spent travelling, over a year, and all the dangers I had faced and all the times I had expected to die, that now I was going to be safe. And it washed over me like a feeling of such happiness. And I thought, "This man that save me, he is an angel. An angel has saved me."'

L, from Afghanistan, describes the crossing from Turkey to Greece

'We were brought from Afghanistan to Pakistan to Iran to Turkey and then we were waiting for a boat. Every time you cross a border, or come to a new place, the people watching you change. We were all young, all friends because we had been together for a long time. When we got near the coast, the men left us in an old barn, locked in, for two days and we had no food, we were getting worried. Then the men came on the third day and put all of us, there were ten of us, in a small boat. They waited until it was dark and then they pushed the boat out into the sea. They had shown us how to work the motor and said, make for where you see the lights. The motor of the boat did not work properly and it kept starting and stopping and sending out smoke. When we got near the land and saw the lights, we hoped this is Greece and we should be safe.

'We could see figures of men and some cars or vans near where we were coming in. But then there was shooting, then men were in uniform – army or police. And they shot at the boat. We ducked down and some of the boys jumped into the sea, because they thought then the men wouldn't see them. The boat was hit and began to sink. We were so scared. We tried to hold onto each other, my friend Ibrahim said to us "Get hold of everyone's hand so that we can stay together." We were in a kind of circle in the water. But some of the boys couldn't swim and some were panicking. We didn't know what to do. I could see that some of them were dropping away. I couldn't see Ibrahim any more. I shouted his name but he didn't answer.

'Ibrahim was my friend, from my village.'

Traversing Europe

S, Syrian, 14, tells how he left Italy and set off across Europe

'In Italy they call us bambinos, meaning children. In my country, I thought of myself as quite grown up, because I helped my father in the farm and I helped look after my little brothers and sister. But here I feel I don't know anything. I don't know Italian. I don't go to a school. We live at the station, in the streets behind the station, and it is not safe for us. There are a lot of people who are selling drugs and some they just say, here you can have these drugs. I don't know what the drugs are and I don't take them.

'When we first came it was good, we were given clothes and drinks, and taken to a village that was quite like where I was brought up. The people were nice to us and there was a class every day for teaching us Italian. But my ambition is to go to UK and to be a lawyer or a doctor, and I can't here. So me and another boy, we left the centre and we are trying to get on a train to France and then the UK.'

M, Ethiopian, 16, has been living in the Jungle camp at Calais for 4 months

'I am living here alone, but it is not safe for girls. It really worries me, we sleep separately in the building that is for women and girls only, but we have to come out of there for food and for praying. And then I am worried that the men here don't respect girls and they will hurt us. I would like to get to UK but I don't have family there. They say if you have family you can go. I try every night to try and get on a truck. It's best to get a refrigerated truck because that way you avoid the police, they have a way to know if there is any body-heat in the truck so you let yourself get very cold. And the sniffer dogs can sniff out the smell of smoke from the camp fires so you must wash, and wash your clothes, and not smell like the camp. One day I hope to get to UK, that is my dream.'

Preface to Section 2

Y and R, 15 and 14, make it to the UK illegally from Calais

'We spent six months in the Jungle, and then they pulled the camp down, and they sent buses for children the young people, the bambinos, and we thought we were going to UK, but it was a trick and they sent us to other places in France. We don't want to stay in France because the French hate us, they tear-gas us and attack us in the Jungle. And here at this place they do not feed us, and they said the UK would come to see if we had a case for UK. But when they came they just asked us questions for five minutes and then they left. So after a few weeks we were giving up hope and we all left that place, and we came back to Calais.

'Calais was not the same because now there is no Jungle, no place to find people you know, find food or help from the volunteers. It was cold and we slept in the woods and in a broken-down house. The police would find us and hit us, and make us move on. Every night we tried to get on a truck, but there are gangs now that protect all the places you might get on a truck, and they have knives and guns and they ask you for money or they say they will kill you. But finally one night, we got on a truck and we got to UK.'

Life in the UK

Y and R continue their story after they arrive in the UK:

'We were sent to a foster mum in Kent and she had our hair cut, we were pleased about that, and she let us ride the bikes that belonged to her sons, and we were very happy. But she said we could not stay because there was no room for us in Kent, we have to go to another part of the country. So then we had another foster mum, she had the same first name. We thought that was funny. But she was not so understanding and wouldn't take us to church. Then we have another, a third foster mum and we can't believe she also has the same name! Now we are settled with her, and finally they have found a school that will take us and we go to school. We are happy to be here – but we have been asked so many questions, every time we have to have interviews, and the Home Office interview us in a way that means they don't believe what we say. They look at us all the time like we are lying, they ask us trick questions. We don't sleep very well because we worry about this.

'It hurts us to remember the past. But this week our foster mum made us injera, the bread from our country, which it takes five days to make, as you have to brew the yeast for many days. We know she cares for us because she does this. I have been beaten up by local boys because of my race, my skin colour. I fought back. I don't know if I should have done but I was defending myself. So life is not perfect but we are getting better at English, and we have each other and our new foster family, so it is okay. I do not think about what happens when we are 18.'

On signing

H, Afghan, has now turned 18 and must sign every week at a Home Office centre

'This is so crazy. Now I am 18, I must go all the way from Canterbury to Dover just to say "I am here." It costs so much money. We live in a flat, four of us, and for £36 a week have to pay for food, electricity, phone, fares, school books and clothes. I don't have £5.80 for the train. Every time I go, I think they might keep me there. I have no one back home, my life is here now, I am more and more worried. I have finished school but I can't work. I don't know what will happen to me next.'

A, Afghan, 18 is also afraid of forced removal

'I am very afraid because every Tuesday morning I have to travel to London on the train, and go for signing at a big building near London Bridge station. There is always a queue outside of about 100 or 200 people and everyone is afraid, and some of them are crying, because when you go in, sometimes they say to you "Go wait in that queue over there." And they put you in an office or a special place, and then the guards come and take you to detention and then you get sent back to your country. So deciding to go and sign, is very hard. I have exams coming up at school. I have girlfriend, I get on really well with her family. I go to the pub with her grandad! I push his wheelchair! My girlfriend she has had some difficult times and I have tried to help her. Every Monday night we say that we love each other and she gets upset and then I have to go and sign. Every time I come out I am shaking! My hands are shaking but the first thing I do is phone her and tell her I am safe, this time.'

After the court appeal at 18

P, Afghan, 19, describes his anger and frustration, which is getting out of control

'I am angry with the government. I am angry about everything! I have been to court but they don't believe anything I say. They said my story was not true. They said I might not be from where I said I am from. I told them my family has moved many times, I don't remember all the times and dates. I got angry in the court and then I could see they were never going to let me stay. I am English now, I can't go back. They say there is nothing to stop me going back. That I would be safe. I have a child on the way here, but the judge says you can be a father by Skype. I don't know what I will do, but I will have to run away and work illegally and just not be legal. I don't care now about being legal. I just know this is who I am, I need to stay.'

The road to forced removal

H, an Afghan boy who lived in Dover, was arrested at 18 and then detained prior to forced removal

'I went to visit a friend who was detained when he went to his weekly signing. I was held when I went in to visit him, and locked up, but not with him. Over the next two months I got very sad and depressed. I was moved seven times from one detention centre to another. I could never get to see a lawyer or get to know what was happening to me. I'm feeling sad, lonely. They have taken away our shoes and we are on a bus now entering the cargo terminal of the airport, that's where the plane is going from.

'I've got no-one in Afghanistan. Is there no chance? No last chance? Is there any chance of going to another country, like Canada?

'In Canterbury I'll miss my friends, my teacher, the people, and everything … I felt happy here but now I feel sad. Because I've got no one, no friend in Afghanistan. No chance, there's no way for me to stay here? So then I say I love all of you that you helped me, and I'll miss all of you.'

Life after forced removal

H writes from Kabul, and then the north of the country after his forced removal

'In Kabul I found some of my distant family but they treated me like a criminal because I have been deported. I can't stay here. Everyone is strange to me and I to them.

'A long time ago in my sleep time my parents would tell me stories They said "Humans must be stronger than rocks and more fragile than flowers." I did not know what they meant then, but now I know what they mean. I have to learn to be a man but I don't know where to start. What to do, where to start. My old village has gone. I know no one. I am a refugee in my own country.'

FOUR

Narrating the young migrant journey: themes of self-representation

Sue Clayton

In this chapter I will reflect, from my perspective as a filmmaker and news producer, on ways in which refugee youth has been represented in recent years in the UK media. I consider that such representations have had a material effect on the way these young people are perceived, and perceive themselves. I will draw on my experience of working with unaccompanied children and young people in focusing on the role of film and video to enable them to articulate different narratives that might more fully reflect their challenges and aspirations. I will also consider how we may need to interrogate our own attitudes to adapt to these new refugee perspectives.

Reporting young refugees

Particularly since the so-called refugee crisis of 2015 onwards, a number of surveys have been produced on the press coverage of asylum-seeking refugees in Europe (Berry et al, 2015; Zhang and Hellmueller, 2017). Berry et al identify two contrasting perspectives in media coverage: first, a view of the refugee condition as a global human-rights issue that looks for causes and solutions in the wider politics of conflict and war; and second, in opposition, one that regards refugees *en masse* as something hardly human – threatening, invasive and likely to damage the host country's way of life. The authors find that while the continental European press carry an average of 8.9% of all stories in this latter category, the UK's figures are disturbingly higher, with the *Daily Telegraph* at 15.8%, *The Sun* at 26.2%, and the *Daily Mail* at 41.9%. Berry summarises as follows:

> The most striking finding in our research is how polarised and aggressive British press reporting was compared to the

other countries. In most countries, newspapers, whether left or right, tended to report using the same sources, featured the same themes and provided similar explanations and solutions to the crisis. But in Britain the situation was very different. While the *Guardian* – and to a lesser extent the *Daily Mirror* – featured a range of humanitarian themes and sources sympathetic to the plight of refugees, the right-wing press consistently endorsed a hardline anti-refugee and migrant, Fortress Europe approach (Berry, 2016).

Furthermore, broadcast television is known to rely perhaps uncritically on the larger-circulation print newspapers to identify its viewing cohorts and their preferences, with references to 'the Heartland' and 'the *Mail* reader' (the latter prized as far larger ratings fodder than 'the *Guardian* reader') frequently made in programme briefings and editorial meetings. Thus, broadcasters carry forward the tabloid press narrative, and their argument that 'most people' are against refugees starts to become a self-fulfilling claim. In fact 'most people' according to surveys carried out by the UK Refugee Council, remain woefully misinformed about basic contextual information. A 2012 Refugee Council report found that despite – or perhaps because of – media reporting, the UK public estimated that 100,000 refugees were accepted into the UK per year, when the actual number was 4,000 (McIntyre, 2012). The reports cited above suggest that similar levels of misunderstanding continue today.

Where does unaccompanied migrant youth figure in this narrative? While UK print and broadcast media show rather more empathy on some aspects of child migrancy such as trafficking and child labour, they continue to conform nonetheless to a binary opposition along the lines identified above. That is, the young people are not merely themselves: they must be either victim, or menacing threat. And in the case of children and young people, even the 'positive' victim stories carry certain implicit value judgements that affect our perception of this group. The shocking image of the body of Alan Kurdi, a three-year-old Syrian boy drowned off the coast of Turkey in September 2015, was first released on social media. For several days UK newspapers and television did not report it as it was considered 'too disturbing' (Fahey, 2015). When they eventually did, it triggered a watershed in refugee coverage, with previously hostile state actors such as then Prime Minister David Cameron (who had in July 2015 referred to refugees as a 'swarm') giving personal responses: Cameron himself said he responded to the image 'as a father.' However, this individuating of the image and story of a suffering child, inviting a response of easily-wrought pity, also has a number of negative consequences. First, as Gillian Hughes discusses in Chapter Five of this book, it takes away the sense of collective movements and journeys, and the power and agency associated with these: in this case one appealing child is considered to be moving, but 90,000 of them – the number for instance to have claimed asylum in Europe in 2015 (Eurostat, 2017) – are not. Second, objectifying the image of a suffering child in a manner we associate with coverage of natural disasters and NGO campaigns helps to maintain a sense of 'us and them', because tinged with our pity is a sense of gratitude and guilt that 'we' are not 'them', and that we can discharge our emotions by making a response typical for this context – after feeling moved, perhaps make a charitable donation. This continues to leave unaddressed the underlying questions of why we have a surge of lone child refugees in Europe; what has contributed to the destabilising of their home countries over which we in the West may have influence; and how our government might work with others to find long-term solutions. Finally, 'victim' coverage, even for minors, tends also to exhibit gradations of 'deserving' through to 'undeserving', and there lie further embedded values. In the workaday shorthand of media reporting as I experience it, the most 'deserving' victim to interview for television will for preference be Arabic or Asian not African, visually appealing, speak English, have some physical wounds, and cry. (Angry, exhausted or emotionally unstable young people will be used to feed instead the counter-narratives of 'threat'.)

I have highlighted the issue above because I have become acutely aware in my work across all those who deal with separated young asylum seekers – judges, social workers, teachers, potential foster parents and so on – that all of us are still 'the public' and are still, I believe, both consciously and unconsciously influenced by this backwash of media messages, which at its heart seeks to divide the unaccompanied minors into 'appealing victim' or 'security threat'. This duality shows up as paradox from time to time, as for instance when the Home Office agreed to accept a small number of unaccompanied minors from the Calais Jungle in October 2016 and exhibited them on arrival at Croydon for a photo call (see Chapter One). There was outrage from the UK tabloids that these were young males in their teens, and not the appealing kiddies that would have been considered acceptable (though the older children qualified equally under law). The *Telegraph* responded with uncharacteristic acuity, saying 'sorry these are not as cute as you were led to believe' (Wilkinson, 2016).

The material effects of embedded values

I consider it of great importance that we examine the embedded values with which we may judge refugee cohorts, and the reductive binary oppositions that underlie them – whether we acquire these through the media or through other forms of societal discourse – particularly as they do in my view have both direct and indirect influence on material outcomes for the young people. For instance, I have frequently observed innate value judgements at play in Immigration Court hearings and Home Office interviews where, as York and Warren describe in Chapter Two, in the absence of documented evidence of their situation, unaccompanied minors are assessed on the basis of their 'credibility'. Of course, the Home Office and the courts have the right and the responsibility to examine the material facts of each case, as this will for instance help to elucidate whether the young person qualifies for care until 18 under the Children Act 1989, or for longer-term protection under refugee protocols. But the 'credibility' test is arguably flawed in practice, and exhibits clear signs of being subject to embedded notions of 'deserving' and 'underserving' carried by those who make the assessments. For example, composure and stoicism seem to be required of young refugees in formal situations, as a sort of guarantee of their victimhood. Anger is never perceived as other than dangerous and disrespectful. (One has to remind oneself that we are here discussing vulnerable minors, as young as eight, the vast majority of whom began their horrific journeys at others', not their own, behest). I have witnessed first-hand the reaction of the courts and the Home Office to anyone who is angry or frustrated – perhaps at the lack of an interpreter, or their inability to articulate in English, or answer possibly painful questions put to them about their past. One young person facing their appeal against removal at age 18 who had a partner and a much-loved new baby in UK, when told he could be removed back to Afghanistan and "be a father by Skype" fell silent for a few minutes, and was reprimanded for being 'surly'. Even apparently trivial court exchanges carry the weight of value judgements which play to the axis of 'deserving/undeserving'. I documented one Afghan boy who was asked, in order to prove he was from a certain town, how many mosques there were in that town. After some thought he replied "...As many as there pubs in London" to indicate that there were a great many, very visible, but he couldn't specify a number. This was regarded as a frivolous response, and the judge from then on weighed the boy's credibility as low.

Another, who followed a court clerk out of the hearing as he needed the toilet and assumed that he, like the clerk, could come and go freely, was admonished for disrespecting the court. A third, who had taken great pains to dress what he thought was smartly for court, and arrived in a shiny suit with his gelled hair combed up in spikes, was also treated with distrust and disdain in court from the moment he entered (and incidentally was not considered suitable for a subsequent TV interview because he "looked like an X-Factor reject"). Such simple actions, gestures or silences on the part of the young people are filtered through officials' and administrators' expectations as to what behaviour suggests someone deserving of our consideration, within the very fabric of our law-making and governmental decision-making processes. As Anna Gupta describes in Chapter Three, the same process of received truths and stereotypes influencing concrete process and becoming embedded in policy can be seen at work in the language used around age assessments, with European ideas of what constitutes a child or an adult being transposed onto the assessment of boys and girls from very different cultures.

How then can we begin to recognise and change these patterns? Given that I have argued that the media both generates and feeds many of the seemingly 'normal' ideological assumptions that we seem to carry, can a radical media practice be brought into service to help present a different positioning, a different view of child migrants and their journeys? One that takes account of many of the issues raised elsewhere in this book – self-determination; aspirations; a more nuanced understanding of affect and agency? Below I will present a brief account of my film work with young asylum seekers, and then reflect on how we might build new narratives from the tropes and themes that emerge.

Researching identity and representation through creative practice

I began my work with young asylum seekers as I was interested as a filmmaker in issues of identity, and the young migrants' construction of complex identities as they move from one political, cultural and linguistic locus to another. How does a child of ten or twelve or fourteen, stepping off a truck and into an alien country, create a sense of self that will sustain him or her through both cultural assimilation and integration, and potential conflict and trauma around future removal? How will this developing self process issues of, for instance, nationality, ethnicity, religion, sexuality and family?

My first work with unaccompanied minors was alongside volunteers at after-school groups, social evenings for unaccompanied minors at the Refugee Council, and with the young people's theatre company Project Phakama on a performance project working with the issue of refugee self-representation – *Strange Familiars* and *Breaking the Glass Box* (Project Phakama, 2004). Here I offered my video skills to help lone young asylum seekers find ways to articulate their identities and concerns. As most arrivals to the UK do not speak English, I discovered that performance and audio-visual work provided valuable tools for their self-expression, and would often, in addition, indicate to those concerned with their welfare subtextual issues (trauma, loss, anxiety for the future), which could later be articulated in therapy. This led me to collaborate in participatory video work in refugee psychotherapy sessions at the Tavistock and Portman Hospital, along with clinical psychologist Gillian Hughes whose practice engages with refugee subjects. As she describes in Chapter Five, she and I were able to articulate our findings in a research framework around liberation psychology, referencing the pioneering work of Martín-Baró (1996), which considers the need to confront and deconstruct political and ideological value judgements on the path to personal liberation. We were able to further explore the notion of the split self, and the unresolved conflicts around identity and wellbeing, which we conclude can only be resolved by ourselves participating as listeners or witnesses, and being open to observe and interpret suppressed feelings and help give them voice (Clayton and Hughes, 2015). I applied this strategy in directing the play *Mazloom* (2013) on the topic of forced removal of refugee youth at age 18. Based on young people's testimonies, we created a film backdrop of action and images that portrays a subtext of unarticulated fear and anxiety, and fragmented memories and dreams, as a boy waits alone for night-time arrest and removal.

I have also, from 2004 to the present day, filmed extended interviews with over 200 young people – some longitudinally over several years – and facilitated many of them to film for themselves. Extracts of these interviews are quoted in the preface to this section of the book, and illuminate many of the points raised not only in this chapter but in those that follow. Facilitating young people in developing auto-ethnographic skills had important results when one of these young people, Hamedullah, was forcibly removed by the UK Home Office to Kabul at the age of 18. The footage he filmed of his traumatic return to Afghanistan, edited and added to by me, became the documentary film *Hamedullah: The Road Home* (UK, 2011) which has since been requested at numerous Immigration Court appeal hearings and Judicial

Reviews, where it offers unique and nuanced first-hand evidence of the harsh conditions faced by those forcibly removed at 18. I have applied a similar approach when filming in Italy, Belgium and France where I followed young refugee arrivals to produce the documentary *Calais Children: A Case to Answer* (2017), which also seeks to highlight not only the 'voices' of the young people themselves – what they are able to articulate – but also what conflicts and silences are going on beneath the surface, and also unpick what narratives we the host country may be trying to impose on them, because of our own embedded belief-systems. (*Calais Children* was submitted as evidence in a High Court Judicial Review *ZS versus the Secretary of State for the Home Office* (February–March 2018) where my legal team argued that the Home Office was acting unlawfully in its failure to consider these children under the Dubs Amendment.)

Representing the self: loss, anger, mourning and survival

I have described above various practices using creative and psychotherapeutic tools that can be used to better understand some underlying factors that shape these young people's perspectives; how we might better interpret their actions and behaviour, and therefore how better aid them in building an authentic and robust sense of self and survival. Below I offer a number of potential themes or tropes that have emerged across my work of many years in film, theatre and UK news and current affairs, I hope these will contribute to the development of new and more humane refugee narratives and perspectives, aid young people in forming a healthy sense of self, which can encompass shades and contradictions, and help disrupt the crippling stereotypes of media, and the public perceptions of these young people. I have had the advantage of working with many of the young people on their journey to the UK, and observing these stages has allowed me further insights.

Stopping and starting: problems with time

Refugee journeys are often represented by experts and media pundits as a line on a map from home to here, traversing perhaps five or six countries and a couple of seas. The line may be animated so that progress looks as smooth and regular as train or airline route, implying order, purpose and progress. But refugee life – particularly that of lone young people – is better understood as a series of stops, starts, reverses and circularities. While at interviews on arrival the young people will dutifully list in order the countries they passed through, they continue to unscramble for years after, what might or must have happened to friends, how they may have ended up not where they intended, where or how they lost agency. For example, many still struggle to understand why in October 2016, approximately 1,500 of them in the destroyed Calais Jungle camp were put on buses which they thought were bringing them to the UK, but instead took them with no explanation to accommodation centres all over France, some 15 hours south in the wrong direction. "We were taken by force" says Jamal, 13, in my film *Calais Children: A Case to Answer* (2017)

Just as their ideas of space become problematised, so do notions of time. Their lives on the journey here comprise bursts of high-adrenaline action, set against long periods of stasis. Most young people will have been held at borders waiting for the next agent to collect them. They may end up doing months of labour. They may be woken in the night and told to get into a truck. They may be jailed, let out and jailed again. Those referred to above, who lived for months or years in the Calais Jungle, were for the most part highly active and thrived on movement. The boys would nightly run at the border fence, only to be pushed back by riot police and tear-gas; girls chose a more arduous route, walking six or seven hours a night through woods outside Calais, to reach a place easier to access vehicles to stow away. And every day involved surviving a chaotic unregulated camp of 10,000 people. When with the camp's closure they were moved to temporary and remote accommodation centres in France, they fell back into stasis. "We cannot go by boat" says Elias, 17, over and over again, as he stands alone and stares at the sea at Le Havre, where he was re-located. "We cannot go by walking. We cannot fly. Only the sea, but we don't have boat. We cannot go by walking…" Time passing slowly is what they cannot stand. "We are wasting our time needlessly" he says. Time away from home, spent unproductively, is time wasted. And time when painful memories can no longer be held at bay.

When young people finally reach the host country, again time is a double-edged blade. A few precious years will flash by until the feared coming-of-age at 18 which they soon learn may lead to the end of their protection in the UK. When Y and R, Eritreans aged 15 who reached UK as stowaways, received the news that they had been granted five years' leave to remain in UK, their foster mother reports that they went wild with joy. "They were hitting the ceiling!" Then Y's face fell, as he realised he was also perversely celebrating not seeing his mother and his homeland for five long years. He expressed this at first indirectly, describing a beach near his home village where he had played all his life, saying he wasn't sure he could bear not to see it for so long.

Thus young refugees must somehow hold in parallel number of contradictory timelines: first a notion of the life they had before whatever crisis made them leave – a life which can seem to them like a mythical and timeless Utopia; second, the journey with its ellipses and confusions its stops and starts; and finally the rhythms of life in the host country, more orderly and regulated but always rushing towards a precarious outcome at 18 – one which will hardly ever lead back to that precious safe remembered childhood place. This where the work of Louise Drammeh (Chapter Six) and Gillian Hughes (Chapter Five) is so important in identifying ways of supporting young people to build a sense of identity that can cope with these fractured timelines, and generate a sense of continuity across the stages of life. In the play *Mazloom*, I show how they must hold together this sense of split time by contrasting its oppositions: on stage a recently turned-18 boy, his case for adult asylum refused, is alone in his room at night, acutely in the present, knowing that the Home Office may arrive at any moment to detain and remove him. On the screens around the stage fade up sequences of his other 'times' – memories of his mother's kitchen, the vast empty deserts he crossed, the sharp movements of springing with others from a suddenly-opened truck. These past times haunt the space around him. What is harder to represent – both for him, and for us as facilitators – are any clues as to his future. In *Hamedullah: The Road Home*, I represent this slippage, this complexity of time and place, by showing Hamedullah's repeated visits to his old village which is bombed beyond recognition. The ruined village provides a sharp image of the sudden brutality of war, but Hamedullah can only circle around it, stuck in his own time-loop, his own stasis. He can't move forward, or back.

Grief and the symbolic mother

Following from the above, I was struck by how, in France, young people I had known in the Calais Jungle changed significantly when placed in a position of 'stasis' over the winter of 2016–17. In those long winter months in remote French villages or in segregated parts of towns, young people who had seemed independent, feisty and used to living by their wits, seemed to enter a period of regression and grieving.

Now they took stock of what they had lost, and this inevitably played out through the symbolism of the mother. "I miss my mum" was their commonest simple expression. From my research I have drawn the conclusion that many of the young people still have mothers surviving in their home country, with the father either deceased, missing, or away seeking work or possibly other routes to asylum. It is the women and smaller children who are less likely to undertake the long journey to Europe, and they are missed. In the theatre work I did with Project Phakama, I noted that when asked collectively to create an image or an object representing the security they wanted from the UK, they constructed a huge hovering kite in the form of a massive mother-like woman that would fly over them and protect them. In camps and welcome centres I have visited in Palermo, Catania, Paris, Calais and Dunkerque, it is women most often who greet the arrivals and women who make up the larger part of the volunteers. Young people tend to call any of us aged over 30 or so "Mammy" partly as they no doubt have trouble remembering our names, but also I would argue from a need to have such a figure in their lives (I have never heard male volunteers referred to as "Daddy"). In addition, they may well see us women in opposition to armed forces, traffickers, border officials and police, who are overwhelmingly male. Filming children over the winter of 2016–17 in the temporary centres in France, I would find myself with strings of interviews where these young people – many albeit streetwise, surly, near adulthood – broke down and cried, or talked about crying. "We can't sleep, we are all crying", says E, from Eritrea. "Every night when I sleep I see child crying, baby crying" says ZS, from Afghanistan. Every day I write "Mom, Dad, I love Mom and Dad, I love…." In filmic terms, I did not attempt to be proactive or ask 'interview'-type questions in such a process, I simply recorded it. I saw it as privilege earned from having followed them across France, to be a familiar face, a little continuity, after their expulsion from Calais. There is further debate to be had around issues of gender and volunteering, and what is the exchange that takes place between the female volunteer or support worker and the refugee child. Some women feel uneasy about the burden placed on them by the word Mum or Mammy; others, like me, accept it as a kind of functional shorthand for a psychological need that the boys in particular would struggle to otherwise express.

    I have observed a related and complex response when young people arrive in the host country and are placed with foster parents. While fostering is on balance a very desirable outcome for them, there is nonetheless a kind of taking stock, where young people may accept that they are in a family, but are aware that it is not actually their own family. This can prompt further grieving for the family they miss. Papadopoulos refers to this state as 'nostalgic disorientation' in the important collection *Therapeutic care for refugees: No place like home* (2002). Moreover, the new arrivals may also discover that there are limits to their new family's ability to love and protect them. For instance M, from Afghanistan, was treated by his foster parents as "one of the family", and said he hoped some people might think by appearance he was their own child. When he neared 18 and the end of local authority care, he assumed he'd continue to live with them. He was deeply shocked when they said that much as they cared about him, they could not continue to support, unpaid, every child they fostered beyond the age of 18.

Thus, unpacking the word 'mother' shows another split or complication for the young refugee – beneath a superficial bravado, most seek out the closeness of a nurturing relationship which they identify as a maternal function. But when they find it, they can be torn between feeling disloyalty to those mothers and grandmothers they left behind and for whom they grieve, and fear that the new mother or family will in any case reject them. This places a heavy burden on women who work in this field: every woman I have interviewed, whether social worker, volunteer or foster mother, has found it challenging to keep a line when faced with this complex set of needs.

Friendship between and beyond refugees

Perhaps as a direct counterpoint to the above, unaccompanied young asylum seekers on the journey make extremely strong bonds of friendship. These are relationships which replace, but do not carry the complexity of, familial ties. They also crucially function to protect the group against outside abuse and other forms of danger. My research suggests that friendships flourish across the boundaries of language, nationality and religion. At a small camp in the woods near Dunkerque in 2016–17 with around 100 refugees in total, the boys and men built their own small shacks, but the women and girls, though of different religions and ethnicities, created a living-structure that they all shared and which was a relatively safe place at some distance from the men. Institutionally, these informal friendship networks are supported in some countries in the early stages of processing new arrivals – for instance in at the reception centres of Catania and Palermo, such as Santa Chiara and Centro Astalli, young people are accommodated together when they arrive and remain in peer groups through the first stage of settlement. However, as I discuss later in this section, other systems place little or no value on these crucial peer relationships, and indeed may actively discourage them.

As well as friendships between the young people, there are also those with local communities and supporters. Faced with the task of receiving over 100,000 lone minors between 2015 and 2017, European governments have responded with diverse levels of support – but in all cases, the deficit in their response has been filled by mainly young activists and volunteers; and they do not tend to work in the same formal 'us and them' mode as governments and official NGOs. The volunteer activist-based support for refugees all over Europe since 2015, particularly among younger people, has led to friendship networks developing between refugees and their supporters, maintained through contact and social media. Particularly in refugee 'hotspots' such as Athens, Lesvos, Idomeni, Sicily and Northern France, groups such as Lighthouse, Help Refugees, the Hummingbird Project, Refugee Youth Service, Care4Calais, Calais Action and others have a practice of working inclusively with young refugees, and in many situations the volunteers have, like the young people themselves, been subject to state brutality and arrest. (For instance in March 2017, the Mayor of Calais declared it a criminal offence to offer food or shelter to refugees in the Calais area. Volunteers from Calais Refugee Community Kitchen and Utopia 56 went on delivering food to the young people and faced daily police harassment for doing so.) The closure of the Calais Jungle brought an interesting reversal: for the refugees, this was just another move from another camp on their interminable journey; but among the volunteers, there was real distress that they had failed to secure a future for the minors, and it was the young refugees who consoled their friends the volunteers. This is another refugee perspective on social relations and integration which the media does not find relevant or important, preferring to report either the individual or the mass, or the 'us' or the 'them'.

My approach as a filmmaker to highlight these relationships and friendships, both within refugee cohorts and between them and their supporters, has been to become immersed in the group as a witness or relatively passive protagonist. (A parallel project, Nina Kusturica's excellent *Little Alien* (2009) uses a similar strategy.) Thus instead of standing outside the group and posing the 'closed' questions of television reporting, I would participate and witness debates and decisions even if I and my crew had no idea what was being said until we subsequently had the dialogue translated. I have filmed with young people as they have talked and debated which route to take; whether to wait and try for legal status or stow away on a truck; in the UK;

whether to go 'sign' at the Home Office each week and face potential detention; and after removal, whether or not to risk doing the entire journey all over again. But it is most of all from the reactions of friends – the faces turned in thought, the unspoken gestures of affection – that I learn the most. I would argue that the tropes of friendship – little groups, helping each other survive through rough times, with warm involvement from local and international volunteers – are some of the most positive to come out of the current 'crisis' and yet they are rarely shown in the mainstream media. And those nations who ultimately host the arrivals place no value on these networks, on the grounds of guarding against potential association with traffickers. It was made a condition for one boy E, 17, who sought to claim asylum in France, that he move to a new district, give up his phone for several months and not contact any other asylum seekers. He found this very painful. In the UK, some local authorities also seek to restrict young people's contact with anyone they knew before arrival, which cuts then off from painstakingly-acquired and valuable networks. However, thanks to social media, and to the shared values of friendship and solidarity among the new generation of activist volunteers, these networks continue to prevail.

Misplaced feelings of guilt

I sensed over many years conducting interviews with young refugees settled in the UK that there was an emotion they experienced which I could not place; I thought at first it was a kind of melancholy, or some type of anxiety. It was only when I knew some of the young people very well that I understood that it was guilt. Their guilt operates on many levels and is for the most part misplaced and left unresolved. First, as I have discussed earlier, many young separated migrants experience a kind of fundamental guilt at leaving their mothers and their family, even if it was the family who decided they should leave. (In the exhibition *Odisseo: Arriving Alone* (2017) in Palermo in which young people drew portraits of family members they missed, one was simply a blank cut-out paper shape, as the girl who made it simply could not remember what her mother's face looked like, and this caused her considerable grief and guilt.) And as I discovered during sessions at the Tavistock and Portman Hospital, young people also can experience guilt when enjoying life in the UK as their families are not sharing their pleasures. It could be argued that all adolescents and teenagers go through a form of these emotions – gradually separating from parents, being happy to be independent, while perhaps nervous of becoming 'more' than the parents. However, lone refugee youths in addition experience a kind of survivor guilt, as they know they left many behind on the journey who did not make it across the borders, deserts and seas that they crossed. As L from Afghanistan describes in the 'Voices' preface, only half of his group survived the crossing – and years on, that remains the defining fact of his narrative and his life.

Many of the young people also experience guilt as they settle into UK life, as they acquire new values which may affect or drastically alter their cultural and religious views, their politics or their sexuality. It is challenging for them to navigate our western culture with its seemingly liberal-democratic values, while retaining a core sense of self, and still feel supported by values from their primary culture. J, from Iraq, 15, says "I don't know how to be myself but also at the same time, be someone that everyone would recognise if I was back home". For Hamedullah, who did go home, there was no chance that he could fit in; too educated to be a farm labourer, not educated enough to get a professional job and in appearance quite western and metrosexual, he feels as foreign walking around Kabul as a westerner would. He is despised for having been sent back, as it is assumed he must have committed a crime to warrant something so serious. He cannot overcome a sense of guilt and failure. "I am like a refugee in my own country" he says. He changed, and now he can't change back.

Helpless rage and therapeutic anger

As discussed earlier, the media and arguably many of the public do not expect to see anger from young refugees – they want to see gratitude or nothing at all. On the other hand the young people, whatever their ultimate status, have endured a journey where they have seen danger and death, experienced abuse and suffered appalling hardship. Anger needs to be discharged. I have identified in my research and filming two broad types of anger: the first expressed as frustration and hopeless rage – at the weekly signing, at being detained, at assiduously becoming 'British' and then being removed anyway – and the second, a more eloquent and righteous voice that signifies the young person or young people have at last found a platform. Those who were removed from Calais to Le Havre after months of little food and no Home Office visits left their hostel *en masse* and marched to the train station to try to board a train back to Calais. They were promptly arrested and send back to their hostel. When I filmed Y at the station days later narrating these events, he responded to the sudden opportunity of being filmed and being in a public place, and segued into a declaratory speech saying "We have suffered enough. People don't want us here. They don't even look at us. They don't feed us, and we don't want to stay." H from Afghanistan, recently turned 18 and detained in the UK awaiting forced removal, committed to going on hunger strike as he was so helplessly angry that his case had been refused, and he said he would rather die than go back. Those of us supporting him – unofficial, untrained and simply filling in a gap that no state service would provide – were advised by a specialist charity that as an adult, H had the right to make this decision and it was not up to us to persuade him not to do it – and we could not know what perceived worse fate he would face on return to Kabul. In the end, some rather amateur hugging and crying, and telling him that we would miss him if he died, prevailed over his determination to take his life – a decision which had seemed to us to be based mostly on a sense of rage and helplessness. He began taking fluids and food, and with a lawyer we assigned to his case, he was able to appeal his forced removal. This coincided with demonstrations against forced removals at his and other UK detention centres, and he found a voice alongside others, demanding the UK recognise that Afghanistan is not safe for young returnees. In both these examples, the young people found a way to present their argument, though at some personal cost (arrest, hunger strike) and so generate a sense of agency and momentum. The ability to speak straight to the camera (not the polite convention of 20 degrees off, addressing the nodding interviewer), to own their own image and articulate a position is not one which they all acquire. But some do.

Pride and aspiration

Within the contradictions of selfhood, it is a challenge for these young people to envisage a future. Allsopp et al (2015: 4) note that

> existing scholarship has demonstrated that the wellbeing of young people subject to immigration control, particularly as they transition to "adulthood", is intrinsically linked to the notion of "ontological security", a clear sense of a projected self within a future trajectory.

Across my research I found substantive evidence that the uncertainty of being accepted into the UK at all, followed by the uncertainty of remaining after 18, hinders the development of that 'projected self'. What is apparent, however, is that this recent generation of young refugees understands quite well the politics of what is happening in

Europe (*The New Arab*, 2016; NBC, 2014). They follow international news and are aware of the EU deal with Turkey, and Italy's deal with Libya, both of which have closed down the substantive numbers of refugees entering Europe since 2015. And few young asylum seekers now expect the UK to be a paradise, but they have seen enough racism and police violence on their way through Europe to realise that they will no doubt continue to be an underclass in many ways even if they acquire status. The comment below was made to me by E, one of a group of Afghan boys, as they headed to truck-stops to risk their lives for the UK, having given up on the process of UK law. He is speaking of his younger friend, who had a legal case to be in the UK.

> 'They said they'd take him – but they're just playing with them. They promise but they don't do.' (*Calais Children: A Case To Answer*, 2017)

But within this realism is a sense of political awareness which suggests that they have a resilience and realism that will support them.

> 'We were something in our country. We were not homeless, or something like that. We left because of war, because of problems. But what can you do. It's politics. Politics kills the humanity.' (*Calais Children: A Case To Answer*, 2017)

There were E's final words to us as he and his friends walked off into the night.

Any representation of 'journeys' is bound to be full of shots of people travelling and moving. I found increasingly I was filming people walking away from, and not towards, the camera. They had pride enough to talk and engage, but also pride enough to walk away.

Conclusion: on not being able to sleep

To conclude, what I have done here is to seek to understand how one person effectively becomes another, and must reframe their references in so many fundamental ways – all before they are even formed as adult personalities. This can only fully happen when we, the hosts, stop seeing ourselves as 'us' and fully empathise and participate in 'their' situation. I have welcomed the chance during the process of co-editing this book to share these insights with those at the more cutting edge of policy and care practice. Many of us who work in creative fields, such as filmmaking, performance and art therapy, have been trained to consider and use our own experiences as a way to build empathy with others, in order to gain a more nuanced understanding of their condition, see for example the work of groups such as Art Refuge[1] and the Protestimony project,[2] as well as Gillian Hughes' creative projects detailed in Chapter Five of this collection. In this spirit I'd like to end on a personal reflection.

Throughout the process, I have had as an almost subliminal reference in my mind, a work by feminist theorist and critic Jacqueline Rose. Her book is not directly to do with the 'refugee issue' – it is concerned more with issues around public lives and reputations in the modern world. But its title, and the conceptual framework behind it, resonates with points that I have discussed here. The book aims to consider '… how to understand the link between public and private worlds, between our collective histories and the innermost, hidden components of our lives and minds' (Rose, 2004: 1).

Young refugees, no less than the artists and intellectual celebrities she writes about, need to do this work too – relate their public and private worlds, reconcile the contradictions of their position, go on inventing themselves anew. In that sense, this trope – of not sleeping – inflects and encompasses all the others: loss, excitement, anxiety, grieving. I have never met a refugee who says they sleep well. A great number of those in the UK with access to healthcare take sleeping pills. In part, this can be seen as a consequence of the irregular lives they have led, usually sleeping during the day and travelling, attempting to cross borders, or simply surviving their environment, at night. But it is more than this; the work, as it were, of their night-time hours (as I first learnt from the young people who contributed to the Mazloom play) is to grieve, to contact friends and family in different time zones, to play and be distracted, and to constantly attempt to reconcile, to triangulate, the kinds of contradictions of their lives that I have tried to characterise here. I offer this as an example: When I was grieving for a much-loved family member, I also could not sleep. Like all volunteers, I am used to the young refugees whether in UK, Europe, or further afield, texting or phoning in the night, as this is when their carefully-assembled front, their bravado, seems to slip away and their emotions are more raw. A, from Afghanistan, was also unable to sleep. He had always said that one day he would tell me his whole true story – not what he'd been told to say to the Home Office, nor what he parrots to friends at school, nor even what he tells himself as a sort of sustaining shorthand to get by. We agreed in a late-night call that he and his carer would drive across London in the early hours (luckily the carer was a night-owl) and he would tell me his whole story. He knew it would be painful but he was ready to tell it – to maybe offload it in some way – and fully share it. He wanted, in other words, a witness, to whom he could express memories and feelings that he had not felt able to articulate before. He did so, I filmed, and then his carer drove him home again. The filmed interview was the fullest account of all the above themes that I am ever likely to achieve. And for one night at least, both of us could sleep.

Acknowledgements

Sue Clayton would like to thank Alessandra Rizzo and the Palermo Festival delle Letterature Migranti for hosting her to write this chapter.

Notes

[1] www.artrefugeuk.org/calais

[2] www.platforma.org.uk/pf_events/protestimony/

References

The New Arab (2016) 'Paradise no more: the asylum-seekers want to leave Europe', 26 January, www.alaraby.co.uk/english/society/2016/1/27/paradise-no-more-the-asylum-seekers-want-to-leave-europe

Allsopp, J., Chase, E. and Mitchell, M. (2015) 'The tactics of time and status: Young people's experiences of building futures while subject to immigration control in Britain', *Journal of Refugee Studies*, 28(2): 163–82.

Amoruso, M., Cipolla, N., Piraneo, C. and Salvato, V. (curators) (2017) *Odisseo: Arriving Alone* Exhibition Catalogue, Palermo: Palermo University Press.

Berry, M. (2016) 'British media coverage of refugee and migrant crisis is the most polarised and aggressive in Europe', Cardiff University journalism, media and culture blog, 14 March, www.jomec.co.uk/blog/new-report-finds-british-media-coverage-of-refugee-and-migrant-crisis-is-the-most-polarised-and-aggressive-in-europe/

Berry, M., Garcia-Blanco, I., and Moore, D. (2015) *Press coverage of the refugee and migrant crisis in the EU: A content analysis of five European countries*, Geneva: UNHCR, www.unhcr.org/56bb369c9.html

Calais Children: A Case To Answer (2017) film, directed by Sue Clayton, UK: Eastwest Pictures, www.calais.gebnet.co.uk and https://vimeo.com/230595898

Clayton, S. and Hughes, G. (2015) 'The use of film and creative media to liberate young refugee and asylum-seeking people from disempowering identities: A dialogical approach', in T. Afuape and G. Hughes (eds) *Liberation practices: Towards emotional wellbeing through dialogue*, London: Routledge, pp. 89–100.

Fahey, J. (2015) 'The Guardian's decision to publish shocking photos of Aylan Kurdi', *Guardian*, 7 September, www.theguardian.com/commentisfree/2015/sep/07/guardian-decision-to-publish-shocking-photos-of-aylan-kurdi

Eurostat (2017) 'Asylum applications considered to be unaccompanied minors', Eurostat press release 80/2017, 11 May, http://ec.europa.eu/eurostat/documents/2995521/8016696/3-11052017-AP-EN.pdf/30ca2206-0db9-4076-a681-e069a4bc5290

Little Alien (2009) film, directed by Nina Kusturica, Greece, Morocco, https://mubi.com/films/little-alien

Martín-Baró, I. (1996) *Writings for a liberation psychology*, Cambridge, MA: Harvard University Press.

McIntyre, P. (2012) *Refugee Council – Leveson Inquiry: submission of evidence*, February, http://webarchive.nationalarchives.gov.uk/20140122145147/http:/www.levesoninquiry.org.uk/wp-content/uploads/2012/03/Submission-by-Refugee-Council.pdf

NBC News (2014) 'Europe's Border Crisis'. NBC News, 7 November, www.nbcnews.com/storyline/europes-border-crisis/asylum-seekers-chasing-better-lives-u-k-face-immigration-mess-n227136

Papadopoulos, R. (ed) (2002) *Therapeutic care for refugees: No place like home*, Tavistock Clinic Series, Karnac books.

Project Phakama (2004) *Strange Familiars*, play, http://projectphakama.org/strange-familiars/

Rose, J. (2004) *On not being able to sleep: Psychoanalysis and the modern world*, London: Vintage.

Wilkinson, A. (2016) 'Child refugees deserve our help – even if they're not as cute as we were led to imagine', *Telegraph*, 21 October, www.telegraph.co.uk/news/2016/10/21/child-refugees-deserve-our-help---even-if-theyre-not-as-cute-as/

Zhang, X. and Hellmueller, L. (2017) 'Visual framing of the European refugee crisis in Der Spiegel and CNN International: Global journalism in news photographs', *International Communication Gazette*, 79(5): 437–58.

FIVE

From individual vulnerability to collective resistance: responding to the emotional impact of trauma on unaccompanied children seeking asylum

Gillian Hughes

'Haseeb', an Afghan teenage boy, sits clenching a damp tissue in a therapy session at the Tavistock Centre in London. He is saying through gritted teeth how violently angry he feels at getting another refusal for asylum from the Home Office. He has endured weeks of anguish, nightmares and flashbacks returning with a vengeance, while waiting for the fateful day of his court hearing. He has tried so hard at school to be the brilliant student that he was back home, but has so struggled to concentrate that his grades have been poor. He has some friends, but the racism he faces from many of his peers makes him feel lonely and inadequate. He misses Afghan food as his foster family are African, and none of them come with him to the mosque as they don't share his religion.

A central challenge for separated young people seeking asylum is to reconstruct their identities in the context of a new home, new culture, an entirely new set of relationships with no shared history, a new language. In sum, they have none of the anchors that they have grown up with that tell them who they are, and what their purpose is in life. This momentous task of identity reconstruction has to take place alongside the process of mourning for the loss of everything and everyone that they have known and relied on, and at the same time their having to navigate the usual developmental tasks of adolescence. These extraordinary challenges so often take place in environments that are hostile and rejecting, and where sources of positive reinforcement are very sparse. Our job as mental health and social care practitioners is not only to support young people through this minefield, but also to help them reconnect with positive identities, to take hold of hopes and dreams for their future, and help them draw on available communities who can support these.

The risks of individualistic problem-focused interventions

Negative accounts of refugees abound in our national media, as Sue Clayton discusses in Chapter Four, and refugee children are often subjected to racism and social marginalisation in their schools (Rutter, 2006). Added to this, the experience of being uprooted from family, community and homeland, of witnessing terrifying events, and often of having had to endure violence and abuse, means that the emotional wellbeing and identity of separated young people can be profoundly disrupted. Even those who attempt to help can compound this assault on their emerging identities by viewing them as primarily vulnerable and traumatised individuals. If these young people are to grow into healthy functioning adults, they have an enormous task ahead of them both in learning to navigate the vulnerabilities that their traumatic experiences have opened up, but also, crucially, to develop a view of themselves that is enabling, positive and hopeful. Many mental health services fall into the trap of focusing only on the former and, in so doing, can leave young people with the belief they will be permanently vulnerable and irremediably damaged.

Those separated young people that do make it into psychological services invariably receive individual assessments and treatments. Assessments often include a diagnosis of PTSD (post-traumatic stress disorder, as defined by the American Psychiatric Association's *Diagnostic and Statistical Manual of Mental Disorders*). Young people are invited to talk about their experiences and the effect this has had on them, framed in terms of symptoms such as flashbacks and intrusive memories, hypervigilance, sleep disturbance, persistent negative emotions, and avoidance of stimuli that may trigger memories, among others. They are supported to develop strategies for responding to these effects which build on their individual resilience – a now widely used concept (Agaibi and Wilson, 2005). All good, seemingly. But there are some serious problems with this approach for a number of reasons.

First, these therapies have been developed with people whose trauma is in the past and who are now in positions of safety. They have their roots in work developed with war veterans returning from the First World War (whose symptoms were later described by the diagnostic label of 'post-traumatic stress disorder'), who were subsequently unable to reintegrate and function as productive members of society (Trimble, 1985). For separated children seeking asylum, their trauma is usually ongoing – where they are living with the uncertainty about whether their families are safe, or whether they will ever see their parents again. Only a minority are granted leave to remain in the UK beyond their 18th birthdays, so most have to return to the Immigration court to re-present their case as they near this time (Home Office, 2016). This can be hugely traumatic: going back over experiences they have tried to put behind them; having their account picked apart in court and not being believed; living with the terrifying prospect of losing the security and social networks they have built up in the UK; and ultimately, the prospect they may be returned to the dangers from which they had originally fled (Hughes, 2015). So trauma is not 'post', and interventions with someone who has not established a safe and secure base yet require a very different approach.

Second, the commonly used trauma models (such as trauma focused cognitive behavioural therapy (CBT), eye movement desensitisation and reprocessing (EMDR) and narrative exposure therapy) do not take account of these political contexts, which are fundamental to emotional wellbeing. As Waldegrave et al (2003: 34) highlight, where people's distress arises from oppression and abuse, it is problematic offering therapy that does not acknowledge the political meanings behind this distress and instead focuses purely on the individual. Coupled with the experience for separated young people of their personal accounts being undermined in court, and the negative reporting within mainstream media, this can have a devastating impact on how separated young people view themselves, and on their emotional wellbeing (Hughes, 2015). As White and Epston (1990) suggest, marginalised groups tend to internalise the negative discourses told about them and unaccompanied young people in therapy very commonly blame themselves for what they understand as their personal weaknesses as they struggle with day to day life.

Third, the notion of individuality has been derived from western culture and is not a universal concept (Bracken et al, 1997). Separated children often come from collectivist cultures which construct the 'self' in connected and communal ways. Here in the West, therapy is primarily offered to individuals, which can undermine preferred and known ways of being. Thus, the dominant discourses of expert therapeutic knowledge can silence discourses of how mental or emotional distress is understood within marginalised cultures, and can thereby undermine the identity of those we are attempting to help. It can also undermine community structures that are likely to be a crucial source of protection against the effects of trauma (Ungar, 2011). Also, western therapeutic models assume that all cultural groups will respond to trauma in the same way, and that symptoms and signs of distress can be universally understood and treated. However, there is no consensus in the research literature about either different cultural responses to trauma in refugees, or the best treatments for a diagnosis of PTSD (Crumlish and O'Rourke, 2010).

In summary, individualistic problem-focused interventions can have an unintended negative impact on identity. These approaches risk concealing acts of resistance to abuse which open alternative vistas to richer descriptions of identity (Wade, 2007; Yuen, 2009). As described, the refugee experience and particularly that of separated young people, represents a profound attack on identity. Therefore, a crucial task in re-establishing a life elsewhere is re-building 'home', reconnecting with who they are in a foreign context and developing a set of relationships in which their identity can be securely established. Any intervention designed to improve emotional wellbeing needs to have these aims at its core. I would therefore argue that the therapeutic process cannot be separated from the social and political context of separated young people's lives, and also needs to involve young people's communities and social networks. Our identities are created through our relationships with others, through our interactions out there in the world and not by an isolated internal process.

Vulnerablility and 'resilience'

While holding in mind the potential pitfalls of traditional trauma intervention models, it is nevertheless important to acknowledge the ways in which trauma can make separated young people feel vulnerable, and to offer help with addressing this. Young people can have dramatic physical responses – such as flashbacks, intrusive memories, very disturbed sleep, poor concentration, bodily pains, to name but a few – which are thoroughly documented in many research studies (Caffo et al, 2005; Ehntholt and Yule, 2006). Trauma has an isolating effect as it is so often accompanied by difficult emotions such as shame and guilt which invite people to retreat into themselves. Some forms of trauma such as rape can also lead to severe social stigma and rejection by local communities, as research in many African countries has highlighted (Turshen, 2001). As Po Lin Lee argued, trauma can be seen as seeking to rupture ourselves from our bodies, our relationships and our communities (Po Lin Lee, personal communication, 2017). Our work as therapists needs to address these effects, and help people to view their responses as understandable reactions to extreme experiences.

However, there has been a growing interest in the concept of resilience and the importance of also helping separated young people to reconnect with stories of strength, survival and hope in order for them to go on in their lives. Unfortunately, 'resilience' is often used to shift responsibility onto individuals to learn to cope with unacceptable social conditions. However, if resilience is thought of as something that exists both within an individual, within their personal relationships, within communities, and on a social and political level, then interventions can be focused in ways that help people re-build identities that are connected to others and embedded in cultural references. Michael Ungar (2011) has challenged the notion of individual resilience through his research into the potential for whole communities to promote resilience. He illustrates how relationships and services offer communities the potential to recover from dramatic change, support their adaptability and encourage new growth. Therefore, I would argue that recovery from trauma needs to include the harnessing of both personal and social resources and the building of resilient communities.

Given these considerations, I have developed a 'Narrative Liberation' therapeutic framework to guide work with separated children who are suffering the consequences of trauma. This framework is based on social constructionist systemic theory, and narrative therapy (informed by the work of Michael White[1]). The young person is understood within the context of the multiple relationships that have shaped their life over time, from close family and friends to more distant relationships which play out in societal structures. The narratives that develop around these relationships, shaped by power, history and politics, are crucial in understanding the choices available to young people in how they can go on in their lives, and the possibilities for how their emotional world can strengthen and grow. I also draw on ideas drawn from community psychology (Nelson and Prilleltensky, 2010), and liberation psychology which has its roots in the work of El Salvadoran scholar and social psychologist, Ignacio Martín-Baró (1994). These approaches directly address the political social and cultural contexts of separated young people's lives. They separate the problem from the individual person and offer ways of connecting young people to others, thus counteracting the isolating effect of trauma. In addition, they focus on identity and how to re-connect young people with their cultural roots and social history, and draw on ideas of resistance to dominant and oppressive ways of knowing and being.

A Narrative Liberation framework

When supporting separated young people it is important to recognise that they come with their own histories and ways of responding which may render them more or less vulnerable to the effects of trauma and abuse. Within their personal histories will be opportunities for discovering responses that have sustained them over time, and relationships that have supported them. As argued above, it is also important to identify collective accounts and responses to trauma which are sustaining of the individual, and help to counter the isolating impact trauma can have.

I am proposing that the types of interventions offered to support young people on this journey can be divided into four broad domains, arranged along two axes:

1. Interventions that focus on addressing vulnerability and which involve witnessing and acknowledging young people's accounts of abuse at one end, through to interventions that focus on resources and skills developed to resist the effects of abuse at the other.
2. Interventions that centralise individual experience through to those that have a collective and wider community focus.

Although this scheme may suggest fixed methods and techniques, in reality interventions will be fluid, criss-crossing back and forth between different domains as conversations progress. The Narrative Liberation framework is intended to help practitioners to keep all areas of intervention in mind and avoid some of the traps described earlier that therapeutic interventions can fall into. The chapter now describes what interventions in each of the different domains may look like.

Working with individuals to understand and acknowledge abuse (Domain 1 in Figure 4)

Most trauma interventions take place in Domain 1 of the framework, which involve conversations with separated young people to help them make sense of what has happened to them, and find ways of dealing with their experiences. However, in order to avoid locating the problem within the individual it is necessary to help young people 'decode' the broader social and political contexts. Paolo Freire (1973) describes this as a process of critical consciousness (or 'conscientisation'). He argued that when people critically reflect on their experience in the light of social and political contexts, the

Figure 4: Narrative Liberation framework for responding to trauma

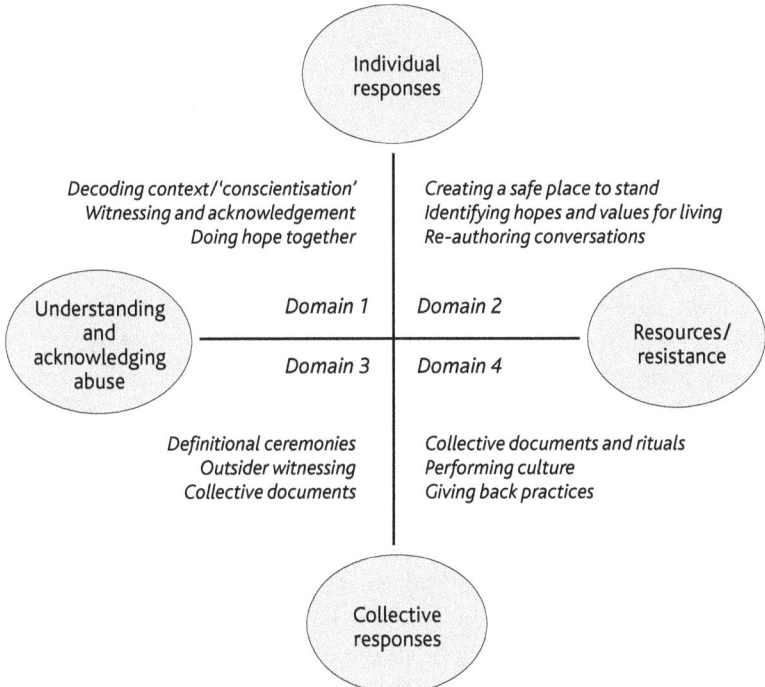

technologies of oppression can be made visible and new possibilities for action emerge. By acquiring new knowledge about their social world and their place within it, people can begin to connect with more positive versions of their identity and are able to envisage new possibilities for action within their multiple relationships. Freire was interested in critical pedagogy and how this process could function within an education context, but it can equally take place within a therapeutic relationship. As a liberation psychologist, Martín-Baró (1994) proposed that it is this dialectical process through which people can make sense of the mechanisms of oppression and decode their world, in order to facilitate new understandings of themselves and of their social identity.

Drawing on communication theory, Cronen and Pearce (1985) developed a framework called the 'coordinated management of meaning' (CMM) as a structure for conversations that enable people to identify the layers of context which have impinged on their experience (Pearce, 1994). These frameworks can be used to help locate abuse and trauma within the context of specific relationships, but also of family, community, cultural group, religions groups, social and political trends and the history of nations – thus facilitating a critical understanding of how abuse came about. From this position of understanding, people have more choices about how to act in relation to the abuse.

Working within what is referred to as Domain 1, I often have conversations with unaccompanied young people about the social and political forces that led them to flee their countries. This might include hearing about the political affiliations of their families, what this meant in their village or town, how gender relationships might have made them particularly vulnerable (for example, boys being expected to take up arms), what the significance was of them being sent away, what the families' hopes were for them, and so on. These contexts are important in shaping the identity of the young person, and will be the site of many of their beliefs about themselves and their hopes for the future. An Afghan teenager I met talked about how all the boys in his family were at risk of being recruited by the Taliban, who had already murdered his father, and that unless they escaped the country, they would be forcibly taken. His family had spent all their savings sending him away with traffickers to a place of safety, with the hope that as the eldest son, he would be able to make a life in the UK and send for his younger brothers and the rest of the family. This was a terrible burden for him as he was struggling to secure leave to remain, was unable to focus on his education, and was trying desperately to get safely settled while knowing that his family were still in danger. This context needed to be acknowledged and understood as the frame for his responses to the traumatic events he had witnessed. Our conversation helped him view his responses (guilt, anger, sadness) as reasonable reactions to extreme circumstances, and a communication about what had been violated, rather than a personal weakness.

Another important dimension of therapeutic conversations within Domain 1 is witnessing and acknowledgement of abuse and injustice. Weingarten (2003) suggests that as carers, therapists need to demonstrate 'compassionate witnessing'. This includes acknowledging painful losses while remaining emotionally present to support mourning and grief. They also need to be able and prepared to stay with the discomfort of witnessing people's pain, and be prepared to be changed by the stories they hear in order to counter the isolating and depersonalising effects of trauma. As Weingarten urges, they must draw on as much compassion as they can muster to connect emotionally with the people they are working with. 'It [compassion] is founded on an ability to recognize and express a common bond with another' (Weingarten, 2003: 2). Bergum and Dossetor (2005) describe 'relational ethics' as embodying respect, engagement and being present. These are crucial elements in how practitioners respond to the dehumanising context that separated young people face when they arrive in the UK. Many have also been through the refugee camps in Northern France where racism, suspicion and police brutality are rife (Burck and Hughes, 2018; see also Chapter One in this collection), adding to the corrosion of their identity.

I noticed when working with separated young people in the Tavistock Refugee Service, that sometimes they would refer to me knowing their story (of trauma) when in fact very little detail had been shared. One Congolese teenage girl (I will call her 'Candice') wanted me to talk to her new key worker to explain why she did not want to answer any of their questions about her family. Candice had been imprisoned, raped and tortured and did not know what had happened to either her parents or younger sisters. She sometimes commented that I knew everything about her. Although she always made it clear she didn't want to talk about her past, she clearly felt some refuge in the knowledge that someone else knew, and was able to go on in their relationship with her. Weingarten (2000) proposes that witnessing is not a passive process, but enables connection with the other person and validation of their story. In our emotional responses, practitioners can convey that they have been touched by what the other person has said and that they are not alone in their distress.

Weingarten also talks about how this process of witnessing allows practitioners to join in *doing hope together*, which is another role for carers within Domain 1. For separated young people, hope is the main thing that keeps them going – hope that their life will have a better future, that they will get asylum and feel safe, that they will be able to complete their education, that they will be able to re-create lasting relationships, and that they will once again be able to experience family life. Hope often feels very precarious and having other people to hold onto this with them is essential in resisting isolation and despair.

One day, Candice told me she was not ready to start trying to trace her family in the Congo as she did not yet feel secure enough to bear bad news if it came, and that she did not dare to hope. But following a conversation about what needed to happen in her life for her to reach this point and when she would know she was there, she was able for the first time to begin tentatively voicing her hope that her family might one day be re-united. This seemed to enable other hopes for the future to also be voiced, and she began to imagine a future in which she herself might be able to start a family. This 'doing hope together' seemed to bring new energy to this young person. It was important that I didn't get drawn into offering hollow reassurances that 'it will be all right', but in joining with her by asking where she currently stood in relation to hope, and centring her experience, this appeared to enable her to let go of some of the huge burden she carried.

The other aspect to witnessing which seems so crucial for healing is acknowledging the violence and multiple injustices that the person has been subjected to, and naming this injustice. I use Cronen and Pearce's (1985) framework of CMM with young people to map the contexts that have given rise to their abuse and oppression (including their experiences in the UK), and talk about the whole range of responses to injustice that might be open to them and to those they are in relationship with. The truth and reconciliation process in South Africa was a large-scale example of the healing potential of acknowledgement. In therapy, it can be very useful to invite others into meetings to hear and acknowledge what has taken place – either those who have experienced similar abuses, or simply concerned onlookers. Denborough (2005) has developed a narrative framework for receiving and documenting testimonies of trauma, which facilitates acknowledgement of abuse, recognising the ways in which the person concerned has resisted the effects, and offering opportunities for others to respond to and learn from their experiences. These practices often represent a move from Domain 1 to Domain 3, as they connect people and allow for the generation of collective accounts of abuse and resistance.

Towards accounts of resistance: uncovering preferred narratives of identity (Domain 2)

One of the significant risks of carrying out 'trauma focused' therapies is taking young people back to memories that repeat their experiences of traumatisation. It is a necessary part of ethical practice to ensure that our interventions do not do this, which is why it is so important to focus on accounts of resistance, and values or relationships that support a strong sense of identity (the work that happens in Domain 2, see Figure 4). White (2005) proposes that therapists need to develop an 'alternative territory of identity', a safe place in which young people can stand as they start to give expression to their experiences of trauma and its consequences, without experiencing an assault on their identity. This safe place is developed through conversations about the multiple ways in which they have responded to trauma in order to minimise the negative effects it has on their lives. Inherent in these responses are skills and knowledges, for example, how to find support in hostile places, how to protect themselves, how to hold onto hope, nurturing and reaching out to others who are also experiencing trauma, discovering ways of healing, and so on. These alternative stories are about the multiple ways that young people have resisted the effects of abuse, and what values they hold which have made that resistance possible. These 're-authoring conversations' help people to identify and give voice to an account of their experiences, which strengthens them and connects them to others. Wade (1997) describes how to help people identify 'small acts of living' – actions that represent small but significant moments of resistance to abuse. These may be private acts of resistance concealed in subtle behaviours, or more public actions, but all speak of that person's refusal to give into the effects of abuse.

The following is one such conversation, where I was working within Domain 2. It is re-created from notes I made of a conversation I had in the Calais refugee camp, with a gentle Sudanese boy, 'Abdul', aged 15 years, speaking ruefully of the violence that seemed to be following him throughout his life. This was the night after a big fight had broken out in the camp between Afghani and Sudanese people, which started in the food queue. Drawing on narrative practices, I helped Abdul reflect on his responses to violence and identify his values for living that lay behind these responses, which were that he was peace loving. I then helped him trace the roots of these values in family and community, so that his responses were not understood as isolated, personal ones, but represented the desires of a whole community.

> Abdul: I am so tired of violence. I left Darfur to get away from violence, but there was more on my journey here, and now there is violence here… so much…
>
> Gillian: It sounds like it has been impossible to get away from it.
>
> A: Yes, I hate violence. I don't like it at all… I am not that kind of person. I don't like to fight.
>
> G: What did you do last night when the fight started?
>
> A: I ran away from it, to the other side of the camp. I got away quickly. I went and sat by the road at the edge of the camp up there (points), just sat in the grass at the edge of the road and waited. It was cold and I didn't have my coat, but I didn't want to go back to get my things.
>
> G: Sounds like you were determined to keep away. Is that what you normally do when there is violence nearby – try to get away from it?

A: Yes, yes... keep away from fights. I don't want to join in with fighting. I don't want to get hurt and I don't like to hurt anyone else.

G: Was there anything else you did last night to keep yourself safe?

A: I just waited, waited almost all night long. I couldn't sleep because it was too cold. I prayed too.

G: Did that help?

A: Yes, it made me feel calmer.

G: When else have you used praying to help you calm down in the face of violence?

A: Back home [in Darfur], my family always used to pray when the fighting started. My mother would bring us all together and we would sit and pray, wait until it was over and hope nobody would come into our house.

G: What did your family think about violence?

A: We all hated it. We did not want to fight anyone. That's why my family sent me away, because they didn't want me to be taken and made to fight... [Pauses, and looks sad]

G: It sounds like your family took a stand against violence when they decided to do that. What would they think now, if they knew you were still keeping away from violence, and praying to help calm yourself down?

A: They would be happy to know that. They would be proud of me.

G: And who else would be happy to know that?

A: My auntie... my cousins... my friends too. None of us liked the fighting. We all wanted to get away.

G: Are most Sudanese people like that? Peace loving, not wanting violence? Or is it just your family and friends.

A: The place, the village where we lived, nobody liked the fighting. We all wanted peace.

G: So when you run away from violence here, this is something that the people in your village would have supported? They would have wanted you to do that?

A: Yes, yes...

G: And is there anyone else you would like to share this with?

In order to strengthen accounts of resistance to abuse and preferred versions of self, they need to be rooted in people's social and cultural histories so that they are seen as central to their identity. Dominant and oppressive discourses often present reality as entirely divorced from the influence of history, which makes it easier to view the status quo as 'just how things are' which we should not challenge – for example, 'we have to severely limit immigration to our country because there are not enough jobs or housing for any extra people'. But as Chimamanda Adiche says in her 2009 TED talk,[2] our history defines us both in our identity and our relationships, and history is important as a reservoir of memories and stories that have the potential to empower us. Stories can break but also repair human dignity. Separated young people usually have difficult relationships with their home and country where they have experienced violence and persecution, and as practitioners we have a role to help them connect with positive aspects of these memories.

The narrative tradition emphasises the significance for our emotional wellbeing as closely connected to our hopes and values for living. White (2003) understands that behind every expression of distress is a value that has been violated, and that the strength of our responses to abuse is testament to the importance of the value which has been violated. In my conversation with Abdul, it was clear that he had a very strong negative response to violence because peaceful relationships were so important to him, and were strongly embedded in his family and home community culture. This reframing helps people to understand distress in more constructive ways, and can free people up to talk about other ways of staying connected to their values, moving them from a position of despair to action.

Collective responses

Collective responses to trauma are important for many reasons: to counter isolation and self-blame; as an opportunity for communal meaning making; to provide an audience for people's preferred accounts of themselves; for public witnessing and acknowledgement of abuse; for solidarity and joint action to resist the effects of abuse; and to enable people to re-position themselves from victim to helper/activist. These collective responses can lie either within the domain of understanding (meaning making) and acknowledging abuse (Domain 3 of the framework), or that of identifying shared resources and building resistance to the effects of abuse (Domain 4).

Collective understanding and acknowledgement (Domain 3)

When we talk with others, our ideas shift and develop, and suddenly new possibilities emerge for how we understand and respond to our experiences. The process of communal meaning making that takes place in group conversations can be a powerful illustration of this process.

I ran a group at the Tavistock Centre for eight separated young people from Eritrea, Congo, Vietnam, Afghanistan, and Albania, aged 15–18, both boys and girls. We had a conversation one afternoon about 'suffering'. It began with one boy talking about how much suffering had featured in his life, a statement with which others quickly agreed with. We began to talk about the effects of suffering on the young people's lives – that it isolated them from others, made them angry, tired, unmotivated, and made others resent or even hate them. But as I started to enquire about their responses to suffering, and what they had learnt from others about how to live with this, alternative (more hidden) accounts began to emerge which brought to light many personal resources and abilities. They described how they thought suffering had made them stronger; helped them discover bravery; made them kinder and more sensitive to others; made them smarter and wiser; and showed them their capacity to survive in extreme circumstances. They also talked about how they believed that suffering was good for developing dignity and about the importance of forgiveness, which can be a source of power and strength for them. The richness of this moving conversation came from the many voices that contributed to it – as one person spoke, others made connections, until a powerful shared story had developed. Individual conversations with these young people would never have generated such richness or the sense of solidarity that this conversation generated. This process and its outcomes illustrate what is possible through collective activity and how important it is to create opportunities during therapeutic work for these types of conversation – the work within Domain 3 (meaning making), which also moves into Domain 4 as people identify their resources and resistance to distress.

Burton (2004) highlights the importance of bringing people together so that suffering can be transformed from a secret distress to a social and shared experience. Taking this a step further, through the process of joint meaning making, possibilities are created for joint action. As Freire (2001) suggests, solidarity is more than joining others in naming oppression, it involves action that will 'transform oneself, institutions and the world'. Reports from people who engage in collective action have shown how this impacts positively on their sense of belonging and personal worth (Kagan et al, 2001).

But the other task within Domain 3 is collective acknowledgement and witnessing, and clearly, the power of this can be magnified by increasing the size of the audience. There are numerous ways that public acknowledgement and witnessing of preferred accounts can be facilitated. Narrative practices offer ways to structure conversations which facilitate this. For example, Michael White's (2007) 'definitional ceremonies' are rituals that enable people to tell or perform their personal accounts of their lives in front of others – the 'outsider witnesses' – and hear how these accounts have influenced others. Those witnessing respond to what they have heard by sharing: what has touched them in the person's story; what images this has evoked for them; what it says about the values that person holds; how this resonated with their own experience; and how their lives have been touched by hearing this account. This ritual enables people to not only have their story heard, but they receive validation of their account through hearing how it has touched the lives of others.

David Denborough's (2008) book *Collective Narrative Practice* is a rich description of many such practices which bring people together in their collective response to difficulties they face in their lives. He uses collectively created documents in the form of letters, checklists of psychological and social resistance, timelines and maps of history, as well as rituals and songs to help people respond to trauma together in ways that strengthen and connect them. Another example is how the digital world has been used to connect people through virtual communities as with the 'anti anorexia league' and the archive of resistance against anorexia and bulimia, developed by the online community 'Narrative Approaches'.[3]

These offer many ideas for how to connect the unaccompanied young people practitioners work with to supportive communities that go beyond the life of therapy (but extend the developments in their lives achieved through this). There are numerous small drama and arts organisations that have run projects which offer these opportunities. One such initiative is Project Phakama, a London based group that aims to bring young people from diverse communities together through drama and provide a platform from which to express, grow and perform. They have worked with separated young people seeking asylum to create performances of their experiences which are used to educate the general public (Clayton and Hughes, 2016).

Collective resources and accounts of resistance (Domain 4)

As therapeutic work takes place in Domain 3 of the framework, this usually leads conversations directly into Domain 4, where accounts of resistance to abuse develop and resources are named. In the Child and Family Refugee Service, we have run a number of 'Tree of Life' groups (Ncube, 2006; Hughes, 2014), and also 'Team of Life' groups (Denborough, 2012; Hughes and Kaur, 2014) based on a narrative methodology that offers a way of mapping out alternative territories of identity using the creative metaphor of a tree or football team. These groups have offered young people ways of talking about traumatic experiences, and creating meaning together about what has happened to them, alongside their accounts of resistance which are embedded in their preferred identities. For example, one group of separated Afghan boys talked about their experiences of racist abuse at school and on the housing estates where they lived. They described how they had learnt to protect themselves by holding their heads up high and not responding to the insults. They traced these skills back to cultural expectations and to Pashto-speaking people, saying that when you do respond to abuse with further insults and violence you are doing no better than 'barking like a dog'. Together they voiced an alternative account of themselves as strong and proud Afghans, who were honouring their traditions in their responses to racist abuse.

These initiatives crossed the activities in both Domains 3 and 4. They initially brought people together to give voice to their personal stories, for others to witness their accounts and create opportunities for shared meaning making – but they also sought to develop accounts of resistance to abuse together. During one Tree of Life group, there was an animated conversation about why it is so difficult to gain asylum in the UK and how inhumane the legal system feels at times. It started with anger and incomprehension but turned to a discussion about how the system is supported by accounts in the media and on social platforms of the dangers of immigration. "You turn on your phone and it is all there, saying how bad we are and how to keep us out." They began to make sense of this as arising from ignorance and fear, leading to racism, and how human weaknesses invite people worldwide to guard their territories at the cost of human compassion. The conversation appeared to help the young people feel that the system was not designed to persecute them personally, but instead reflected inequalities and abuses that even western democracies had not managed to resist. The conversation connected them in this shared experience, and ended with them saying that they were determined to keep going with their gruelling asylum claims and not allow others' ignorance to stop them reaching for what they were entitled to.

Within Domain 4, a powerful way of embedding a person's connection with their resources is by enabling 'giving back practices', which involves re-positioning people from someone requiring help to themselves becoming a helper of others. Schwartz and Sendor (1999) found that when chronically ill patients have the opportunity to offer support to other patients, this led to a significant improvement in their confidence, self-esteem, mood and role functioning. Richard Sennett, the American sociology professor, describes in his book *Respect* (2004) how we gain respect from society and a sense of self-worth by helping others – by giving something back, but that the opportunities for doing this are severely limited by prevailing conditions of social inequality. For asylum seekers, not being allowed to work is a stark example of this, and not being fluent in the host language also makes it much more difficult to be socially useful. However, if therapy can be a place for people to move from the position of helped to helper (even in small ways), this can have a huge impact on self-esteem. Definitional ceremonies offer the opportunity for this as people can hear how their personal account has the power to touch and transform the life of others in positive ways.

When we have run groups for separated young people (both in the Tavistock Child and Family Refugee Service and with the Refugee Resilience Collective[4]), we have placed a significant emphasis on participants sharing the knowledge and skills that they have developed in resisting the effects of trauma, and being consultants to each other. The feedback we consistently get from the different groups is that not only is it good to receive that support from peers, but that it has a powerful impact on the young people's sense of self-worth to know that they have something valuable to offer others. Also, that it helps to reframe their negative experiences as an opportunity to develop special skills which they can use to benefit others.

Another function of bringing people together (as described in Domain 4) is what liberation psychologist Martín-Baró (1994) described as assisting people with the recovery of their 'historical memory'. He understood this to be the development of a liberating account of a person's identity, recovered through an examination of social, interpersonal and collective memories. This cultural remembering helps to uncover resources and skills held across communities which offer opportunities and choices for action. Martín-Baró proposes that by helping people discover the roots of their identity, it will help them connect to their hopes for what they might become in the future. This connecting with cultural roots and performing of culture can be most powerfully done collectively.

In the Tavistock Refugee Team, we set up a number of initiatives where people could perform their culture together, share memories of cultural rituals and talk about what these said about the values that they held to be important. We collaborated with an organisation called the Social Kitchen, which uses cooking as a way of bringing people together to share memories through cooking their favourite food together. We ran a project that included adults from the local Congolese community and unaccompanied Congolese youth, who prepared a meal together of food that had particular symbolic meanings, and then shared it. They talked about what memories the food evoked and why particular dishes were eaten, which in turn brought forth memories of hardship and survival in extreme times. They also talked about celebrations and happy times, and how these rituals represented cultural beliefs and values. Talking about shared values created a sense of solidarity, connecting people, and represented a deeply held resource for people to draw on in the future.

With the Narrative Liberation framework I have proposed, although I have presented the different domains in a chronological order, the framework is intended to be more flexible than this. It is important when practitioners meet a separated young person seeking asylum in a caring capacity that therapists evaluate where they are in relation to the trauma they have experienced. Many young people do not want to talk about what has happened to them and I believe it is ethically problematic to ask probing questions about this if explicit permission to do this has not been given. Therapists need to hold in mind that it may be more appropriate to start with collective practices in Domains 2 and 4. Similarly, young people may want to share their accounts of trauma in the privacy of a one to one relationship, but not wish to have these shared more publicly. In which case the communal witnessing practices would not be appropriate. Young people may prefer more of the activities in Domain 4 where they enact positive aspects of their culture with others, developing their identity which is separate from the abuse they have experienced. Whatever domain practitioners choose to work in, it is essential that this is carefully negotiated with the young people, and it should not be assumed that every practice described will be useful for everyone. Also, the reality of conversations is that they are fluid, and likely to move back and forth between different domains over time and as relationships between the young person and carer evolve.

Conclusions

Much good therapeutic work is done with individual separated young people seeking asylum to help them overcome the effects of trauma and abuse. However, there are dangers to many of the individual trauma focused interventions where young people can become defined by their vulnerabilities, stuck in relationships which position them as damaged, vulnerable and needing help, and dogged by the belief that their social position and distress are signs of their personal failure. Therapists therefore urgently need to reflect on how attempts to help these young people are positioning them. I argue that it is necessary to draw on practices that enable abuses to be acknowledged and recognised within the social and political contexts in which they occur – practices that fall within Domain 1 of the Narrative Liberation framework I propose. To then move young people onto more solid ground where they are able to connect with personal accounts of survival and resistance to abuse, and connect with their hopes and dreams for their future (Domain 2).

In order to counter the isolating effects of trauma and abuse, therapists' role must also be to connect people with others, to enable shared meaning making and expand opportunities for witnessing and acknowledgement (Domain 3). Finally, working within Domain 4, therapists need to facilitate collective practices where people are able to connect with life affirming aspects of their cultural and social histories, and build this together through collective remembering. Also, to offer opportunities for giving back practices so that young people can be repositioned as experts on resisting the effects of trauma and abuse, and have the experience of using these skills to help others.

The Narrative Liberation framework is intended to enable practitioners to reflect on what they are doing in their care of separated young people, and to help guard against isolating and unhelpful therapeutic practices. It also proposes how practitioners can explore and work within the powerful and all defining social, political and cultural contexts shaping the lives and identities of separated young people, and indeed, any person who has suffered trauma and abuse. Talking therapies need to routinely incorporate these practices if hopes for a better future which young people feel they have the means to shape are to be ignited.

Notes

1. Michael White is credited with developing the founding principles of Narrative Therapy, (White 1995; 2004; 2007), based at the Dulwich Centre in Adelaide.

2. TED is a media organisation founded in 1984, which posts talks online for free distribution, using the slogan 'ideas worth spreading.'

3. See www.narrativeapproaches.com/resources/anorexia-bulimia-archives-of-resistance/

4. The Refugee Resilience Collective (RRC) was set up in March 2016 by a group of systemic therapists and psychologists to support refugees and volunteers in the refugee camps of Northern France. Facebook: Refugee Resilience Collective.

References

Adiche, C.N. (2009) 'The danger of a single story', TED Talk, www.ted.com/talks/chimamanda_adichie_the_danger_of_a_single_story

Agaibi, C.E. and Wilson, J.B. (2005) 'Trauma, PTSD and resilience: A review of the literature', *Trauma, Violence and Abuse*, 6 (3):195–216.

American Psychiatric Association (2013) *Diagnostic and Statistical Manual of Mental Disorders*, 5th edition, Arlington, VA: American Psychiatric Publishing.

Bergum, V. and Dossetor, J. (2005) *Relational ethics: The full meaning of respect*, Hagerstown, Maryland: University Publishing Group.

Bracken, P., Giller, J.E., and Summerfield, D. (1997) 'Rethinking mental health work with survivors of wartime violence and refugees', *Journal of Refugee Studies*, 10(4): 431–42.

Burck, C. and Hughes, G. (2018) 'Challenges and impossibilities of 'standing alongside' in an intolerable context. Learning from refugees and volunteers in the Calais camp', *Clinical Child Psychology and Psychiatry*, 23 (2): 223–37.

Burton, M. (2004) 'Liberation social psychology: Learning from the Latin American experience', *Clinical Psychology*, 38, 32–7.

Caffo, E., Forresi, B. and Lievers, L.S. (2005) 'Impact, psychological sequelae and management of trauma affecting children and adolescents', *Current Opinion in Psychiatry*, 18(4): 422–8.

Clayton, S. and Hughes, G. (2016) 'The uses of film and creative methods to liberate young refugee and asylum seeking people from disempowering identities – a dialogic approach', in T. Afuape and G. Hughes (eds) *Liberation practices: Towards emotional wellbeing through dialogue*, London: Routledge, pp 89–100.

Cronen, V. and Pearce, W.B. (1985) 'Towards an explanation of how the Milan Method works: An invitation to a systemic epistemology and the evolution of family systems', in D. Campbell and R. Draper (eds) *Applications of systemic family therapy. The Milan Approach*, London: Grune & Stratton.

Crumlish, N., and O'Rourke, K. (2010) 'A systematic review of treatments for Post-Traumatic Stress Disorder among refugees and asylum-seekers', *Journal of Nervous & Mental Disease*, 198(4): 237–51.

Denborough, D. (2005) 'A framework for receiving and documenting testimonies of trauma', *International Journal of Narrative Therapy and Community Work*, 3 & 4, part 2, 34–42.

Denborough, D. (2008) *Collective narrative practice. Responding to individuals, groups and communities who have experienced trauma*, Adelaide: Dulwich Centre Publications.

Denborough, D. (2012) 'The Team of Life with young men from refugee backgrounds', *International Journal of Narrative Therapy and Community Work*, 2: 44–52.

Ehntholt, K.A. and Yule, W. (2006) 'Practitioner review: Assessment and treatment of refugee children and adolescents who have experienced war-related trauma,' *Journal of Child Psychology and Psychiatry*, 47(12): 1197–210.

Home Office (2016) '6. Unaccompanied asylum-seeking children', www.gov.uk/government/publications/immigration-statistics-july-to-september-2016/asylum#unaccompanied-asylum-seeking-children

Hughes, G. (2014) 'Finding a voice through 'The Tree of Life': A strength-based approach to mental health for refugee children and families in schools', *Clinical Child Psychology and Psychiatry*, 19(1):139–53.

Hughes, G. and Kaur, P. (2014) 'Young men from refugee communities score goals for their future using the Team of Life', *Context*, 134, 25–31.

Freire, P. (1973) *Education for critical consciousness*, New York: Continuum.

Freire, P. (2001) *Pedagogy of freedom: Ethics, democracy and civic courage*, Lanham, MD: Rowman and Littlefield.

Hughes, G. (2015) 'Our asylum system is forcing vulnerable teenagers to re-live their trauma', *Guardian*, 11 November, www.theguardian.com/commentisfree/2015/nov/11/asylum-teenagers-refugees-mental-health

Kagan, C., Caton, S., and Amin, A. (2001) *The need for witness support. Report of feasibility study of a community witness support scheme for Heartlands, North Town*, IOD Occasional papers, 1/01. Manchester Metropolitan University.

Martín-Baró, I. (1994) *Writings for a Liberation Psychology: Essays, 1985–1989*, edited by A. Aron and S. Corne, Cambridge, MA: Harvard University Press.

Ncube, N. (2006) 'The Tree of Life Project: Using narrative ideas in work with vulnerable children in Southern Africa', *The International Journal of Narrative Therapy and Community Work*, 1: 3–16.

Nelson, G. and Prilleltensky, I. (2010) (eds) *Community Psychology. In pursuit of liberation and well-being*, 2nd edition, Basingstoke: Palgrave Macmillan.

Pearce, W.B. (1994) *Interpersonal communication. Making social worlds*, New York: Harper Collins.

Rutter, J. (2006) *Refugee children in the UK*, Milton Keynes: Open University Press

Schwartz, C.E. and Sendor, M. (1999) 'Helping others helps oneself: response shift effects in peer support', *Social Science and Medicine*, 48(11): 1563–75.

Sennett, R. (2004) *Respect: The formation of character in an age of inequality*, London: Penguin.

Trimble, M.R. (1985) 'Post-traumatic Stress Disorder: History of a concept', in C.R. Figley (ed) *Trauma and its wake, Vol 1, The study and treatment of Post-Traumatic Stress Disorder*, Brunner/Mazel Psychosocial Stress Series, Bristol, PA: Brunner/Mazel.

Turshen, M. (2001) 'The political economy of rape: An analysis of systematic rape and sexual abuse of women during armed conflict in Africa', in C. Moser and F. Clarke (eds) *Victors, perpetrators or actors: Gender, armed conflict and political violence*, London: Zed Books, pp 55–68.

Ungar, M. (2011) 'Community resilience for youth and families: Facilitative physical and social capital in contexts of adversity', *Children and Youth Services Review*, 33: 1742–48.

Wade, A. (1997) 'Small acts of living: Everyday resistance to violence and other forms of oppression', *Contemporary Family Therapy*, 19(1): 23–39.

Wade, A. (2007) 'Despair, resistance, hope: Response-based therapy with victims of violence', in C. Flaskas, I. McCarthy, and J. Sheehan (eds) *Hope and despair in narrative and family therapy: Adversity, forgiveness and reconciliation*, New York: Routledge/Taylor & Francis Group, pp 63–74.

Waldegrave, C., Tamasese, K., Tuhaka, F., and Campbell, W. (2003) *Just Therapy – a Journey. A collection of papers from the Just Therapy Team*, New Zealand. Adelaide: Dulwich Centre Publications.

Weingarten, K. (2000) 'Witnessing, Wonder, and Hope', *Family Process*, 39: 389–402.

Weingarten, K. (2003) 'Compassionate witnessing and the transformation of societal violence: How individuals can make a difference', *Common Shock, How we are Harmed, How We Can Heal* New York: Dutton.

White, M. (1995) *Re-authoring lives: Interviews and essays*, Adelaide: Dulwich Centre Publications.

White, M. (2003) 'Narrative practice and community assignments', *International Journal of Narrative Therapy and Community Work*, 2: 17–56.

White, M. (2004) *Narrative practice and exotic lives: Resurrecting diversity in everyday life*, Adelaide: Dulwich Centre Publications.

White, M. (2005) 'Children, trauma and subordinate storyline development', *The International Journal of Narrative Therapy and Community Work*, 3 & 4: 10–21.

White, M. (2007) *Maps of Narrative Practice*, London: W.W. Norton & Co.

White, M. and Epston, D. (1990) *Narrative Means to Therapeutic Ends*, New York: W.W. Norton & Company.

Yuen, A. (2009) 'Less pain, more gain: Explorations of responses versus effects when working with the consequences of trauma', *Explorations: An E-journal of Narrative practice*, 1: 6–16.

SIX

Spaces of belonging and social care

Louise Drammeh

Introduction

Unaccompanied young people are in a precarious situation but, despite this, they can and do create some feelings of belonging. In this chapter, I draw on my own experience as a social worker and researcher to explore the forms and spaces of belonging that young people create, and the ways in which social workers and others can support this process.

The first section examines the concept of belonging in relation to an asylum system designed to exclude, within an environment where preventing refugees from accessing safety is developing beyond a covert agenda into stated policy, and where internal barriers and restrictions form part of the 'production of discomfort' (Lewis, 2013). Unaccompanied young people have a close structural relationship with social care, being recognised as 'abandoned children' and thus looked-after under Section 20, Children Act 1989 and supported into early adulthood through the Children (Leaving Care) Act 2000 (see also Chapter Three). Rather than objectifying them as 'service users', however, the chapter seeks to depict *their* views and perceptions and the complexity of their individual lives. Accordingly, the chapter draws on the work of many disciplines and goes well beyond the literature on 'children', which as well as objectifying them further – and overlooking the fact that most are over 16 (Home Office, 2017) and on the cusp of adulthood – often relies on westernised assumptions around chronological age, which can lead to infantilising and to a denial of agency and autonomy.

The chapter's main section considers how, despite structural constraints, young people strive to create some spaces of belonging, focusing on accommodation, schools and colleges, places of worship, social networks and local neighbourhoods. Alongside existing literature, whenever possible points are illustrated through glimpses into the real lives of some of the young people with whom I have the privilege to work, who kindly consented to take part in my PhD research, which explores their experiences of the UK asylum system and its interaction with social care. Qualitative data was collected between 2013 and 2017 from 21 participants, including 12 young people, plus carers and other professionals, using participant observation and interviews. The local authority is in south-west London and all but one of the young people live in London and the south-east. Wherever an account or speech is not attributed to a published source it refers to 'my' participants, anonymised through pseudonyms.[1] The chapter aims to put social care in proportion, as part of young people's lives but not always central and also to demonstrate how it can both impede and help create 'spaces of belonging'.

Suggestions are then made as to some ways in which, through creative and assertive use of existing processes, social workers[2] *can* stand alongside young people, challenge oppression, overcome barriers and strengthen their opportunities to create and sustain those experiences of belonging. The chapter concludes that although unaccompanied young people do, in many ways, create some spaces of belonging, unless structural inequalities are addressed these will be contingent, incomplete and fragile. Social care can tacitly accept this as 'good enough under the circumstances'. Or it can rise to the challenge and play a greater role in creating a fairer society.

'Belonging is a puzzling term...'

As Sarah Wright continues, 'the term is at once slippery and axiomatic, flexible and self-evident' (2015: 391). Rather than rigid theories, she suggests broadening its possibilities through concepts such as affect, process, performance and change. Crucially, belonging is not just about 'being' in the present but also 'longing' for that 'being' (Probyn 1996).

Yuval-Davis depicts belonging as 'feeling at home', which she differentiates from the politics of belonging, but she agrees with Hage that 'home is an on-going project entailing a sense of hope for the future' (1997: 103 in Yuval-Davis, 2011: 10). This clearly links the everyday belongings of unaccompanied young people to their migration status. Antonsich is clearer in pointing to 'the realm of power' (2010: 649) as the thread which runs throughout the concept of belonging, as it ranges from 'a personal, intimate, private sentiment ... [of] place ... [to] a discursive resource which ... claims, justifies, resists forms of socio-spatial inclusion/exclusion' (Antonsich, 2010: 645). This chapter takes a diffuse, Foucauldian view of power, to include that of individuals throughout society, including 'street-level bureaucrats' (Mountz, 2010; Baba, 2013) not only in immigration offices but also in social care. If, as Allan (2015) argues, in its focus on the personal or psychosocial aspects of belonging, social care neglects the structural, it risks losing sight of how belonging 'is at once emotional and political and personal and societal' (Wright 2015: 400). It also risks obfuscating its own power.

Belonging is at its most poignant when threatened (Yuval-Davis, 2011: 10). Nothing could better depict the situation of unaccompanied young people, as they attend interviews, await decisions, often face refusals and appeals (even 'permission to appeal') and sometimes find themselves 'appeal rights exhausted' (see Chapter Two).

Unaccompanied minors are not shielded from asylum processes, despite guidelines on processing claims from a child: 'every applicant, regardless of age, has to show to the same standard ... that they have a well-founded fear of persecution for a Convention reason' (UK Border Agency, 2013: S.16). With 'enforced temporariness' forming part of immigration control (Anderson, 2013), fears and anxieties over the future overshadow many asylum claimants' lives, including children (Heptinstall et al, 2004; Sigona, 2012; Teather et al, 2013). Clinical psychologists Groark et al find that, among unaccompanied young people, 'high levels of post-migratory stress have been linked to uncertainty about asylum status...[and] constant negotiation with the authorities...' (2010: 422). Chase (2010: 2051) talks of the 'stresses and uncertainties placed on refugee children as a result of the asylum-seeking and immigration processes they are subjected to'. The enforced state of limbo impacts on wellbeing and the capacity to deal with the past, despite efforts to grasp some hope and sense of control (Wade, 2011; Chase, 2013). Sue Clayton also explores issues of time, of stopping and starting, or enforced limbo, in Chapter Four of this book.

Even if or when asylum claims are successful, stigma and rejection persist in an environment increasingly hostile to refugees (Rutter, 2006; Anderson, 2013; Teather et al, 2013, Tyler, 2013). Some may have difficulties of the kind faced by citizens, such as racism or exclusion. There is always a political aspect to belonging.

As an act of becoming, belonging overlaps with identity construction. Like belonging, identity is best understood as a process rather than a label, which risks equating it with destiny. Hall suggests that identification better encapsulates its dynamic nature. He describes:

> the meeting point, the point of suture between on the one hand the discourses and practices which attempt to

'interpellate', speak to us or hail us into place as the social subjects of particular discourses, and on the other hand the processes which produce subjectivities, which construct us as subjects which can be 'spoken' (1996: 6–7).

Unaccompanied young people exemplify this interaction between discourses, processes and subjectivities very effectively. Faced with many processes, many discourses, from the most exclusionary to the most welcoming, they find themselves with labels ranging from 'looked-after child' to 'person liable for removal'. They are situated at an interesting point in terms of lifecycle, separated, sometimes for the first time, from the direct influence of families. As migrants, they are adjusting to new environments and as *forced* migrants applying for asylum, they must constantly justify their 'right to belong'. Living through the paradoxes or acceptance and rejection, young people experience ever-changing forms of suturing, resulting in unique, personal and contextual forms of self-construction and self-representation. In the midst of this, they strive to construct spaces of belonging, both in the sense of feeling 'at home' and in the structural/legal sense of attempting to secure those emergent belongings and feelings of safety.

Performance forms part of discourse, identity, identification, belonging and claims to belong. Young people experience and respond to Home Office processes: thus we see the work of 'policy, regulations, institutions in performing, mobilising and constraining belonging' (Wright, 2015: 400). Social care is also a performance, with its rituals, jargon, procedures, role-designations, acronyms, categories and labels which all have the capacity to both constrain and mobilise belongings. The legal and policy contexts of social care provision are discussed by Anna Gupta in Chapter Three.

Creating spaces of belonging

Some years ago I spent some time in an impoverished West African country. One day at a fishing village, a heavily-laden boat was spotted off the coast. As it approached, the villagers realised it was carrying refugees from a war-torn country further south. The young men waded in and carried the elderly to shore on their shoulders. The villagers were all very, very poor, but many dashed to the local shop and bought what they could, handing bananas or sweets to the many toddlers carried by their mothers. The villagers hadn't gone on a training course; they had never heard of 'social care'. The villagers and boat people didn't speak the same language, but they didn't need to. This was the language of common humanity.

Support is more officially structured in the UK but that shouldn't make Britons forget that they are all part of that common humanity. Social care in itself does not necessarily provide 'a space of belonging' but through their actions and the relationship established with the young people, social workers can and do influence their capacity to build spaces of belonging. In a managerialist, process-driven organisation, a procedural approach gets things demonstrably done. Alternatively, social workers can try to imagine being alone in a strange place with official-looking people asking questions. That first-day meeting may set the scene for years to come. Will the young person remember an interrogation, or someone saying "welcome", asking if they're well, if they're tired, offering water, maybe a biscuit – simply acknowledging them as another human being? Will they remember someone explaining who they are and that a few forms are necessary, but perhaps making a conspiratorial little joke about the paperwork? Will they remember someone who listened, even if their story was jumbled, who listened also to their silences, realising that they too were part of their story?

In a practice-focused outline of approaches to working with unaccompanied young people, Kohli depicts three broad responses to 'silences and fractured narratives' (2009: 108), the thin stories which they often present to fit the expectations of the asylum system. In the first model, social workers are less interested in individual lives than in the practicalities of the present, while in the second they take a therapeutic approach, working with silences until the young person can talk about the past. The third type aims for a companionable relationship, with young people recognised as complex individuals whose lives cannot always fit the narrow categories of the asylum system. Categories and labels within social care could be added, particularly those in IT systems which insidiously mould records into clear but simplistic products. Kohli's 'companionable' social workers see not only vulnerabilities but also real, resourceful, multidimensional people, rather than carriers of labels such as 'asylum seeker' or 'refugee' – or, in the context of social care, 'looked after child'. Kohli's three models probably overlap and shift more than he suggests, so that even social workers in that 'third type' offer practical support and listen, sometimes therapeutically, but I find much to agree with his view that they 'tended to make the young people feel welcome' (p 120).

Chase too, considers young people's silences and 'selective disclosures' but sees them as an effort to establish agency and control, in the face of scrutiny from both immigration and social care systems. Young people in her study describe themselves as 'catapulted into a series of interlocking systems of surveillance and control ... set up to identify, label, oversee and monitor' (Chase, 2010: 2055). Faced with variable or 'procedural' support, small wonder that some were 'mistrustful of the interplay between social care and immigration services' (Chase, 2010: 2060).

The main structural relationships[3] of unaccompanied young people in the UK can be represented as a triangle (see Figure 5). The assumption that social care is always an inclusive force masks the risk of existing power imbalances between social workers and young people being exacerbated by overlaps between social care and the Home Office. Social workers can, however, consciously resist that pull and instead stand alongside the young people and help sustain their emergent belongings.

Figure 5: Structural relationships of unaccompanied young people

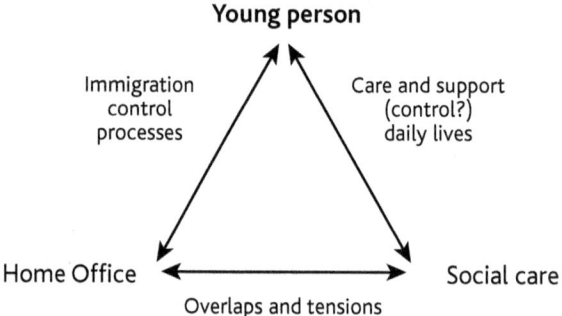

The following sections focus on different spaces in which forms of belonging are created; the home, schools and colleges, religion and spaces of worship, and the wider locality. This links with Gillian Hughes' writing in Chapter Five about facilitating collective practices where young people are able to connect with life affirming aspects of their cultural and social histories.

Foster care: A 'home' or (just) a 'placement'?[4]

"She said ... 'Do you want any food?' ... and ... 'Do you want to go to sleep? ... I went to sleep and ... I was feeling so nice' (a young person's recollections of his foster carer's welcome, cited in Sirriyeh, 2013: 9). Compare this heartfelt reaction with jargon such as 'safe and appropriate accommodation', which all too often reflects process-driven, service-led decisions.

In the UK, fostering is usually arranged for under-16s, with various forms of semi-independent accommodation also possible for 16 and 17-year-olds, depending on 'vulnerability'. Ideally, the social worker will have grasped something about the young person's 'wishes and feelings', probably one of the better bits of social care jargon. I remember a traumatised 17-year-old who was a clear candidate for fostering, but he was adamant that he would not live with a family as that would be a betrayal of his parents, whose violent death he had witnessed. Despite efforts to explain that no one would try to replace them, he insisted on semi-independent accommodation. It was only after some months that he decided, *in his own time and of his own accord*, that perhaps he would like to live in a 'household' after all and he went on to develop a good rapport with foster carers who were caring but non-intrusive and always led by him. It was significant that just before that he was granted asylum, which could not obliterate his loss but perhaps helped him look towards the future.

Drawing on Derrida's notion of hospitality, Sirriyeh (2013) suggests three broad models of foster care for unaccompanied minors, from the distant, rule-governed 'lodger' model, then a 'guest' model based on 'visitation', to the most inclusive, based on 'invitation', which she describes as 'like-family'. I find that situations and perceptions change across time and context, but the model, which directly reflects the views of young people in her study, is a good reference point.

This is clearly demonstrated through the narratives of young people and foster carers:

> 'Ha! [grins] … I had to pop out yesterday and when I came back I found Sara along the road – walking the dogs!' (Alan, a foster carer in my study)

I felt I understood that "ha!", especially as Sara had initially been wary of the boisterous puppies. Alan and I looked at each other and smiled: we both perceived this as a small but landmark moment in Sara beginning to feel that she played a part in that household, that family.

> 'She [Mai] insisted on washing up after dinner, then she started tidying up the kitchen and ended up reorganising all the cutlery and crockery cupboards. It was really funny!' (Kate, another foster carer in my study)

Another tale told with a smile. I was delighted by Kate relaying this as an amusing tale rather than being territorial about 'her' kitchen or resenting Mai claiming 'mastery of the house' (Sirriyeh, 2013). As Mee and Wright (2009) point out, through 'everyday performances' (p 774), 'belonging is an actively practised and highly political activity' (p 776).

Mutual trust plays a large part in this: "At [first, unsuccessful 'placement'] ... I was not allowed to have the [house] key. But Kate gave me a key straight away! I thought: 'ok, *this* is my home'." (Carl)

The goal of young people trusting 'professionals' is often mentioned but less is said about professionals trusting young people. House keys or family dogs can be a good start.

Reciprocation plays a similar role: "Yes, Keith [Kate's husband] was in hospital last week, so Kate was with him a lot ... *of course* I helped ... " (Carl again).

That was the response when I thanked Carl for going shopping, sorting the rubbish and walking the dog when they were faced with an emergency. He was amazed that I should thank him: "They helped *me* ... Now I help *them*." Here was a young man moving beyond the 'vulnerable child' label and making a mundane but natural contribution to *his* household.

Food is highly symbolic. Having food available as a household member may be particularly evocative for young people who have suffered shortages (Kohli et al, 2010). Beyond basic needs, being able to express preferences over food, activities or interests gives a sense of being respected and listened to. Belonging is about feeling 'at home' and 'secure' but also 'recognised and understood' (Wood and Waite, 2011: 201).

Being not just a 'looked after child' but also a young refugee is important and a sense of belonging can allow suppressed stories to emerge in a trusting and supportive atmosphere. As Kate explains:

> 'You know, something happened when we went camping. It was a nice evening, by the beach ... He just started to talk about how scared he was, locked in the lorry, how he thought he'd never make it ... It was the first time he'd spoken about any of it directly to us ... He just came out with all this ...'

That little tale encompassed so much. Kate had identified it as a landmark moment, not because the information was new, but because Carl had spontaneously started to talk about difficult experiences knowing and trusting that they would understand.

Beyond keys and dogs, trust includes listening and simply 'believing', which can turn into a desire to help. This is echoed by Sirriyeh, who found that carers' involvement with asylum processes 'contributed to, and resulted from, the building of close bonds' (2013: 11). Belonging is developed both through routine and times of crisis (Yuval-Davis, 2011).

Some months after Carl helped out, he was the one finding himself vulnerable and frightened at his asylum appeal. Kate and Keith accompanied him and Kate spoke as a character witness. She would have done so regardless of the hospital episode, but perhaps it felt natural because they had built a relationship based on trust and respect beyond that of 'appropriate placements'. As Sirriyeh (2013) also argues, the attitude and actions of carers is valued more highly by young people than over-professionalisation.

In Sara's case, Jo and Alan had never fostered an unaccompanied minor and were anxious around asylum processes so initially I alone supported her through those, until she was called for her interview, when I suggested they might come. They readily agreed and we all set off together on a cold, dark morning. The interview was not handled sensitively, and Sara rushed out very distressed. Jo and I comforted her as she clung to us, sobbing, until she felt ready to continue. After the interview, asked if she was OK, she said she just wanted to "go home". Exhausted, she slept in the car, on the way to her *home* (not 'home' as in country of origin, as depicted by the interviewer), her refuge, where she felt in-place, not in-the-wrong-place, as she had been made to feel that day. Jo later reflected on her own emotional response: "That was … a very, very hard day…because – you know, seeing her so upset, really upset me. Just like … if it had been one of my girls …".

That was an episode of shared emotional bonding, although of course the stakes were highest for Sara. Jo had starkly realised that Sara's safety could be brought to an end at a keystroke. Jo hadn't cried in front of Sara, but Sara knew Jo was upset and knew she cared. Initially daunted by asylum processes, Jo and Alan had become very involved, having first got to know Sara as a person, rather than the bearer of a label.

One of the debates within fostering relates to the relative merits of 'culturally-matched' placements. Deeta, a social worker in my study, who had many years' experience with unaccompanied young people and who had herself come to the UK as a refugee simply stated, "It doesn't matter where they're from, what matters is that they're kind". In considering whether 'matched' or 'cross-cultural placements' hinder or support a sense of belonging, it is important to ask: what culture, whose culture? Who defines it and how? Is this about simplistic labels and stereotypes such as country of origin, religion or ethnicity? Does it neglect intersecting aspects of identity, as Ni Raghallaigh and Sirriyeh (2015) warn? I am reminded of a highly-educated Middle Eastern young person's frequent hints about her co-national foster carers' 'working class'. When she moved, for unrelated reasons, she developed a close and enduring relationship with her Black Caribbean carer.

Even if it is accepted for a moment that 'a culture' could be defined or described, the assumption that the young person wished to maintain all its aspects conflates culture with destiny, limiting autonomy by enhancing the power differentials which inform 'where and how identity and categorical boundaries are being or should be drawn …' (Yuval-Davis, 2011: 18). Some young people may prefer living with people who 'understand' them, in various senses. Equally, assumptions around 'loss' or 'identity' disregard how, as refugees, some have fled parts of 'their' culture, such as forced marriage, honour-based violence or blood feuds; some even fear co-nationals. Is this simply social care being comfortable with its templates of 'loss', perhaps relying on procedural responses that fail to recognise young people as individuals, or is it substituting one form of oppression for another? If so, is it harder to recognise the seemingly benign but insidious labelling depicted as 'matching' than more visibly violent oppression?

Echoing Deeta's views, Ni Raghallaigh and Sirriyeh's respondents repeatedly referred to the carer's personality. Some appreciated an interest in 'their' culture and others preferred more autonomy: "Umm, I don't know, getting you to join things … that involve your cultural stuff or something … it's up to you how you want to keep your culture" (2015: 269). I too find that young people appreciate an interest in *their* explanations about food, language, 'culture' or beliefs, thus validating their knowledge and interpretation. Sometimes this leads to 'fusion' meals that not only please the palate but also act as an allegory for integration.

Some of Ni Raghallaigh and Sirriyeh's informants valued being able to express themselves in their original languages, while others preferred the educational benefits of an English-speaking household. Still others appreciated the efforts of English-speaking carers to try and speak their language, as I found when I introduced Mai, the young woman with the penchant for kitchen reorganisation:

> They were welcoming but Mai was stiff and wary. Then Keith produced a little notebook, cleared his throat and

said something, not in English, directly to her. She looked puzzled. He repeated it. Still puzzled. Then he said: "it's 'welcome', in *your* language!" The interpreter exclaimed: "ah!" and repeated the word, which to me sounded just like what Keith had said, but to them it clearly didn't. Mai and the interpreter burst into giggles. Keith persisted, trying to say things like "I hope you'll be happy here" and soon we were all rolling around with laughter. I could not have planned a better ice-breaker. (My notes)

'Semi-independent' settings

Many young people who have arrived in the UK as unaccompanied asylum seekers live in semi-independent settings, which are not permanently staffed, but keyworkers attend at intervals. Being less regulated, there are marked differences in standards and commitment: this section refers to well-respected and caring providers who participated in my research, as well as the young people accommodated with them.

Such settings often focus on practical tasks such as registering with a doctor, which may not initially make sense to the young person, but they can demonstrate that they are entitled to the same rights as others and that this is more than a temporary stopping-off point: they are like little rootlets, little pieces of evidence that the young person 'belongs'. Many young people have proudly shown me their public library cards, evidence that they are 'officially there' and valued all the more because, unlike Home Office registration cards, they do not carry the word 'asylum'.

Such settings offer more freedom and independence and young people typically build up many ties and connections unmediated by foster carers. They tend to develop their own peer networks locally and through co-residents, perhaps comparing notes on the experience of arrival or the frustrations of the asylum system. Social belonging often plays a big part in their lives and enduring friendships develop, sometimes across diverse backgrounds, reflecting life in a mixed society. Conversely, if there is a predominance of young people from the same country or region, exclusive, bounded groups can form, impacting on more isolated individuals. For example, Modou observed:

> 'I like this house, my room is good, I go to college on the bus ... Here are shops, and it's ok. It's ok, but – all the guys ... they all speak their language. They are not bad

> people, they give me no problem ... but I am the only one ... Well, if you can find me a room in another house, I'll be very happy.'

Modou had witnessed ethnic genocide and experienced violent racism before arrival. He was visibly Black among a group of White young people and maybe there was some veiled racism, but compared to what he had suffered, for him this probably felt tolerable, hence his tentative tone. He is now much happier in a more diverse house.

Young people can also form close bonds with keyworkers, particularly when the latter display the kind of empathy akin to that of Sirriyeh's (2013) 'like-family' foster carers. With many years' experience, keyworkers are proactive in supporting young people through the practicalities and emotional roller-coasters of the asylum system, even acting as character witnesses at appeals. Like foster carers, keyworkers can become emotionally involved: "A young person I've been working with for 4 years ... you can see he's very, very anxious, very emotional. And when ... he talks about his concerns, it really gets you down ..." (David, keyworker). On a happier note, shared fun experiences can help young people develop a relaxed sense of day-to-day belonging as demonstrated in this interaction between Michael and David at Michael's looked-after review:

> Michael: Look, this is my kirar! David helped me...
> David: Yes, he said he wanted to make a kirar, a traditional instrument from his country. First we got some wood from a builder's merchants, then for the strings I suggested a music shop but he said no, we need a bicycle shop! I was confused but off we went and he got some brake wires...Then I got my tools from home and we set to – and here it is!

That triumphant tale of discovery and success, with Michael playing his homemade instrument, was a moment to treasure for us all.

As in foster care, sometimes bonds persist, with young people who have moved on 'returning to base', to visit past keyworkers, especially when they have good news, such as graduating, getting married or becoming UK citizens – knowing that they will share their joy. David's pride in 'his' young people is evident:

> 'We've got ... young people ... that are very well settled and now have ... small families of their own [smiles] ...

One who's now ... at university ... said 'I want to help other people in my circumstances' ... Definitely, when I see people that have done really well then I feel very happy.'

Beyond the 'placement': schools and colleges

Having something to get up for in the morning provides routine and 'normality', particularly following chaotic experiences. A school uniform is a visible sign of 'ordinary' belonging and simply walking through the entrance with all the mainstream students defies the stigma of being 'an asylum seeker'. Sometimes it allows the creation of an alternative persona, with young people describing themselves as 'international students'. The right to remain in the UK may be a dream but, locally, the ID pass gives a right of entry to a significant site and is a tangible symbol of that right, with young people sometimes wearing their passes even on non-college days, thus proclaiming their status as 'students'.

Whether looking through the tentative letter formations of a newcomer who had never been to school, or the confident work of a high-flyer, I am always heartened by the pride and purposefulness in the words "Do you want to see my work?" Many young people have gone on to shine, obtaining excellent jobs and making wonderful contributions to society, and I am tremendously proud of them. Schools and colleges do provide 'the scaffolding for later success' as Kohli (2011: 314) points out, but I am wary of his distinction between those who later obtain documentation and the 'sojourners' – a rather dismissive label – partly because the categories can shift, and also because there is more to education than academic success. Academic status cannot replace migration status, but it can provide some means of gaining control in the present, coping with past trauma and future uncertainties (Groark et al, 2011; Kohli, 2011; Chase, 2013). The short-term goals of structured education can extend those 'spaces of the present' in an otherwise dark forest of uncertainty.

As sites for extra activities, schools and colleges provide more rootlets of belonging, more anchorage. When asked what he liked best about college, Modou stated, "It's not just lessons – today is the 'Link' [counselling] group and tomorrow I have boxing!" On-site services such as this counselling group can avoid the stigma of a clinic setting and are often preferred because of the 'feeling of safety and familiarity' found there (Fazel et al, 2016: 4). Teachers and tutors often provide pastoral support and advocate for young people, sometimes writing letters in support of appeals.

Schools and colleges are ready-made sites for forming the friendship networks vital for wellbeing, belonging and mental health (Kia-Keating and Ellis, 2007; Bloch et al, 2009; Ni Raghallaigh and Gilligan, 2010). Whether made in the classroom, cafeteria or college gym, each connection forms part of overall social belonging, providing further anchorage and potentially long-lasting friendships.

'Mastery of the house' is supplemented by 'mastery of the school site': guiding newcomers, perhaps showing social workers or carers around is an opportunity to move beyond vulnerability, to display efficacy as the expert guide. Real loyalty can develop: "This is definitely the best college in London!" was proclaimed by a young person who had not been in London long enough to make comparisons, but that is irrelevant – her beaming pride, as we headed to her first parents'/carers' evening, made it the best college for her. I was reminded of Kirsty, who relished inter-school team sports. Many times her eyes lit up as she proclaimed: "we're through to the area finals!" or "we've won the cup!" with as much pride in that *we* as in all her academic successes.

Structural challenges and barriers and the interplay between processes can, however, impact on school or college belongings. Mohammed aged 17 asked me "Why does everybody have a [16–19] bursary and not me?" He had been age-disputed by the Home Office but I had accepted his age through a "Merton-compliant" age assessment. The Home Office accepted this but, despite reminders, they neglected to replace his registration card with one showing the correct age. The college also accepted my age assessment, but with the wrong age on the card he could not register for the bursary to which he was entitled. Eventually, to avoid discrimination the local authority agreed to provide him with the equivalent but the feeling of rejection remained: "hmm ... maybe [the college] don't want me ..."

Purpose and recognition cannot be assumed, of course. Some students may be satisfied with basic functional skills. Some may have other obligations, such as debt repayments or family remittances. Some lose interest as the hope of documentation fades. For some over 18s who find themselves 'removeable', disengaging from education, consolidating informal networks and making contingency plans for remaining in the UK undocumented is a rational choice – although social services may describe that as 'going missing' rather than a tactic of survival.

Some intrinsically value education, doggedly persisting despite uncertainties, only to find the path to higher education seemingly blocked. This can be doubly difficult when co-students are busy making plans for university (Sirriyeh, 2010). Occasionally, determination, advocacy, and perhaps luck, can prise the door open, as they did for Kirsty, our sporty student.

Having sought asylum as a young child, Kirsty was denied it but granted a series of three-year discretionary leave periods, as it then was,[5] and had made an 'in-time' application for an extension of the final such leave aged 17.5. Immigration regulations indicated that she was entitled to indefinite leave by virtue of her length of 'lawful stay', which included over half her childhood, but aged 18.5 and in year 13, the paperwork was caught up in bureaucratic delays. Kirsty's National Insurance number was still valid, she had a Saturday job and her 'difference' was not visible. A gifted student, her goal had always been to become a doctor and with high grades predicted, she received various offers to study medicine but due to changes in guidelines, and despite the possibility of discretion, the universities insisted on considering her an international student, thus denying her access to student finance. Kirsty refused to give up and focused on what she could control: "OK ... Maybe the answer will come in time ... I have to get on with it, I have exams ..." At the 11th hour, by chance I met a trustee of a little-known charity, which led to it funding her fees on a year-by-year basis. The local authority agreed to pay her accommodation and living costs, Kirsty obtained top grades in all her A levels and confirmed her place at university. Only then did she reveal how anxious she had felt. Excitedly talking about student accommodation, she suddenly paused, took a deep breath, shook her head and said: "I don't believe this is happening. I didn't think I would ever be packing my bags and going off to [university]. It doesn't feel real ..."

The smile that followed told of sheer relief following years of frustrations. Kirsty remained in administrative limbo for two more years before the long-overdue documentation arrived, but it was many more months, phone calls and letters before her university reclassified her so that she could access student finance. Throughout, she continued to shine academically and in her hospital placements, achieving her potential and building her contribution to society. Ultimately, a combination of determination and chance averted what Sigona describes as 'the waste of precious human capital' (2012: 23).

Religion and places of worship

Social care's role around accommodation, school or college is clear but not everything is down to social care: young people also forge spaces of belonging through their own exploration, social networks and agency. The possibilities are endless but this section focuses on religion and places of worship because for many young people they are significant spaces of belonging, for differing, personal and contextual reasons. This is illustrated by reference to three young people in my broader study.

John describes himself as Catholic and he was shown the nearest Catholic churches but soon found one he preferred a 45-minute bus ride away, where most worshippers are from Eritrea, his country of origin, and services are in Tigrynia and English. John now speaks English well, is busy studying and, with refugee status, he is making plans for the future. His version of Catholicism is country-specific, but it does not reflect the nationalism demanded by the Eritrean state in its control of adherents there. The relationship between the Eritrean state and 'permitted' and 'not permitted' religions is too complex to discuss here, but as Hepner summarises, 'religious settings ... [in countries of refuge or settlement] ... provide a way for people to practice Eritreanness beyond its tortured politicization' (2003: 279). John does not usually have time for after-service social activities, but he enjoys familiar prayers in his first language, in a setting which offers continuity with aspects of the past which he enjoyed, while rejecting those he fled from. For John, the church is a once-a-week, loose diasporic space, which alongside other elements is part of the jigsaw of belonging he is tailor-making for himself.

Yonu is from a Middle Eastern country affected by years of violence. Having been in the UK for six years, Yonu speaks English well, studies, works part-time and has friends from many backgrounds. Now aged 21, he is still facing anxieties over his asylum status. As a practising Muslim, he too selected the place of worship where he felt most comfortable. He cites his chosen mosque as one of the best things about 'his' area and passionately describes it as an inclusive, welcoming site: "There are people from *many* countries ... from everywhere, we all help each other ..." The mosque is part of the global umma but is also very local, with advice offered on secular aspects of life in the UK, including work, benefits, housing or schooling. It is also a port in a storm for people who find themselves destitute, often following unsuccessful asylum claims. There, they can get a free meal after services: "they just put their name down ... so they know how many will come ... No, no, they don't have to explain why they need it ..." Yonu also prays at home and religion would be an important part of his life whatever his circumstances, but as Ni Raghallaigh (2011) shows, religion can offer a coping resource, particularly for unaccompanied young people at times of stress and anxiety. Yonu attributes his generally calm demeanour – despite prolonged frustrations – to a belief in God, a constant throughout his life. For Yonu, religion is simultaneously social and private. Unlike John, it is not linked to a particular nation or region and the mosque allows him to feel globally connected through its various worshippers and also to feel a local belonging in a neighbourhood which is itself globally connected in a manner reminiscent of Massey's (1994) depiction of Kilburn.

Stella is Eritrean. As Pentecostalists, she and her parents were forced to practise in hiding as, unlike John's Catholicism, it was not an 'authorised' religion. Following a raid on their covert prayer meeting, when she lost her parents, Stella was saved by Orthodox relatives who acted as guarantors that she would no longer practise Pentecostalism, but she eventually fled as she could not accept giving up her beliefs. Like John, she is studying and building a new life in the UK, but she suffers from nightly flashbacks and chronic tiredness. Nevertheless, she rises early every weekend to travel to her chosen church. Services are in Amharic, Tigrynia and English, but when asked whether most worshippers were from Ethiopia or Eritrea, she grimaced:

> 'No! Our church is for *everybody*, Eritrean, Ethiopian, anybody, even English ... It doesn't matter where people come from, we are all the same, all together, with God ... This business of Eritrea and Ethiopia, it's all politics, we don't want that, people are killed ...'

Stella's global view seems more akin to Yonu's appreciation of his mosque than John's enjoyment of his church. Stella and her parents had spent some years in Ethiopia before being deported to Eritrea due to the war, which may inform her visceral rejection of nation-state labels. Stella first chose the church on linguistic grounds, but having made many friends there she continued to attend as her English improved, although there are other Pentecostal churches more conveniently located. In a later conversation, she mused that because many worshippers *were* Eritrean, she did not have to explain upsetting events of the past: "if people say 'pray for me, I had a problem', *everybody* knows what they mean, they don't have to cry and be upset, explaining it all again." This seems like a diasporic belonging through the shared past experience of being-Pentecostal-in-Eritrea rather than 'being Eritrean' as a national affiliation.

Stella's church also offers a secular diasporic space. Particularly on special occasions, people bring what she describes as "cultural food" for all to share and, in echoes of Yonu's mosque, those who can't afford it need not contribute. There are many and interrelated aspects to Stella's story. Prayers may be a coping strategy and a tribute to her parents. There is comfort in being with like-minded people, sometimes through 'cultural' activities but mainly through shared beliefs, which Stella describes as her "main identity". Through her church she connects with people with whom she identifies: "We all understand each other." Stella often says that she and her co-worshippers appreciate the shelter and freedom to practise in the UK: "Here we can be free … We won't waste our chance!" Alongside that, she points to Pentecostalism's emphasis on work, study and social contribution – these 'fit' the UK's meritocratic model. Belonging to the church, to 'the world' and to the UK are not conflicting, they are mutually supportive. The church provides a space of belonging and an expression of Stella's multi-faceted but far from fractured identity.

Place-belongings

Spaces of belonging are inherently relational (Massey 2004): the area or neighbourhood where young people live is more than the sum of the home, school or college, places of worship, identifiable sites or 'micro-spaces of opportunity … for positive encounter' such as parks (Phillips and Robinson, 2015: 415). It is also about the feel of the area in all its complexity or global connections, the memories made as young people get to know neighbours, shopkeepers and bus routes, as they travel around and explore, tailor-making mental maps of their environment or watching the world go by. As Platts-Fowler and Robinson point out, 'place is not merely a setting in which social life unfolds, but also a medium through which social relations are produced and reproduced' (2015: 478). Socially-deprived areas may be less welcoming and even lead to discrimination and harassment (Spicer, 2008; Teather et al, 2013) but simple indicators of wealth and poverty are insufficient. Cross-cutting these, local history and patterns of inward migration inform how settled residents and migrants react to each other (Hickman and Mai, 2015).

Realising the place matters does not deny that place and space are constantly changing (Massey, 2004), nor depict people as immobile or lacking in agency (Platts-Fowler and Robinson, 2015). Some young people, particularly those with refugee status, choose to move to other areas, for personal, work or study reasons, moving up a scale and spreading their wings as part of long-term aspirations. Place-belonging does not mean place-imprisonment. Conversely, for many young people, particularly those with insecure asylum status, place-belonging entails a strong sense of place-attachment, but internal barriers can deny them agency, reinforcing their dependence on social services and exaggerating existing power imbalances. Already uprooted in traumatic circumstances, some may face the threat of being forced to move once again. To illustrate this we return to Yonu.

Yonu had been refused asylum when he claimed aged 15, but was granted leave to 17.5. Having made an 'in-time' extension request, as a 19-year old college student he was receiving income support but faced barriers in accessing privately-rented accommodation (particularly in light of landlords' suspicions towards those without settled status, reinforced by internal border controls) and was not eligible for public housing. The local authority wanted Yonu to move back to their area, largely to meet performance indicators designed on the generic assumption that care leavers had connections there. At management's request, I approached Yonu regarding a possible move but – arguing that he had never lived in-borough and was settled in his area, which was inclusive and friendly and where he had built a social network – I insisted on giving him a choice. Even then, he was aghast at the thought, gasping with shock and almost crying: "No! No! Please, *please* don't do this to me. I am here with no family ... I can't move! ... Please tell them I can't, I don't know what I would do ..."

As Wood and Waite (2011) point out, not enough attention is paid to the emotional aspects of belonging. This was the first time I had seen Yonu so emotional about what was happening to himself, rather than his family. Feelings of place-belonging are linked to self-formation (Antonsich, 2010) and Yonu was trying to construct not only a 'liveable life' (Wetherell, 2009) but also forging identifications and shaping his identity in relation to the place where he felt he belonged. Despite the fragility of his asylum status, within that neighbourhood, with its 'various practices of ... inhabitation, [its]...particular collection of objects, animals, plants, germs, people ... performances or ideas' (Mee and Wright, 2009: 772), Yonu was creating his version of belonging, and longing for its continuation.

The last thing Yonu wanted or expected was to be reminded that as well as the mighty power of the Home Office there was another power, perhaps disguised as benign, which could also pull the rug from under his feet, that little rug he was clinging to in a sea of uncertainty. Such oppression mirrors that within the dispersal system for adult claimants, which inflicts more forced moves on people who have already been forced to leave their original homes (Teather et al, 2013; Kearns and Whitley 2015). Back in the office, I argued Yonu's case and thankfully he was not uprooted and – thanks also to his accommodation providers, who drew on local contacts – he now rents a bedsit locally. Recently, Yonu told me about an elderly, lonely neighbour, a White British army veteran who had sorrowfully confided that his family rarely visited. Yonu began chatting with him and so began a friendship linked by place rather than ethnicity, beliefs or age. On the man's birthday, Yonu invited him to eat with him: this was the only human interaction the man had on that special day and Yonu enjoys the company of his grandad substitute. In turn, when the man heard that Yonu had to attend an appeal hearing, he expressed dismay at the thought that his young friend could be 'removed' and spontaneously wrote a heartfelt handwritten letter to the courts.

Phillips and Robinson remind us that community is 'constructed through close and weak ties, social interaction…and feelings of place-belonging' (2015: 409). Place, they continue, is '… subjective and practiced – created and re-created by its users and their interactions' (2015: 410). Yonu is not just experiencing the place, he is also part of its constant re-creation, through the mosque, the elderly neighbour, the local shopkeepers or the myriad other people and practices he takes part in. This is his space of belonging.

Back to social care: resisting barriers, fighting injustice

A welcoming 'home', school or college, social relationships, religious groups, place-attachment – all help to create spaces of belonging, but without long-term documentation there's a better-than-nothing flavour. However well-meaning, if social care disregards the elephant in the room, belongings will be fragile and wellbeing superficial (Groark et al, 2011; Wade, 2011; Chase, 2013; Allan 2015). Heeding the mantra of 'child first, migrant second' (Crawley, 2006) cannot mean brushing that 'dark side' under the carpet on the grounds that asylum decisions are 'outside the control' of social services. Social workers *can* take that blinkered view – and thus collude with the oppression. Or they can choose to pay more than lip-service to the ideals of anti-discriminatory or anti-racist practice (Dominelli, 2004; Thompson, 2006) and take responsibility for resisting the 'structural barriers [that] contribute to the perpetuation of inequalities or discrimination … [and] oppression' (International Federation of Social Workers, 2016).

How or why does this matter to young people's sense of belonging? At a subtle level, having a social worker who really *is* your champion is part of the 'belonging' picture. Second, as we saw for example in Yonu's case, action or inaction by social workers *can* affect individual outcomes, enhancing wellbeing and allowing belonging to flourish.

A committed and effective solicitor is also crucial and as Wade (2011) argues, here too social workers must play their part. When workers make the referral their role is clear, but it can be challenging when young people present with a solicitor already appointed. Occasionally these are lucky finds but often the links are made by agents, traffickers or others with a financial incentive (including, sad to say, 'interpreters' lurking near immigration offices). Without evidence of wrongdoing, if the young person has unwittingly gone along with this and given instructions, it can be difficult to redress. Beyond providing support, attending appointments with the young person is doubly important. I recall accompanying a young man to his first meeting with the solicitor he had instructed: unbelievably, the latter had a pre-prepared 'blood feud' template and was intent on simply inserting his name and date of birth and submitting that as the witness statement, ignoring his attempts to tell his story. As I objected, the solicitor waved his hand dismissively: "Pff – we'll put all that in the appeal". Needless to say, I made a formal complaint and we headed elsewhere, but sometimes the issues are less evident, with some solicitors appearing adequate initially then abandoning young people whose initial claim is unsuccessful, leaving social workers to hurriedly hunt for an effective one to pick up the pieces within the appeal window. Others, despite legal aid restrictions, are committed to preparing the strongest case from the outset and persevering in exploring avenues for appeal if necessary. The legal framework for asylum and immigration in relation to unaccompanied young people, including the provision of legal services, is also considered in Chapter Two.

Age assessments represent an area of formal intersection between asylum and social care. I cannot fully explore here the Eurocentric pitfalls (Crawley, 2009), the over-reliance on social work concepts of 'vulnerability' or 'loss' rather than, say, agency or resourcefulness, save to highlight that through age assessments, social care is implicated in immigration control (Crawley, 2009; Chase, 2013), not least because a negative assessment profoundly affects the credibility of the claim as well as the support provided. The 'Merton-compliant' format suggests some kind of science, but ultimately the assessment is made by human beings who circulate in a society where even a parliamentary enquiry points to the 'urgent need to address the public discourse around asylum and refugee issues' (Teather et al, 2013: 4). As Cemlyn and Nye (2012) highlight, age assessments and work with unaccompanied minors overall does not take place in a bubble, immune from general discourses. Social care is certainly not apolitical. The age assessment process is explored in Chapter Three.

In a practice-focused outline, Wade considers the difficulties of Pathway Planning for young people with uncertain migration status. Despite the idea of 'maximising young people's choices and options' (2011: 2248), Wade falls short of challenging the underlying structural inequalities. In many ways however, judicious use of existing processes such as Pathway Plans can help sustain spaces of belonging, redress deeper inequalities such as those around higher education, and challenge oppression and injustice. Social workers *can* act as champions for young people and resist the power imbalances which threaten their fragile belongings, such as those around unwarranted moves. Sometimes they must assert values and ethics, fight the young people's corner and challenge organisational policy.

Social workers can take a deferential attitude towards the administration of the asylum system. They can close their eyes to the weight of evidence pointing to the arbitrary nature of decisions, the delays and their consequences, the gaps between policy and practice, the simple mistakes which can even lead to unlawful detentions (Bohmer and Shuman, 2008; Griffiths, 2012; White, 2012; Campbell, 2013; Tyler, 2013; Refugee Council 2016, 2017). Or, they can deploy their critical thinking skills and refuse to stand by as young people fall victim to injustice.

From the outset, John had explained that having repeatedly failed to cross to the UK undetected, he eventually agreed to purchase a passport with a fake UK visa from a man in the ad-hoc camp near Calais. John had explained that as he tried to use this to board a bus for the UK, he had been caught and fingerprinted, then released, before making the crossing later without the document, which had been confiscated. I had carefully completed a detailed age assessment, acknowledging this and confirming John's age. Almost a year passed while John awaited a decision, then the Home Office suddenly contacted me, requesting that I change the age assessment due to 'new evidence' allegedly showing that he was an adult. The new evidence, it transpired, was the somewhat delayed copy of the fake passport that John had told everyone about. Pointing out that this was not new evidence but confirmation of John's account, I politely refused to change the age assessment. John's age was accepted, he was granted refugee status and is now cementing his spaces of belonging in the UK, contributing to society and looking ahead to applying for citizenship.

Young people who, correctly or not, are recorded as 'appeal rights exhausted' face the greatest challenges. This is where having a social worker standing alongside them is so desperately important, but it is also where it can be easy to accept the 'inevitable' view that young person has 'no right to belong' in the UK. Despite acknowledging the 'conflict between government legislation and the values and ethics which inform social work practice' (2014: 1027), Frances Wright risks sliding into collusion. Mentioning but not respecting the oft-cited concept of service users as 'experts' (Smale et al, 1993), the only options she considers for those in this situation are forced or voluntary removal. She depicts the logical and reasonable response of many unsuccessful claimants – remaining in the UK without documentation – as 'absconding'. She suggests that if the 'voluntary' return option is explained by outside organisations, this 'will help social workers to remain neutral in the eyes of the young person' (Wright, 2014: 1032). Aside from whether social work can and should be neutral, this is a very strange kind of neutrality. In contrast, Humphreys (2004) points out how workers may convince themselves that they are undertaking 'anti-oppressive practice' even as they do the 'dirty work' of immigration control, such as 'enforcement counselling'.

Social workers who take a critical view will appreciate how destitution is arguably designed both as a deterrent to claiming asylum and as an incentive towards 'voluntary' return (Teather et al, 2013; Tyler, 2013). The human rights assessment framework, however, provides an opportunity to fight back. If a young person risks being forced into destitution, homelessness or extreme exploitation, there are valid grounds for continuing support under the Children (Leaving Care) Act 2000, as withdrawal may breach their human rights. This can also provide some valuable time: in the context of bureaucratic inefficiencies and errors, some young people may eventually acquire documentation even after being classified as 'appeal rights exhausted'. Abdullah, for example, endured many years of Kafkaesque fiascos, sometimes going in and out of such status, with threats of judicial reviews and referral to the European Court of Human Rights juxtaposed with narrowly avoiding detention and potential removal. He is now a UK citizen.

Conclusion

Belonging is a flexible term but, however defined, it carries within it the concept of longing, the hope or prospect of being nurtured and sustained. Despite fears about the future and an asylum system designed to exclude, young people do strive to create some spaces of belonging, sometimes assisted by social care, through welcoming foster care or accommodation and inclusive schools or colleges, sometimes also through their own agency, networks and explorations. Social care adds an extra dimension to their relationship with the state, which can play out in different ways. Social workers may limit themselves to their narrow comfort zone, deny any role in addressing that difficult, fragile, sometimes terrifying side of young people's lives and tacitly accept that belongings may be transient rather than sustainable, poignant rather than joyful – and social care will thus collude with the structural oppressions it was designed to challenge. If, however, they choose to stand alongside the young people and deploy their critical and creative skills, they can play a role in mitigating, challenging, resisting and sometimes overcoming oppressions. Some may go about this quietly, powerfully affecting individual lives; others may speak out more widely, which is a topic for another day but no less important. With will and determination much can be done to support, strengthen and sustain the spaces of belonging which young people try so hard to create. In rising to the challenge, social care can help create a fairer, more inclusive and just society for us all.

Notes

[1] My research, which is ongoing, takes place through the University of Sussex, which also granted ethical approval.

[2] To avoid professional hierarchies meaningless to the young people, I use the term social worker to include not only qualified and registered social workers, but also personal advisors and workers in similar roles.

[3] Of course this is only part of their lives, which include many other connections and relationships.

[4] 'Home' is used here in the positive sense. The term 'placement' encompasses the power imbalances inherent in social care. We *place* an ornament or a chess piece. We don't 'place' human beings.

[5] This was replaced by UASC leave in 2013, reflecting its incorporation into the immigration regulations.

References

Allan, J. (2015) 'Reconciling the 'psycho-social/structural' in social work counselling with refugees', *British Journal of Social Work*, 45: 1699–716.

Anderson, B. (2013) *Us and them? The dangerous politics of immigration control*, Oxford: Oxford University Press.

Antonsich, M. (2010) 'Searching for belonging – An analytical framework', *Geography Compass*, 4(6): 644–59.

Baba, M.L. (2013) 'Anthropology and transnational migration: A focus on policy', *International Migration*, 51(2): 1–9.

Bloch, A., Sigona, N. and Zetter, R. (2009) *'No right to dream': The social and economic lives of young undocumented migrants in Britain*, London, Paul Hamlyn Foundation.

Bohmer, C. and Shuman, A. (2008) *Rejecting refugees: political asylum in the 21st century*, London and New York: Routledge.

Campbell, J. (2013) 'Language analysis in the United Kingdom's refugee status determination system: seeing through policy claims about "expert knowledge"', *Ethnic and Racial Studies*, 36(4): 670–90.

Cemlyn, S.J. and Nye, M. (2012) 'Asylum seeker young people: Social work value conflicts in negotiating age assessment in the UK', *International Social Work*, 55(5):675–88.

Chase, E. (2010) 'Agency and silence: Young people seeking asylum alone in the UK', *British Journal of Social Work*, 40: 2050–68.

Chase, E. (2013) 'Security and subjective wellbeing: the experiences of unaccompanied young people seeking asylum in the UK', *Sociology of Health and Illness*, 35(6): 858–72.

Crawley, H. (2006) *Child First, Migrant Second: Ensuring that Every Child Matters*, London: Immigration Law Practitioners' Association.

Crawley, H. (2009) 'Between a rock and a hard place: negotiating age and identity in the UK asylum system' in N. Thomas (ed) *Children, politics and communication: Participation at the margins*, Bristol: Policy Press, pp 89–107.

Dominelli, N. (2004) *Social work: theory and practice for a changing profession*, Oxford, Polity Press.

Fazel, M., Garcia, J. and Stein, A. (2016) 'The right location? Experiences of refugee adolescents seen by school-based mental health services', *Clinical Child Psychology and Psychiatry* (published on line prior to print):1–13

Griffiths, M. (2012) ''Vile liars and truth distorters': Truth, trust and the asylum system', *Anthropology Today*, 28 (5): 8–12.

Groark, C., Sclare, I. and Raval, H. (2011) 'Understanding the experiences of emotional needs of unaccompanied asylum-seeking adolescents in the UK', *Clinical Child Psychology and Psychiatry*, 16(3): 421–42.

Hall, S. (1996) 'Introduction: Who needs identity?" in S. Hall and P. du Gay (eds) *Questions of cultural identity*, London: Sage, pp 1–17.

Hepner, T.R. (2003) 'Religion, nationalism, and transnational civil society in the Eritrean diaspora', *Identities*, 10(3): 269–93.

Heptinstall, E., Sethna, V. and Taylor, E. (2004) 'PTSD and depression in refugee children: Associations with pre-migration trauma and post-migration stress', *European Child and Adolescent Psychiatry*, 13: 373–80.

Hickman, M.J. and Mai, N. (2015) 'Migration and social cohesion: Appraising the resilience of place in London', *Population, Space and Place*, 21: 421–32.

Home Office (2017) 'Asylum data tables immigration statistics April to June 2017 volume 3', Table 8, www.gov.uk/government/statistics/immigration-statistics-april-to-june-2017-data-tables

Humphreys, B. (2004) 'An unacceptable role for social work: Implementing immigration policy', *British Journal of Social Work*, 34(1): 93–107.

International Federation of Social Workers (2016) 'Global Definition of Social Work', http://ifsw.org/get-involved/global-definition-of-social-work/

Kearns, A. and Whitley, E. (2015) 'Getting there? The effects of functional factors, time and place on the social integration of migrants', *Journal of Ethnic and Migration Studies*, 41(13): 2105–29.

Kia-Keating, M. and Ellis, B.H. (2007) 'Belonging and connection to school in resettlement: Young refugees, school belonging and psychosocial adjustment', *Clinical Child Psychology and Psychiatry*, 12(1): 29–43.

Kohli, R. (2009) 'Understanding silences and secrets when working with unaccompanied asylum-seeking children', in N. Thomas (ed) *Children, politics and communication: Participation at the margins*, Bristol: Policy Press, pp 107–122.

Kohli, R. (2011) 'Working to ensure safety, belonging and success for unaccompanied asylum-seeking children', *Child Abuse Review*, 20: 311–23.

Kohli, R., Connolly, H. and Warman, A. (2010) 'Food and its meaning for asylum seeking children and young people in foster care', *Children's Geographies*, 8(3): 233–45.

Lewis, H. (2013) 'The increasingly hostile environment: discomfort as a policy goal', Plenary Lecture delivered to Undoc.Net, End of project conference, London Metropolitan University, 6 December.

Massey, D. (1994) *Space, Place and Gender*, Cambridge: Polity Press/Blackwell.

Massey, D. (2004) 'Geographies of Responsibility', *Geografiska Annaler B*, 86(1): 5–18.

Mee, K. and Wright, S. (2009) 'Guest editorial', *Environment and Planning A*, (41): 772–9.

Mountz, A. (2010) *Seeking Asylum: Human Smuggling and Bureaucracy at the Border*, Minneapolis and London: University of Minnesota Press.

Ni Raghallaigh, M. (2011) 'Religion in the lives of unaccompanied minors: An available and compelling coping resource', *British Journal of Social Work*, 41: 539–56.

Ni Raghallaigh, M. and Gilligan, R. (2010) 'Active survival in the lives of unaccompanied minors: coping strategies, resilience and the relevance of religion', *Child and Family Social Work*, 15: 226–37.

Ni Raghallaigh, M. and Sirriyeh, A. (2015) 'The negotiation of culture in foster care placements for separated refugee and asylum seeking young people in Ireland and England', *Childhood*, 22(2): 263–77.

Phillips, D. and Robinson, D. (2015) 'Reflections on migration, community and place', *Population, Space and Place*, 21: 409–20.

Platts-Fowler, D. and Robinson, D. (2015) 'A place for integration: Refugee experiences in two English cities', *Population, Space and Place*, 21: 476–91.

Probyn, E. (1996) *Outside Belongings*, New York and London: Routledge.

Refugee Council (2016) *Asylum Backlogs*, March, www.refugeecouncil.org.uk/assets/0003/7146/Asylum_Backlogs_Mar_2016.pdf

Refugee Council (2017) 'The truth about asylum', www.refugeecouncil.org.uk/policy_research/the_truth_about_asylum/facts_about_asylum

Rutter, J. (2006) *Refugee children in the UK*, Maidenhead: Open University Press.

Sigona, N. (2012) 'Deportation, non-deportability and precarious lives, the everyday lives of undocumented migrant children in Britain', *Anthropology Today*, 28(5): 22–3.

Sirriyeh, A. (2010) 'Home journeys: Im/mobilities in young refugee and asylum-seeking women's negotiations of home', *Childhood*, 17(2): 213–27.

Sirriyeh, A. (2013) 'Hosting strangers: hospitality and family practices in fostering unaccompanied refugee young people', *Child and Family Social Work*, 18: 5–14.

Smale, G. and Tuson, G., with Biehal, N. and Marsh, P. (1993) *Empowerment, assessment, care management and the skilled worker*, London: NISW.

Spicer, N. (2008) 'Places of exclusion and inclusion: Asylum-seeker and refugee experiences of neighbourhoods in the UK', *Journal of Ethnic and Migration Studies*, 34(3): 491–510.

Teather, S. with Carmichael, N. Dakin, N. Dinenage, C., Sharma, V., Avebury, E., Lister, R., Packer, J., Finch, N., and Reed, M. (2013) *Report of the Parliamentary Inquiry into Asylum Support for Children and Young People*, London, The Children's Society.

Thompson, S. (2006) *Anti-Discriminatory practice*, 4th edition, Basingstoke: Palgrave Macmillan.

Tyler, I. (2013) *Revolting subjects: Social abjection and resistance in neoliberal Britain*, London and New York: Zed Books.

UK Border Agency (2013) *Processing an asylum application from a child*, www.gov.uk/government/uploads/system/uploads/attachment_data/file/257469/processingasylumapplication1.pdf

Wade, J. (2011) 'Preparation and transition planning for unaccompanied asylum-seeking and refugee young people: A review of evidence in England', *Children and Youth Services Review*, 33: 2424–30.

Wetherell, M. (2009) 'Introduction: Negotiating liveable lives – Identity in contemporary Britain', in M. Wetherell (ed) *Identity in the 21st Century: New trends in changing times*, Basingstoke and New York: Palgrave Macmillan, pp 1–18.

White, C. (2012) '"Get me out of here": Bail hearings of people indefinitely detained for immigration purposes', *Anthropology Today*, 28(3): 3–6.

Wood, N. and Waite, L. (2011) 'Editorial: Scales of belonging', *Emotion, Space and Society*, 4: 201–02.

Wright, F. (2014) 'Social work practice with unaccompanied asylum-seeking young people facing removal', *British Journal of Social Work*, 44: 1027–44.

Wright, S. (2015) 'More-than-human, emergent belongings: A weak theory approach', *Progress in Human Geography*, 39(4): 391–411.

Yuval-Davis, N. (2011) *The politics of belonging*, London: Sage.

SEVEN

'Durable solutions' when turning 18

Lucy Williams

Durable solutions for unaccompanied asylum-seeking children

This chapter considers the life options open to unaccompanied asylum-seeking children (UASC) who have sought asylum alone and have reached the legal definition of adulthood in their country of residence. These options ideally represent the potential and possible futures that any young person, no matter their immigration status, could hope for as they launch themselves into the adult world. These futures should reflect a young person's confidence in themselves and in their potential to achieve, participate and be valued in the world. Unfortunately, however, most young people reaching adulthood after a childhood as a migrant or an asylum-seeking child will have a limited range of opportunities open to them. Professional and volunteer workers have a role in supporting unaccompanied asylum-seeking children into adulthood, but contested expectations of possible futures prevents consensus on what these futures might be.

With their status of asylum seekers forced into migration, it is most likely that social care providers, immigration enforcement bodies and other statutory agencies will see young people's futures delineated by the United Nations High Commission for Refugees' (UNHCR) three 'durable solutions' – resettlement, local integration or repatriation – all of which tend to constrain outcomes for young people rather than promote them. The assumption that asylum-seeking children will eventually return to their country of origin (through repatriation) is accepted as self-evident by many but challenged by other advocates who seek to support young people to integrate into the countries they have settled in.

Beyond the UNHCR's technical definitions of 'durable solutions', this chapter seeks to consider how independent migrant young people can prepare and be prepared for the variable realities they meet on reaching adulthood. It considers the many assumptions popularly made about young migrants and seeks ways to promote the kind of 'ontological security' (Giddens, 1991; Chase, 2013; McMichael et al, 2016) that children need to grow into resilient and rounded adults with positive and contributory futures ahead of them. As discussed in Chapters Two and Three and in the following international chapters, many young migrants in Europe, North America and Australia will be granted a form of international protection that can lead to permanent settlement in the country where they claimed asylum, or – in the language of the durable solutions – local integration. Others will establish some form of temporary protection so will enter adulthood hopeful, but not assured, of a future including education, employment and protection from their adopted country. A relatively few young migrants will be resettled as refugees through family reunion programmes, while a much greater number, refused international protection, will be facing either return to a country they feel distant or estranged from or destitution in the country that has been their home for the past years.

Academic literature on child migrants includes much discussion of the problematic category of the 'refugee child' (Watters, 2007; Crawley, 2011; Bhabha, 2009, 2014) but I take it as a given that migrant children have the 'right to have rights' in the Arendtian sense (Arendt, 1966 cited by Bhabha, 2009), a concept which is discussed more fully later in this chapter.

In refugee-receiving countries of the Global North a gulf exists between the preferential protection of child migrants and the difficulty those same young people have achieving protection as adults (see Chapters Two and Three). Rights conferred by a child's minority, rather than by political activism or by another individually-based cause, are lost when children cross the bureaucratic but fluid divide between childhood and adulthood. Such young people move between entitlement and disentitlement at the same time as negotiating the changes in personal identity that are part of anyone's growing up. Child migrants move between bureaucratic categories that confer or refuse legal status and rights, meaning that finding a fixed point to determine a 'once and for all' durable solution is extremely difficult. This in-between status or 'liminal legality', as defined by Menjívar (2006) and described by Warren and York (2014), shapes young migrants' lives as they cross and re-cross borders between regularity and irregularity.

This chapter begins by considering how the UNHCR's 'durable solutions' and the UN Convention on the Rights of the Child (UNCRC) have been understood in relation to young asylum seekers and refugees. The chapter then moves on to a brief discussion of the often uncomfortable classification of children within political asylum frameworks. A consideration how social workers and other advocates have approached the difficult business of preparing young people for a range of uncertain futures follows, with a further section focusing on evidence from young people themselves. Finally, the chapter includes a section on best practice, highlighting how professionals and informal advocates have found ways to support young people. Throughout this chapter, despite the problems inherent in the phrase unaccompanied asylum-seeking children (UASC) as discussed in Chapter One (see also Chase and Allsopp, 2013), this abbreviation will be used and will include UASC who have turned 18.

Durable solutions for unaccompanied asylum-seeking children

The phrase 'Durable Solutions' has a technical definition referring to the UNHCR's three Durable Solutions to the problem of refugee displacement – repatriation, resettlement and local integration. More informally, durable solutions can refer to the stability and security a displaced person needs to build a productive and participative life. This section will look firstly at the UNHCR's Durable Solutions[1] and then at durable solutions from a more informal viewpoint.

Durable Solutions for refugees and displaced persons have been a key goal of the UNHCR since its inception and have their origin in the 1951 Convention, the 1967 Protocol and subsequent documents (UNHCR, 2003). This search for a 'solution' to the problem of displacement fails to acknowledge the life-long effects of exile. It implies that this rupture, especially at an early age, can be overcome and that these simple solutions are enough to establish a new and purposeful life. The availability of the UNHCR's Durable Solutions depend on a person's country of origin, their country of settlement and the individual refugee's personal circumstances. For example, repatriation (return) is only feasible if a refugee can and is prepared to return and rebuild their life where they were born. Local integration can only be a solution if the country of settlement permits refugees to settle permanently: the EU, for example, allows and indeed requires refugees to integrate and become fully participating citizens, but many other countries that receive much greater numbers of refugees – for example Turkey and Egypt – allow an only partial form of local integration. The legal status of a migrant is also crucial as being accepted as a Convention refugee (under the Geneva Convention on Refugees 1951) grants individual rights and options beyond those of unrecognised refugees, migrants or displaced people. International protection may open a route to resettlement, to join family members under family reunion schemes, and refugees may be eligible for resettlement in the relatively few countries (for example, the US and Australia) that accept refugees from outside their borders.

Of the three UNHCR Durable Solutions, repatriation has undoubtedly been most favoured by refugee-receiving countries and return 'home' has been normalised as the preferred option for refugees refused asylum in countries of the Global North. The reasons for this reflect deep-seated views about citizenship (Castles, 2005) and a worldview based on the nation state. In many receiving countries there is also a presumption against movement (Chatty, 2016), assuming that a person 'belongs' where they are born. Building on these assumptions, or perhaps hiding behind them, are the more prosaic imperatives to reduce migration and to keep refugees and migrants out, seeing them as unwanted others, rather than future citizens. Repatriation is often controversial as, to be a durable solution and to avoid breaking the international prohibition on returning refugees to places where their lives will be in danger (the principle of 'non-refoulement'), repatriation must be voluntary. 'Voluntariness' can be in doubt if consent to return is only achieved after social and legal forms of pressure, such as restrictions on access to social benefits or threats of detention, have been applied. Forced returns will not be durable and it is probable, or at least likely, that forced returnees will migrate again to become a refugee, or displaced person once more. While durable solutions clearly should be acceptable to refugees themselves and should be the result of an informed and open consideration of a variety of options, in reality things are different. Refugees may have to accept 'least-worst' solutions in many situations and, as the UNHCR accepts, decisions about where displaced people live are largely dictated by the capacity or willingness of receiving states to grant them protection (Crisp and Long, 2016).

In relation to former UASC, the same durable solutions are promoted with the caveat, respected in most countries of the Global North, that a young person without protection as a Convention refugee eligible for local integration or resettlement, should not be repatriated until they have reached adulthood and therefore have capacity to live an independent life. The claims of young asylum seekers are often slow to reach final determination – but temporary protection until adulthood is granted automatically in most countries of the Global North (see Chapter Two). Delays in decision making however, can mean that notwithstanding the strength of individual asylum claims, many UASC turn 18 without a final determination of their immigration status. The lack of a clear and final decision on young people's cases at 18 means that UASC have to contend with uncertain futures.

As discussed in earlier chapters the UNCRC is the guiding statement on child welfare and has been widely ratified. Importantly for UASC, it relates to the best interest of *children*[2] rather than of young people. UASC are a group whose age, physical, psychological and emotional maturity are unknown so it is reasonable that the UNCRC guidelines should be blind to how a child arrives in the country of settlement. It might be hoped that the guidelines could take a flexible approach to calendar age but as discussion will show, biopolitical imaginaries and ideas about childhood interfere with assessments of a child's 'best interests'.

The UNCRC requires signatories to use clearly formalised processes (best interest assessments, BIA, and best interest determinations, BID) to ensure that the UNCRC principles are adhered to. These processes should determine a child's best interest through holistic, multi-disciplinary, impartial and independent processes which allow and encourage the child to participate. However, the European Migration Network (EMN) Synthesis report (2014: 27) confirms a lack of country-specific legislation in relation to durable solutions for separated children. The EMN emphasises that a durable solution assessment must '… include a determination of the child's best interest in line with international and EU legislation' (EMN, 2014: 9) but they find little consistency in how best interest is determined across member states (EMN, 2015). Best interest principles should be applied throughout a child's progress through asylum systems but as the question of durable solutions is most often raised post-18, the power of the UNCRC to enforce 'best interest' is reduced.

Family tracing, with or without a view to family reunification, is clearly important for the wellbeing of a child so has a key role in all 'best interest' work. Finding family is also important in establishing a durable solution for unaccompanied children and can also result in the resettlement of young people with family members in third countries. Within the EU, the Dublin III Regulation (see Chapter One) provides a mechanism for UASC to move between EU countries to join family members and have their asylum claim, and thus potential durable solutions, determined there (Gregg and Williams, 2015; FRA, 2016: 13).

The UNCRC states that: 'the search for a durable solution commences with analysing the possibility of family reunification' (2005: 21) but family reunion is not inevitably in the best interest of a child.

Family reunification in the country of origin should not be considered where there is a 'reasonable risk' that return will lead to the violation of the child's fundamental human rights (UNCRC, 2005: 21). The best interest principle thus introduces strong protections on returning a child to countries of origin and the UNCRC (2005: 22) lists factors, including the views of the child, the child's identification with the country of origin and their post-return care, to consider before return becomes an option. Other forms of international protection including under trafficking protocols, human rights and children's rights grounds should also be considered as there may be broader reasons for a young person to remain in the country of settlement beyond political ones (EMN, 2014: 9). Wilding and Dembour (2015: 35) have argued that in practice, in the UK at least, best interest is only considered once a decision has been reached on international protection:

> If a child is granted asylum or humanitarian protection, no further consideration of best interests is made. If international protection is refused, there is a presumption that it is in the child's best interests to return to the country of origin...

Such binary options for young people do not allow for the complexity of determining durable solutions or the best interest of the child or young adult.

In countries of the Global North, decisions to return children (under 18) to countries of origin are rare. Projects at EU level, however, have sought to develop return programmes, most notably the ERPUM project (European Return Platform for Unaccompanied Minors) (Lemberg-Pedersen, 2015), which eventually failed to get support from countries expected to receive the children. Efforts to return children continue (European Commission, 2017a) and currently (as of July 2018) there are plans to repatriate children to Albania (Gregg and Williams, 2015: 41–2) and to Morocco (Gazzotti, 2017). Increasingly the return of migrants is facilitated by bilateral agreements aiming to streamline returns. One project aims to return Afghan migrants living across the EU and 'paves the way for a structural dialogue and cooperation on migration issues' (European Union External Action, 2016) including the return of Afghans living in the EU on either a voluntary or non-voluntary basis. Re-admission agreements are also being sought with African countries including Libya and Nigeria (European Commission, 2017b).

When young migrants pass 18 without permanent leave to remain in country of settlement, they have rarely been supported to consider their future in a methodical way. Arnold et al's (2015: 22) survey across EU countries found that national reports 'commented on the lack of a mechanism to determine a holistic durable solution in the child's best interests'. As a result, durable solutions may only emerge after many years and by default rather than by plan. Agencies with the power to decide, or at least influence, young people's future have neglected to positively advocate and work towards durable solutions in good time. Decision making has been deferred, either deliberately or accidentally, resulting in children reaching adulthood when their cases and circumstances have become more complex and their access to legal protection reduced. For many young people, especially those who are repatriated forcibly, a durable solution may be an irrelevant concept as they continue migrating, seeking sanctuary or simply living a permanently peripatetic life (Schuster and Majidi, 2015; Gladwell et al, 2016).

Children and young people in asylum systems

If we accept Hannah Arendt's assessment that the plight of the refugee is defined by rightlessness and the lack of effective protection from a nation state (Arendt, 1966), then durable solutions for UASC rest upon (re)gaining the protection of a functioning nation state. For any of the UNHCR's three Durable Solutions to be valid, a young person must gain the protection of either the country of resettlement – as a participating and rights-bearing person; authorities in a third country where they are legally settled; or by the authorities in the country that they are returned/repatriated to. Finding protection through repatriation requires a migrant to be confident of successful re-integration into a country they left years before. The decision to return is difficult enough for someone who migrated as an adult but, for a young person, without experience of adult life in the country of origin, who is without supportive family and community ties, return may seem impossible. For many young people, the thought of return is also terrifying and bound up with a sense of rejection and failure (Robinson and Williams, 2015). See also Chapter Five in this volume.

Much of the debate around the UNHCR's Durable Solutions, and particularly around repatriation, have at its heart the issue of where a person 'belongs' (Allsopp and Chase, 2017). From a state's perspective, establishing belonging may be framed as deciding which place or political entity should take responsibility for a person – the place where they were born, where they have 'roots' or where they have family members. This view of belonging is problematic in the case of refugees, who by definition cannot claim protection from their countries of origin, and is complicated further as many UASC and child migrants have been born into displacement away from their ancestral or traditional homes. For example, many Afghan UASC have spent much of their young lives displaced in Iran or Pakistan before travelling on towards Europe. They may have little or no experience of Afghanistan, a fact that not only undermines the credibility of their asylum claim but also makes a nonsense of any idea of a return 'home' to Afghanistan. Further, as explained by a young person interviewed in Kent, even for those UASC who did spend their formative years in Afghanistan, their disadvantaged status in the country will undermine their chances of successful reintegration:

> 'In Afghanistan we are targeted by other majorities, we have been targeted for centuries before the British came to Afghanistan ... Our lands were taken, 60% killed, 20% escaped and the rest were chased to the mountains. Their lands were all taken, we have suffered for centuries.' (Young Afghan asylum seeker in Kent, in 2016)

Determining belonging by subjective categories such as ethnicity, religion or culture betrays a reductionist view of the potential of young people (see also Chapter Six). It implies that these essentialist categories are more important than self-identified ones. Establishing where a young person belongs depends very much on the length of time a person has been displaced, how long they have been settled, their experiences of settlement not to mention deeply individualised feelings about themselves and their attachment to people and places. Referring back to a dimly-remembered childhood home, often further clouded by the effects of trauma, is counter-intuitive especially when UASC are so frequently encouraged to integrate and connect with their countries of settlement rather than their countries of origin. When UASC are granted refugee status, the decision as to which state will assure their rights is largely settled.[3] Subsidiary and temporary forms of protection, however, require young people to regularly renew or renegotiate entitlement meaning that, as young people advance into adulthood, a durable solution and their chance to be fully incorporated into a state is deferred.

The problems of establishing credibility as a *bona fide* refugee within the 'cultures of disbelief' that pervade asylum-recognition systems affect children as much as adults. These problems, evidenced powerfully by Warren and York (2014, and York and Warren, Chapter

Two in this volume), have been compounded by poor representation and advocacy and a system led by bureaucratic imperatives. Children are perceived as unreliable, unable to speak for themselves or to know their own minds, and social care providers have failed to ensure that young people's individual cases have been heard properly, fairly and in a timely manner. The rejection of a claim for international protection, however, can never be a once and forever decision as not only can mistakes be made in assessing evidence but also fresh evidence can come to light.

The following quotation from a young person illustrates some of these issues:

> 'Three times I was refused and every 2 weeks I had to go to sign – for maybe 2 years. They told me that they didn't believe my story and they said I was too young, they didn't believe I had escaped from military service. I was fed up I didn't know what they were going to do with me – even deport me ... When I get refused I got my case from the office – I met an interpreter he helped me – you need to talk to your social worker and you need to change your solicitor and when I did that I got my paper!' (Young Eritrean asylum seeker interviewed in Kent, in 2016)

All the time a young person remains in the country of settlement there is a possibility for their claim to be recognised but claims become increasingly difficult to establish as they progress through the judicial system (see Chapter Two). Even a 'final' refusal of protection does not guarantee rapid repatriation and young people continue to live in often extended periods of limbo, or legal liminality (Menjívar, 2006). This is obviously extremely stressful for young people who see their citizen friends moving into adulthood and independence while they lose entitlement to statutory support, employment, education and their aspirations. This period of reducing entitlement and security has been recognised in many studies as a particularly difficult time for young people leading to social dislocation and the risk of mental illness (including Chase, 2013; Chase et al, 2008; Robinson and Williams, 2015; Williams, 2017; see also Chapter Five).

Professional practice and durable solutions

Promoting durable solutions for UASC would be challenging even without the hostility to migrants experienced in many countries.

Social workers and others supporting UASC may aspire to the same durable solutions for their migrant clients as for any other young person in their care but their chance to advocate is limited by decisions made elsewhere. Arnold et al's survey found that 'Care providers … felt that their role in the determination of durable solutions was ultimately limited by immigration and asylum decisions' (2015: 22). This overruling by distant immigration officials is a profoundly dispiriting experience (Robinson, 2014).

There are many different actors involved in the care of UASC including guardians, foster carers, voluntary sector workers, social workers, teachers, health professionals, lawyers, judges and immigration officials (Gregg and Williams, 2015: 14–16; Chapter Six). The complexity of this supporting cast may actually hamper a young person's space to advocate in their own best interest as many young people lack a clear, central person (like a guardian or a foster parent) they can rely on. It is little wonder that young people are often distrustful and express confusion about who to call on for support. Such confusion is surely increased by the lack of shared vision for young people among this large cast of supportive services whose relationships with immigration control bodies range from confrontational and antagonistic to compliant and unquestioning.

The role of a guardian is specifically mentioned by the UNCRC (2005) and the UNHCR (2014). Guardianship schemes are in place in some European countries, albeit that some, in Greece, Slovakia, Belgium and Malta, are undermined by lack of resources (Arnold et al, 2015). In Belgium, the Guardianship Act legislates for the role of a guardian as an intermediary between the child and officials. The Scottish Guardianship Service Project[4] has been evaluated positively for providing good support and for putting the needs of young people 'rather than the processes to which they were subjected – at the centre' (Crawley and Kohli, 2013: 89–90). Even in this seemingly exemplary service however, the project's capacity to influence and work towards durable solutions was evaluated as 'less developed' than the rest of its work partly because the short term needs of young people took priority.

The child or young person should be the most important person in determining best interest and durable solutions especially as they approach adulthood and are coming to understand their personal and cultural identity, their sexuality, and their aspirations and desires. International guidance on determining best interest and durable solutions all emphasise the centrality of the child's voice. The appropriate use of interpreters, child-friendly environments and the presence of children's advocates, guardians and representatives are all recommended (UNHCR, 2014:31). Vervliet et al (2015) have described the desire of UASC to build a future and found, unsurprisingly, that 'these young people have multiple, intersecting identities, beyond just being "a refugee"' (Vervliet et al, 2015: 341). Young migrants are often aspirational and highly focused (Kohli, 2011) and will not accept a durable solution that obstructs their progress towards personal goals. They may also face pressure to pay debts or support family that they cannot publicly articulate. Mai has described state narratives and interventions that assume the passivity of UASC arguing that infantilising interventions that address young people as children without personal agency 'are bound to fail, adolescence being a phase of life marked by the subject's need to negotiate his or her passage into adulthood' (Mai, 2010: 84).

Durable solutions from a young person's perspective

Social workers and others working with UASC are working to support a group of young people living with uncertainty. Young people, especially those who are Appeal Rights Exhausted (ARE) or who have only temporary protection, may experience feelings of uncertainty, fear and worthlessness which have profound effects on the mental and physical wellbeing of young people (see Chapters Five and Six). Interviews carried out with UASC care leavers in Kent (Williams, 2017) refer to experiences in countries of origin as well as in the UK where the age assessment process, being refused asylum, court appearances, reporting and detention affected them as crisis points *and* as long-term sources of anxiety and stress. For this group of young people, the notion of a *choice* of durable solutions was irrelevant. Their asylum claims had been refused so the Home Office,[5] and many in local authority social care services, assumed that they would return 'home' to their country of birth or heritage, even though they felt that the UK was their home:

> 'I had made friends, made a life and then I lost my case in 2011. I'd been given many opportunities and they took all of it back. They stopped financial support, I'd been given a house and they took the house away and I start facing the issues again. I ended up on the street ...' (young person quoted in Williams, 2017)

Above all these former UASC believed that return was dangerous. As one young man reported: "It was worrying me like if they send me back to Afghanistan, what would I do? Who would I ask for help? I don't have any connection and I worry mostly about my safety" (Young person quoted in Williams, 2017).

Return, or repatriation, under these circumstances can hardly be countenanced as a sustainable durable solution. When young people reach this impasse, refused protection but resisting return or effectively unreturnable, there are few institutional responses to their situation. Unless they can prove particular vulnerability, above and beyond the 'normal' mental distress of homelessness and destitution, there will be no state support forthcoming even though they had been in the care of the state as children. In cases where young people are able to regain support due to their extreme illness, support is only temporary unless international protection or another form of permanent status is granted. One young person interviewed had been granted a temporary visa because of a severe psychotic episode; he had a breathing space but no long-term security:

> 'maybe they have a new rule that people who are mentally fucked up or ill or anything – I don't know – give them 2 years see if they get better, if they get better you can send them back. How can you expect them to get better when you put this thing in their head? It means – here's a piece of candy and we are going to slaughter you later on – it means that thing.' (Young person quoted in Williams, 2017)

Best practice in promoting durable solutions for independent migrant young people

One potentially positive approach to finding durable solutions for UASC has been the Council of Europe's Life Projects Planning Framework (the Life Project), adopted by the Council of Europe in 2007. Life Projects place the participation of the young person at their centre and are designed as a tool to be used whether interventions take place in country of asylum, country of origin or are leading towards family reunion in a third country. Life Projects, however, aim to support UASC in achieving their goals and to empower professionals 'whilst not denying states the right to control their borders' (Drammeh, 2010: 8). They are 'a mutual commitment by the unaccompanied migrant minor and the authorities' (FRA, 2010: 79) so, while they allow the participation of young people, they ultimately assert state sovereignty.

The Life Project approach has been endorsed by EU states and Nordic nations and, while it aims to find ways of building positive futures for young people, its vision of best interest maps clearly onto normative views of what is best for young migrants. According to Allsopp and Chase, these normative views are based on two assumptions: 'that European host states share a common understanding of "best interests" with the young people for whom they are responsible' and 'that young people will comply with the institutionally-defined version of their "best interests"' (Allsopp and Chase, 2017). Thus the Life Project approach fails to appreciate that young people have their own 'deinstitutionalised' life projects and have goals and motivations that are quite separate from those social workers and others are prepared to countenance (Chase and Allsopp 2013). This point is echoed in the work of Wells (2011), Mai (2010) and Robinson and Williams (2015), all of whom have found that, while UASC may lack useful connections and skills, they are not without personal and social resources to resist the undesired futures planned for them by others.

The problem remains, however, that many UASC will not be granted international protection, and support workers have to acknowledge and work with this in mind. This uncomfortable reality can undermine relationships between the young person and care providers. Young people are not unaware that 'the same statutory actors looking out for them now may abandon them when they turned 18' (Allsopp and Chase, 2017). Thus, establishing and maintaining supportive relationships is extremely challenging when young people firmly, and realistically, believe that it is in their best interests to withdraw from statutory support and 'go underground'. The cases of former UASC and young people whose local integration has not been assured should be routinely reviewed beyond 18 but, all too often, the most assiduous review of these cases is carried out by border enforcement agencies who keep in contact with young people through regular immigration reporting and other forms of surveillance and compliance monitoring. This is not the sort of review demanded by the UNCRC as it is in no way open to the shifting needs of a young person. Rather it reviews progress towards repatriation – the durable solution determined by immigration control. Advocates supporting young people waiting for appeals to be heard and decisions made may have little to offer young people as support is cut and entitlements reduced. Waiting is debilitating, emotionally draining and undermines educational chances. The danger to children and young people's mental health of long periods of waiting is clear and widely accepted and this situation continues into young adulthood where feelings of loneliness, rejection, anxiety and depression are compounded by very real threats of destitution, detention and deportation. As one young Afghan interviewed in Kent in 2016 said,

> 'When I was refused ... I couldn't think of anything, I was undone, they will send me back. I just didn't know what to do or what to think of – you know when your mind freezes and you don't know what to do, what to think – I was very, very upset at that time'.

Advocates of migrant rights may struggle to acknowledge that there are cases when return might be in the best interest of the young person. Returning 'home' on a temporary or permanent basis may sometimes fit into a young person's life plan especially when they have not felt able to tell their supporters about family or community members who they want to reconnect with. With this eventuality in mind, young people should be supported to explore their cultural heritage and maintain the social skills and links that could support return. This has been referred to as a 'cultural approach' by Robinson and Williams (2015) who argue that appropriate cultural skills can equip young people for futures in the UK *as well as* in their country of origin (see also Matthews, 2014). Sensitive acknowledgement that a young person's future may not only be in the country they have grown up in may support the ontological security of young people and their chance for durable solutions as citizens of world (Chase, 2013; Chase and Allsopp, 2013). Matthews' research (2014) heard from young people who felt they had lost cultural knowledge and skills while they had been away from countries of origin and that this had limited their future choices and chances at finding their own durable solutions.

'Triple planning' has been suggested as a strategy to deal with three realistic outcomes for young people: 'being able to remain in the UK, leaving the UK (either forced or voluntarily), or remaining without any legal status' (Huegler, 2016: 81). But it is hard to conceive of this third option, of a right-less existence, as a 'durable' solution. However, triple, or multiple, planning does at least recognise and accept the uncertainty that is inevitable in young migrants' lives. It also allows for the 'evolving capacities and unique protection needs' (Arnold et al, 2015: 48) of young people. In practice, however, multiple planning may just prepare young people for the durable solutions envisaged by migration control agenda and, like the Life Projects, 'may over rely on the young person's acquiescence in what the state has required for their future and an underestimation of their agency in shaping their own futures' (Matthews, 2014: 81).

Promoting durable solutions

In conclusion, it is clear that the search for durable solutions is rarely a priority for agencies responsible for the care and wellbeing of independent young migrant people. As noted by the House of Lords European Committee, 'The creation of durable solutions, like adherence to the best interests principle, appears to be a mantra rather than an effective guiding principle for EU and Member State action' (2016: 53). The international and EU frameworks and guidance on durable solutions and best interest principles are not rigorously applied, largely because the immigration control agenda, a logic embedded in Theresa May's aim to create a 'hostile environment' when she was Home Secretary, overrides best interest principles for unaccompanied children and young adults. The institutional categories young people move between – for example, child to adult, asylum seeker to refugee to refused asylum seeker or undocumented migrant – and the normative thinking that underpins them are largely to blame for the lack of truly child-centred 'best interest' work.

Durable solutions can only be sustainable after a decision has been made on a young person's asylum or other claim to remain and only after the young person has reached an age and a maturity to decide their future for themselves. Asylum decisions need to be recognised as fair, to be made in good time and to allow for changing protection needs and personal and global developments. Decisions should never be allowed to drag on beyond a young person's 18th birthday (except when they have arrived close to that date) and reasonable consideration should be given to the young person's capacity to understand legal processes and make sense of their own experience. Immigration decisions are beyond the remit of social care providers, but these advocates can insist that young people have access to timely and appropriate legal representation.

Social care workers need to challenge discourses, chiefly propagated by migration control agencies, that categorise post-18 UASC as migrants we have no duty towards. It is a social care worker's role to emphasise their status as care-leavers and as people who belong and are 'one of us'. Guardians specifically tasked with advocating for young people may be particularly well placed for this role. They can stand between young people and publicly-funded social care professionals, who are often subject to political, and managerial, pressure. In the absence of independent guardianship schemes, social care staff need to work towards continuity of support and fostering the trust of young people, the hallmarks of well-functioning guardianship schemes. Social workers and others can draw on their professional values and 'the relationship between social worker and client, shaped by small acts of resistance to dominant discourses and policies, offers practical ways forward for both' (Nelson et al, 2017: 4).

All social care providers have to acknowledge the agency and potential resistance of young migrants to futures imposed on them. Durable solutions imposed will simply not be durable. Return, repatriation in UNHCR's terms, can only be a durable solution when it happens with full, and informed, consent – consent that is increasingly unlikely to be achieved if young people have had to wait long periods under punitive immigration controls with little access to welfare entitlements, education and the workplace. Chase and Allsopp have argued for a shift towards 'a theoretical frame of futures' (Chase and Allsopp, 2013: 4), which would recognise the *potential* contribution of young migrants at least as much as their pasts as exiled children. Looking towards the futures of young people allows recognition of their agency, rather than their vulnerability and would allow countries of settlement to realise the investment that they have already made in supporting independent young migrants. European countries who have 'invested economically and socially in [UASC] ... do not capitalise on these investments; instead, they release into social marginality and irregularity young people who could make a positive economic and social contribution to the world they inhabit' (Mai, 2010: 78). A shift in attitudes to migrant youth, who are often highly motivated to study and work (Rania et al, 2014: 308) might be one way to align state discourses on the durable solutions open to independent young migrants more closely with their own.

The UK government's and state authorities' neglect of these aspirations leads young people to make often risky decisions – to withdraw from systems of support and control and to opt for underground or illegal methods of survival. Acquiring formal citizenship, and the permanent protection of a state is clearly the best and most durable solution for UASC post-18. Formal citizenship allows young people to explore their developing sense of, most likely, multi-layered belonging (McMichael et al, 2016: 8) and a passport, or the prospect of one, allows them to explore complex, transnational identities. Research has shown (Söderqvist, 2014; Carling et al, 2015: 18; McMichael et al, 2016: 8; Nunn et al, 2016) that the granting of citizenship increases the likelihood that migrants will return, permanently or temporarily, to countries of origin as citizenship grants the possibility of mobility across borders.

Within their own fields of expertise, social care providers should always ensure that psychological perspectives are put ahead of the demands of immigration control and that a young person's chronological age and immigration status, for example, is secondary to their psychological need (Derluyn and Broekaert, 2008). Chronological age has a direct impact on the search for durable solutions for young people and the tension between the protection of the 'apolitical child' (Dona and Veale, 2011) and the rejection of the migrant young adult leaves young adults in a particularly vulnerable position. That children and young people need an advocate who is indisputably 'on their side' might seem to be self-evident but the lack of such people, or the compromise of their independence by the institutions they work for, compounds what Jacqueline Bhabha has referred to as the 'radical otherness' of refugee children (Bhabha, 2009: 423).

Overcoming this 'radical otherness' means putting the needs of young people ahead of unimaginative state narratives. It means granting UASC rights to support and protection that change through their life course and lead towards future durable solutions that are based on shared humanity rather than limited by administrative categories. It means:

> 'If you help some migrant emotionally, just being there for them, that means a lot compared to the money you give them or a place to sleep. If you are standing by them, if you consider and think that this person has the same dignity or respect as I do, there must be something wrong if they have travelled all the way from his country. There must be some reason. I just want people to be more considerate, more open-minded, to learn more before doing anything, judging or even trying to help us.' (Young Afghan interviewed in Kent, in 2016)

Notes

[1] Throughout I capitalise Durable Solutions when referring to the UNHCR technical definition.

[2] 'In accordance with CRC Article 1, a child means every human being below the age of 18 years unless under the law applicable to the child, majority is attained earlier. A person who is under the age of 18 is thus to be regarded as a child, regardless of their level of maturity, unless the laws applicable to the child states otherwise' (UNHCR, 2014: 19).

[3] Except if they are convicted of a crime resulting in a custodial sentence of over a year, which can lead to deportation.

4   www.aberlour.org.uk/services/scottish-guardianship-service/
5   Interviews for the evaluation of the Positive Futures project (Robinson and Williams, 2015) made it clear that return was the only option Home Office officials saw for ARE care leavers.

References

Allsopp, J. and Chase, E. (2017) 'Best interests, durable solutions and belonging: future prospects for unaccompanied migrant minors coming of age in Europe', *Journal of Ethnic and Migration Studies*, DOI: 10.1080/1369183X.2017.1404265

Arendt, H. (1966) *The Origins of Totalitarianism*, New York: Harcourt and Brace.

Arnold, S., Ní Raghallaigh, M., Fournier, K., Smith, T., Walst, J., Goeman, M., Gregg, L., Williams, L., Camassa, R., Fajnorová, K., Mittelmannová, M., Guaci, J-P, Cassar, C., Noske, B., Anastasiou, A., Conaty, M., O'Keeffe, E. and Roe, N. (2015) *Durable solutions for separated children in Europe*, Dublin: Irish Refugee Council.

Bhabha, J. (2014) *Child migration and human rights in a global age*, Princeton, NJ: Princeton University Press.

Bhabha, J. (2009) 'Arendt's children: Do today's migrant children have a right to have rights?' *Human Rights Quarterly*, 31(2): 410–51.

Carling, J., Bolognani, M., Bivand, M, Rojan, E., Ezzati, T., Oeppen, C., Paasche, E., Pettersen, S. and Heggli Sagmo, T. (2015) 'Possibilities and realities of return migration', Insight from the research project, *Possibilities and Realities of Return Migration (PREMIG)*, Oslo: Peace Research Institute Oslo (PRIO).

Castles, S. (2005) 'Hierarchical citizenship in a world of unequal nation-states', *Political Science and Politics*, 38(04): 689–92.

Chase, E. (2013) 'Security and subjective wellbeing: the experiences of unaccompanied young people seeking asylum in the UK', *Sociology of Health and Illness*, 35: 858–72.

Chase, E. and Allsopp, J. (2013) *'Future citizens of the world'?: The contested futures of independent young migrants in Europe*, RSC Working Paper Series No. 97 Barnett Papers in Social Research, Working Paper 13-05.

Chase, E., Knight, A. and Statham, J. (2008) *Promoting the emotional wellbeing and mental health of unaccompanied young people seeking asylum in the UK – Research summary*, London: BAAF.

Chatty, D. (2016) 'Refugee voices: Exploring the border zones between states and state bureaucracies', *Refuge: Canada's Journal on Refugees*, 32(1): 3–6.

Crawley, H. (2011) "Asexual, apolitical beings': The interpretation of children's identities and experiences in the UK asylum system', *Journal of Ethnic & Migration Studies*, 37(8): 1171–84.

Crawley, H. and Kohli, R.K.S. (2013) *She endures with me: an evaluation of the Scottish Guardianship Service Pilot*, Edinburgh: Scottish Government, www.scottishrefugeecouncil.org.uk/assets/6798/Final_Report_2108.pdf

Crisp, J. and Long. K. (2016) 'Safe and voluntary refugee repatriation: From principle to practice', *Journal on Migration and Human Security*, 4(3): 141–7.

Derluyn, I., and Broekaert, E. (2008) 'Unaccompanied refugee children and adolescents: The glaring contrast between a legal and a psychological perspective', *International Journal of Law and Psychiatry*, 31(4): 319–30.

Dona, G. and Veale, A. (2011) 'Divergent discourses, children and forced migration', *Journal of Ethnic & Migration Studies*, 37(8): 1273–89.

Drammeh, L. (2010) *Life Projects for unaccompanied migrant minors: A handbook for front-line professionals*, Migration Collection, Council of Europe Publishing.

European Commission (2017a) 'Commission Recommendation of 7.3.2017 on making returns more effective when implementing the Directive 2008/115/EC of the European Parliament and of the Council', C(2017) 1600 final.

European Commission (2017b) *Migration Partnership Framework: A new approach to better manage migration*, https://eeas.europa.eu/sites/eeas/files/factsheet_ec_format_migration_partnership_framework_update_2.pdf

European Migration Network (EMN) (2014) *Policies, practices and data on unaccompanied minors in 2014 Common Template of EMN Focussed Study*, final version 4 June.

European Migration Network (EMN) (2015) *Policies, practices and data on unaccompanied minors in the EU Member States and Norway Synthesis Report: May*, https://ec.europa.eu/anti-trafficking/sites/antitrafficking/files/emn_study_2014_uams.pdf

European Union External Action (2016) *The 'Joint Way Forward on migration issues between Afghanistan and the EU*, 2 October, https://eeas.europa.eu/sites/eeas/files/eu_afghanistan_joint_way_forward_on_migration_issues.pdf

European Union Agency for Fundamental Rights (FRA) (2010) *Separated, asylum-seeking children in European Union Member States: Comparative report*, December, http://fra.europa.eu/en/publication/2012/separated-asylum-seeking-children-european-union-member-states

FRA (2016) *Current migration situation in the EU: separated children*, December, http://fra.europa.eu/en/publication/2016/december-monthly-migration-focus-separated-children

Gazzotti, L. (2017) 'German Plan to Deport Children to Morocco Ignores Lessons of History', *Refugees Deeply*, 3 July, www.newsdeeply.com/refugees/community/2017/07/03/german-plan-to-deport-children-to-morocco-ignores-lessons-of-history

Giddens, A. (1991) *Modernity and self-identity: Self and society in the late modern age*, Stanford University Press.

Gladwell, C., Bowerman, E., Norman. B. and Dickson, S. with Ghafoor, A. (2016) *After Return: documenting the experiences of young people forcibly removed to Afghanistan*, London: Refugee Support Network, www.refugeesupportnetwork.org/resources/after-return

Gregg, L. and Williams, N. (2015) *Not just a temporary fix: The search for durable solutions for separated migrant children*, London: Children's Society, www.childrenssociety.org.uk/what-we-do/resources-and-publications/not-just-a-temporary-fix-durable-solutions-for-separated

House of Lords (2016) *Children in crisis: unaccompanied migrant children in the EU European Union Committee*, 2nd Report of Session 2016–17 HL Paper 34, https://publications.parliament.uk/pa/ld201617/ldselect/ldeucom/34/34.pdf

Huegler, N. (2016) 'Social work with separated young people and human rights: cross-national perspectives on practitioners' approaches', PhD Thesis, London Metropolitan University, http://repository.londonmet.ac.uk/1019/1/HueglerNathalie_SocialWorkWithSeparatedYoungPeopleAndHumanRights.pdf

Kohli, R. K.S. (2011) 'Working to ensure safety, belonging and success for unaccompanied asylum-seeking children', *Child Abuse Review*, 20: 311–23.

Lemberg-Pedersen, M. (2015) 'The rise and fall of the ERPUM pilot: Tracing the European policy drive to deport unaccompanied minors', Working Paper Series No. 108, Oxford: Refugee Studies Centre.

Mai, N. (2010) 'Marginalized young (male) migrants in the European Union: caught between the desire for autonomy and the priorities of social protection', in J. Kanics, D. Senovilla Hernández and K. Touzenis (eds) *Migrating Alone: Unaccompanied and Separated Children's Migration To Europe*, Paris: UNESCO Publishing, pp 69–90.

Matthews, A. (2014) *What's Going to Happen Tomorrow?" Unaccompanied Children Refused Asylum*, April, London: Office of the Children's Commissioner.

McMichael, C., Nunn, C., Gifford, S. and Correa-Velez, I. (2016) 'Return visits and belonging to countries of origin among young people from refugee backgrounds', *Global Networks*, 17(3): 423–40.

Menjívar, C. (2006) 'Liminal Legality: Salvadoran and Guatemalan immigrants' lives in the United States', *American Journal of Sociology*, 111(4): 999–1037.

Nelson, D., Price, E. and Zubrzycki, J. (2017) 'Critical social work with unaccompanied asylum-seeking young people: Restoring hope, agency and meaning for the client and worker', *International Social Work*, 60(3): 601–13.

Nunn, C., McMichael, C., Gifford, S.M. and Correa-Velez, I. (2016) 'Mobility and security: the perceived benefits of citizenship for resettled young people from refugee backgrounds', *Journal of Ethnic and Migration Studies*, 42(3): 382–99.

Rania, N., Migliorini, L., Sclavo, E., Cardinali, P. and Lotti, A. (2014) 'Unaccompanied migrant adolescents in the Italian context: Tailored educational interventions and acculturation stress', *Child & Youth Services*, 35(4): 292–315.

Robinson, K. (2014) 'Voices from the front line: Social work with refugees and asylum seekers in Australia and the UK', *British Journal of Social Work*, 44(6): 1602–20.

Robinson, K. and Williams, L. (2015) 'Leaving care: unaccompanied asylum-seeking young Afghans facing return', *Refuge: Canada's Journal on Refugees*, 31(2): 85–94.

Schuster L. and Majidi, N. (2015) 'Deportation Stigma and Re-migration', *Journal of Ethnic and Migration Studies*, 41(4): 635–52.

Söderqvist, Å. (2014) 'Leaving Care with "Cultural Baggage": The Development of an Identity within a Transnational Space', *Australian Social Work*, 67(1): 39–54.

UNCRC (2005) 'General Comment No. 6 (2005): Treatment of unaccompanied and separated children outside their country of origin', Thirty-ninth session, 17 May–3 June, published 1 September, www.refworld.org/docid/42dd174b4.html

UNHCR (2003) *Framework for Durable Solutions for Refugees and Persons of Concern*, 16 September, EC/53/SC/INF.3.

UNHCR (2014) *Safe and Sound: what States can do to ensure respect for the best interests of unaccompanied and separated children in Europe*, October, www.refworld.org/docid/5423da264.html

Vervliet, M., Vanobbergen, B., Broekaert, E. and Derluyn, I. (2015) 'The aspirations of Afghan unaccompanied refugee minors before departure and on arrival in the host country', *Childhood*, 22(3): 330–45.

Warren, R. and York, S. (2014) *How children become 'failed asylum seekers'. Research report on the experiences of young unaccompanied asylum-seekers in Kent from 2006 to 2013, and how 'corrective remedies' have failed them*, Canterbury: Kent Law Clinic, University of Kent, www.kent.ac.uk/law/clinic/how_children_become_failed_asylum-seekers.pdf

Watters, C. (2007) *Refugee children: Towards the next horizon*, London: Routledge.

Wells, K. (2011) 'The strength of weak ties: the social networks of young separated asylum seekers and refugees in London', *Children's Geographies*, 9(3–4): 319–29.

Wilding, J. and Dembour, M.B. (2015) *Whose best interests? Exploring Unaccompanied Minors' Rights through the Lens of Migration and Asylum Processes (MinAs)*, The UK National Report, Brighton: University of Brighton, www.brighton.ac.uk/_pdf/research/crome/14-oct-15-final-minas-full-report.pdf

Williams, L. (2017) *The mental wellbeing of young former unaccompanied asylum seeking children in East Kent – Final Report*, http://mindinbexley.org.uk/wp/wp-content/uploads/2017/04/The-mental-wellbeing-of-young-former-unaccompanied-asylum-seeking-children-in-East-Kent-Final-Report.pdf

SECTION 3

International perspectives

EIGHT

A relational approach to unaccompanied minor migration, detention and legal protection in Mexico and the US

Mario Bruzzone and Luis Enrique González-Araiza

Introduction

This chapter considers the state systems of protection for unaccompanied migrant minors in Mexico and the US. The transits and arrivals of Central American minors – from El Salvador, Guatemala, and Honduras – offer important opportunities for scholars to consider the sociolegal practices of migrant care, especially how legally-accepted but institutionally-unfulfilled claims might signify something more than system failures. Instead this chapter takes the law and state institutions as sites for power relations to play out, rather than as outcomes of legislative power struggles or as resources for mutual claims by states and individuals (Martin, 2011). Our objective is to analyse the distinctive – and perhaps constitutive – tensions that govern state systems of protection for unaccompanied minors, looking to both legal texts and the empirical realities of state activities in Mexico and the US.

US and Mexican legal systems systematically limit migrant minors' rights and agency, in large part through determinations that children are not full legal subjects. Although migrant minors often make considered decisions as individuals and as parts of a family unit, they are generally not granted legal rights to make decisions regarding their best interests. Writing in the US context, Lauren Heidbrink emphasises a paradox of child agency:

> Without a legally recognized caregiver, the law views unaccompanied children as existing alone, though paradoxically still dependent. Without a recognizable

parent, the child cannot meaningfully access the state to petition for legal relief … Yet as social actors, migrant children challenge conceptualizations of child dependence and passivity, explicitly through their unauthorized and independent presence in the United States, and implicitly in the ways they move through multiple geographic and institutional sites in search of care, education, or employment. (2013: 138–9)

We follow Heidbrink in emphasising the problem of unaccompanied minor migrants' agency for systems that attempt to erase it in legal discourse and minimise it in everyday practices. Our analyses highlight the important work that 'childhood' does as a category and as a legal resource. Yet we also recognise that the contradiction that Heidbrink examines also constrains the state, because one cannot rid minors of agency by judicial or institutional fiat (Martin, 2011: 478).

Through this method, we seek to make several contributions. First, in dialogue with work on humanitarian borderwork (Williams, 2011, 2015; Vaughan-Williams, 2015; Pallister-Wilkins, 2017) and the 'politics of life' – in Didier Fassin's words, 'the evaluation of human beings and the meaning of their existence' (2007: 500–501) – we demonstrate how state systems of unaccompanied migrant minor protection reveal tensions between care for children and policing for undocumented migrants (Heidbrink, 2013), something that is highlighted in other chapters in this book (most notably Chapters One, Two and Ten). Through carework and policing practices, the exclusionary use of borders ('borderwork') can be reinforced, as national organisations carry out their responsibilities in relation to unaccompanied minor migrants as well as by non-state actors challenging the supposed fixity of state-centred boundaries. We emphasise how affirmations of social value may support exclusionary projects, even while the state is disunified and polyvocal. The disunified state's contradictory practices serve as both field of struggle and engine of differentiation in which unaccompanied migrant minors are figured as the most dependent and vulnerable figures in the system, as well as the figures that the system most disprivileges and disadvantages.

Second, and inscribed within our approach, we make a descriptive-interpretive account of the Mexican everyday institutions that serve unaccompanied migrant minors, and their legal bases, accessible to Anglophone readers. At one level, we respond to changes in Mexican law since 2011 that have been inadequately described in English. At a different level, our collaboration works to sketch Mexican legal contradictions and frameworks for scholars less familiar with the complex social practices and understandings associated with Mexican law and political institutions. As scholars have long observed, the law relies on external categories to prescribe and proscribe behaviours, and it further relies on a strategic indeterminacy to invest law-enforcement agents and agencies with a practical power to coerce behaviour (Harcourt, 2005; van Wichelen, 2015; Woodward and Bruzzone, 2015; Gorman, 2017). We put pressure on both the US and Mexican systems' irregularities, where the law fails to recognise adequately the social fields that it attempts to organise as well as where everyday practices subvert the law.

Third, we recognise that unaccompanied minors make decisions in a system that is configured in part by a bi-national effort to restrain Central American migration (Villafuerte Solís and García Aguilar, 2015; Seelke and Finklea, 2017; Vogt, 2017). We argue that migrant protection in North America should be seen as a 'geolegal' space (Brickell and Cuomo, Forthcoming) provisionally unified by minor migrants' mobilities, rather than segmented by national territories. The broader system of US–Mexico state protection of unaccompanied minor children acts to stabilise the potentially chaotic consequences of minor migration and yet is checked and delimited by its own internal tensions. This proposal extends recent works that highlight how migrant minors exhibit agency throughout their journeys (Heidbrink, 2013; Aitken et al, 2014; Thompson et al, 2017; Swanson and Torres, 2016; see also Puga 2016). Few unaccompanied Central American minors enter Mexico with the intent to stay. Rather, through a focus on migrants' access to social services and forms of protection, minor migrants' strategies en route can reveal the series of reciprocities between subnational institutions that take place across borders.

The Mexican system for protecting minor migrants

The Mexican legal framework for protecting unaccompanied migrant minors is broadly oriented to favour migrants' rights, and especially those of unaccompanied minor migrants. However, this pro-claimant orientation in legal texts belies the legal and institutional realities. We offer the story of 'Milton' as a vehicle to explore the severe difficulties for minor migrants to access their rights to remain in Mexico. Finally, we offer a critical analysis of the enforcement of migrants' rights in Mexico by taking departures from statute not as exceptions to the law, but as the law's normal operation.

Legal framework

In June 2011, a Mexican legal reform dramatically reformed the legal framework for the protection of migrant children. The reform's foundation begins in Constitutional Article 1:

> a) All persons present in Mexican territory will enjoy the human rights recognised in this Constitution, as well as all international human-rights treaties to which Mexico is signatory (Article 1, Paragraph I)
>
> b) All related human-rights standards [*normas*] must be interpreted to favour the greatest degree of protection for the individual (Article 1, Paragraph II)
>
> c) The Mexican government as a whole is obliged to "promote, respect, protect and guarantee" the human rights of people in Mexico, in accordance with the principles of universality, interdependence, indivisibility and progressivity (Article 1, Paragraph III)[1]

The reform amended many more of the Constitution's 136 articles, including Articles 3, 11, 15, 18, 29, 89, 97, 102 B and 105. Across these amendments, the reform re-codified the legal recognition of migrants' rights and provided some legal tools for rights enforcement and legal remedies. The Constitutional reform was, however, only the first step. Following the organisation of Mexican law, while each Constitutional Article recognises a specific right, those rights must be specified in application and in their mechanisms through statutory or 'secondary' federal laws (see Figure 6).

Figure 6: Hierarchy of Mexican law

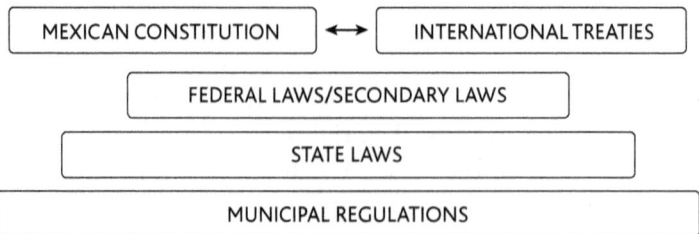

A further reform in October 2011 incorporated 'the best interest of the child' (*interés superior de la niñez*) into the Mexican Constitution:

> In all decisions and actions of the State, the principle of the best interest of the child will be observed and complied with, fully guaranteeing children's rights. Children have the right to satisfy their needs of food, health, education and healthy recreation for their comprehensive development. This principle should guide the design, execution, monitoring and evaluation of public policy aimed at children. (Article 4, Paragraph IX)

As a legal concept, the 'best interest of the child' guarantees children the affective and material conditions for a 'dignified life' (*vida digna*), as well as the material goods and services necessary to their present wellbeing and future growth. Although space precludes a significant treatment of the legal conception of 'dignified life' in Latin American jurisprudence and legal thinking (see Pasqualucci, 2008), it is foundational to understanding the Mexican uptake of the 'best interest of the child'. For our purposes, 'dignified life' implicates a set of affirmative duties or positive obligations that states have to provide for citizens, as well as the converse, that neglect or the failure to provide constitutes a violation of the child's individual rights.

The Constitutional reforms led to three distinct 'secondary' laws relating to the rights of refugees and migrants: 2011's Law of Migration (*Ley de Migración*), 2011's the Law on Refugees, Complementary Protection and Political Asylum (*Ley sobre Refugiados, Protección Complementaria, y Asilo Político*; 'Law on Refugees'), as well as 2014's General Law of the Rights of Girls, Boys, and Adolescents (*Ley General de los Derechos de Niñas, Niños y Adolescentes*; LGDNNA). The Law of Migration and Law on Refugees followed from Article 11, establishing that 'every person has the right to seek and receive asylum' in Mexico (Article 11, Paragraph II). The Law of Migration enables minor migrants to regularise their status for 'humanitarian reasons' (*razones humanitarianas*) and further, if unaccompanied and detained, transfers responsibility for housing and protection to Mexico's national child-welfare agency (*Sistema Nacional Para el Desarrollo Integral de la Familia*, DIF) and out of detention centres (Article 74, Law of Migration). The Law of Migration and the Law on Refugees direct the Mexican Commission for Refugee Aid (COMAR; *Comisión Mexicana de Ayuda a Refugiados*) and the migration-enforcement agency INM (National Institute of Migration; *Instituto Nacional de Migración*) to guarantee the 'best interest of the child' for all minors, including non-citizens (Articles 9 and 20, Law on Refugees; Articles 11 and 120, Law of Migration).

The third law, the LGDNNA, is the main legal instrument for enforcing children's rights in Mexico. Beyond the 'needs' specified in Article 4 (above), the 'best interest of the child' standard has obliged the Mexican Congress to harmonise programmes and obligations for children's wellbeing across federal, state and municipal levels of government. We list the rights recognised in the LGDNNA in full, as part of this chapter's objective to outline the Mexican legal framework for Anglophone social science researchers:

1. Rights to life, survival and development;
2. Right of priority [in relation to others' rights-claims];
3. Right to identity;
4. Right to live as a family;
5. Right to substantive equality;
6. Right not to be discriminated against;
7. Right to live in conditions of well-being and healthy development;
8. Right to personal physical integrity and a life free from violence;
9. Right to health and health-care;
10. Right of inclusion for children and adolescents with disabilities;
11. Right to education;
12. Right to rest and recreation;
13. Rights to freedom of ethical convictions, thought, conscience, religion and culture;
14. Rights to freedom of expression and access to information;
15. Right to participate;
16. Rights of association and assembly;
17. Right to privacy;
18. Rights to legal security and due process;
19. Rights for migrant children and adolescents; and
20. Right of access to information and communication technologies.
    (Article 13, LGDNNA)

In addition, the LGDNNA includes a special section with 12 articles (Articles 89–101) that grant protections to migrant children and adolescents. The LGDNNA, the Law of Migration, and the Law on Refugees act complementarily, and have come to define and even expand the Constitutional protections for unaccompanied minor migrants (see Figure 7).

Figure 7: Laws governing Mexican institutions involved in migrant protection

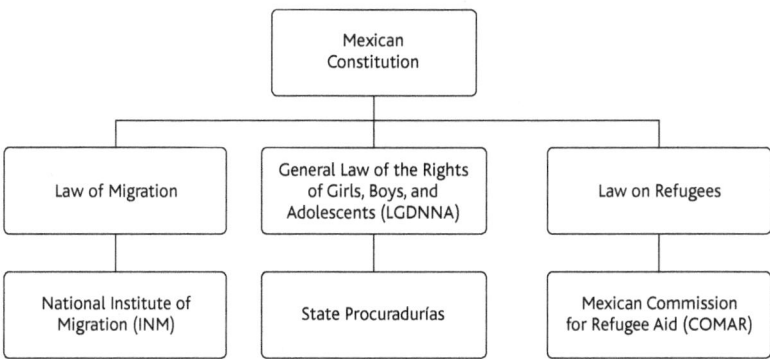

Mexican migrant protection in practice: the story of Milton

This description of minor migrants' legal rights appears to illustrate an orientation that prioritises care of minors over migration enforcement. In practice, however, unaccompanied minor migrants have little practical access to state protection. Here we follow the story of 'Milton' (a pseudonym), to elucidate how the Mexican system for migrant-minor protection militates towards a disinterest in the wellbeing of its charges. Heidbrink's paradox of migrant-minor agency arises as Mexican state institutions treat migrant minors as if they lack functional agency and produce them as legal subjects without rights to make decisions, and yet state protections are unavailable unless minor migrants make use of the very agency they are purported not to have. Further, as this section will detail, minor migrants' access to Mexican state protection is extremely difficult without outside social and legal support.

Milton arrived at the FM4 Paso Libre[2] Shelter in Guadalajara in February 2017 as a 17-year-old travelling alone from Honduras. Similar to many Mexican migrant shelters, FM4 has a formal intake procedure for new arrivals, involving an interview as one step.

In his interview, Milton mentioned two contributing causes for his departure. First, the economic conditions in his community of origin were precarious. Second, the Mara 18 gang had begun forcible recruitment of young men from his neighbourhood into its ranks. Milton had not (yet) been targeted individually; instead he left because the gang "was just about to come for me at my house to take me away". Because he was an unaccompanied minor, FM4 offered to assist him in regularising his migration status in Mexico, cautioning that the process could take months. Both the economic factors –

which negatively impact his right to development in the context of the LGDNNA – and gang-related insecurity offered 'humanitarian reasons' (Law of Migration, Article 52, Section V; and Article 74) for regularisation in Mexico. Milton accepted.

FM4 personnel contacted the Jalisco State Agency for the Protection of Children and Adolescents ('the Procuraduría'; *Procuraduría[3] de Protección de Niños, Niñas y Adolescentes del Estado de Jalisco*) by telephone. The Procuraduría is the legal representative for all unaccompanied minor migrants (LGDNNA, Article 136) and is charged with determining, enacting, and evaluating 'special protection measures' for children under its supervision. Procuraduría employees, however, did not come for Milton. When FM4 personnel contacted the Procuraduría a second time, they were told that the agency "did not have the operational capacity to make it happen" – and directed FM4 employees to deliver Milton to their office themselves. This request to FM4 – which was also a denial of services to Milton – put shelter workers under legal risk. Because the Procuraduría was not yet legal custodian, Milton's legal guardian was not consenting to the transportation, and Milton was legally disqualified from consenting, transport in any private vehicle met the Mexican legal definition for trafficking minors (Mexican Federal Criminal Code, Article 366). Instead, and with Milton's participation, FM4 personnel formulated and presented a legal petition for state protection through the Procuraduría as well as the first steps towards a humanitarian visa.

FM4's senior staff travelled with Milton to present the petition in person. Upon delivery, the Procuraduría chose to leave Milton with FM4, and to leave his guardianship in a state of legal limbo while it decided on Milton's case, continuing the legal risks for the shelter and its employees. A full month passed before the Procuraduría gave its response. The response offered two fundamental decisions: first, it granted Milton 'urgent protection measures', consisting of the safekeeping and legal custody by FM4; and second, it affirmed that legal representation and immigration procedures were the Procuraduría's sole remit, and that FM4 was barred from assisting Milton's regularisation. The Procuraduría did not communicate with Milton nor FM4 to follow up on the case for the next two months.

After those two months, FM4 filed a legal-neglect complaint on Milton's behalf with the Jalisco State Human Rights Commission, responsible for investigating legal violations committed, commissioned or enabled by public servants. Following the letter of the LGDNNA, the complaint listed the Procuraduría's titular heads: the governor of Jalisco and mayor of Guadalajara. Within three weeks, the Procuraduría sent a response for Milton to have interviews with its psychologist, social worker and lawyer in short order. Again, none of these workers showed up for Milton. FM4 staff accompanied Milton back to the Procuraduría offices to force the issue. After the interviews, however, Procuraduría officials demanded a photo identification from the Honduras Ministry of Foreign Affairs. Milton lacked this document, but Procuraduría officials said that they could take the necessary steps to get one on Milton's behalf.

Another month passed without contact from the Procuraduría. The nearest Honduran consular authority to Guadalajara lies in San Luis Potosí, two states and 330 km distance away. FM4 had assumed that the Procuraduría had regular contact with the Consulate and familiarity with its procedures, but after the month, FM4 staff contacted the Consulate directly. The Consulate was willing to speak with FM4 as Milton's legal custodian in Mexico, and staff said that they had no record of contact from the Procuraduría of Jalisco – indeed, they had no knowledge of Milton's case until FM4's communication. The Consulate processed Milton's request and delivered the ID directly to the FM4 shelter.

FM4 and Milton made a strategic decision to bypass the Procuraduría and submit the application for legal status directly to the INM. FM4 recontacted the office of the State Human Rights Commission, to note the Procuraduría's failure to contact Milton's consulate and to charge that this neglect violated Milton's rights under the Vienna Convention on Consular Relations (Article 5, paragraphs e, g, h) as well as a violation of his rights under the LGDNNA. One week later, the Procuraduría summoned Milton and, with staff of both the Human Rights Commission and the INM, finalised his regularisation in Mexico. Milton's 'humanitarian' regularisation had taken just under 11 months. He received his official documentation nine days prior to his 18th birthday.

Understanding minor migrants' claims to protection in Mexico

We find Milton's experience both unjust and infuriating. We hasten to add that Jalisco is widely considered a Mexican state 'friendly' to migrants, both in bureaucracy as well as in cultural discourses and prevailing attitudes. Yet while the impediments were both numerous and drawn out, they were not, and are not, atypical.

Before progressing to discuss the US system of migrant minor protection, we want to draw out three points. Our first point concerns rights. Neither the Procuraduría nor the INM contested Milton's legal claim to a humanitarian visa, as formulated in his initial petition. An account based in liberal political theory might highlight problems of determining and guaranteeing justice for migrants and others outside the state polity (see, for example, Carens, 2015). But we might instead read for the social tensions that exist between the law and its exterior. One law, the LGDNNA, has both mandated the institutions that are to care for unaccompanied minor migrants, including the Procuraduría, and left those institutions unaccountable, or barely accountable, for failing to do so. The toleration of rights violations is indicative of both an economy of rights – differential allocation based in social practices, which manifest in law and institutions – as well as an intimate economy of migration (Hiemstra and Conlon, 2016) to control and distribute who should pay for the social reproduction of some children and all migrants. We should be hesitant to assume that all the individuals carry equal standing, which is a crucial point of departure for liberal political theory. Instead, the organised neglect of Milton enacts a social process that decides whether paperwork is worth filing, a legal status is worth adjudicating, rights are worth protecting, and a life is worth legitimising. Milton's experience describes an agency that shunts off the responsibility for keeping him alive to an NGO, and continually reinforces Milton's lesser status as a certain type of political subject, one who is constructed as – but, we caution, not automatically *lived* as – less 'grievable' (Butler, 2015) and 'less-than-fully-human' (Philo, 2017).

Our second point concerns knowledge. Claiming rights within this system, even rights that all participating agencies agree are due, requires a profound knowledge of both legality and procedure. To receive his legal protections, Milton had to know: (a) Mexican law regarding unaccompanied migrant minors; (b) whether his case qualified under Mexican law; (c) the agency (the Procuraduría) charged with his legal protection; (d) how to write a legal petition; (e) how to petition that agency in particular; (f) how to petition for legal status to a second agency, the INM; (g) how to file a complaint with a third agency, the Human Rights Commission, including who to charge with neglect when the first agency did not fulfil its legal obligations; (h) where to get a Honduran photo ID while in Mexico; (i) how to get a Honduran photo ID while hundreds of kilometres from the nearest consulate; (j) how to fill out the various necessary forms for the application process; (k) how to work around the Procuraduría in order to solicit legal status from the INM, using Human Rights Commission workers for assistance; and (l) how to support himself, without legal authorisation to work, during a process lasting close to a year. Recently both media and UN officials have implied that growing numbers of successful asylum claims in Mexico indicated better state protections for migrants in general and particularly for unaccompanied minor migrants. As the sheer difficulty of managing this system should attest, no valid inferences can be drawn about asylum trends in Mexico if they ignore or elide the actions of the non-governmental organisations that make asylum possible.

Our third point concerns the power relations between and within institutions. Milton barely interacted with any worker or individual in any of the agencies involved as a person. The social norms around reciprocity and respect that 'personhood' typically implies were absent. Rather, Milton was an obligation, a chore, a name on a form, and finally a cause for a lawsuit. Simultaneously the agencies involved all evinced competing, even surprising priorities. The Procuraduría did not help the figure who its entire existence is based around. The INM did not attempt to deport the migrant, contrary to much of its institutional, cultural and funding priorities. The Jalisco State Human Rights Commission assisted with a case only marginally within its legal purview, possibly because of the governor's or mayor's fears of bad publicity. The temporary alliances in Milton's experience are less mission- or morally-driven than related to struggles between and within agencies. Those struggles play out in part across a binary of migrant care and migration enforcement. The claim to the Human Rights Commission against the Procuraduría was that a failure of care was also a de facto form of punishing Milton (Doering-White, 2018): legally Milton was to do nothing but wait. The capacity to use the Human Rights Commission to enforce rights is limited as a tactic; it is less a permanent safeguard than an indicator of a broader power configuration in the moment when Milton attempted to claim his legal rights.

The US system for minor migrants

The chapter now moves to an examination of the US system for minor-migrant protection as well as for the arbitration of unaccompanied migrant minors' claims to state protection. We summarise the relevant legal procedure and agencies briefly, in deference to the many strong accounts elsewhere. Our focus lies in a pair of contradictory state imperatives that inform our account of Mexican state protections. First, US agencies are caught between political directives to punish unaccompanied minors as undesired immigrants and alternatively to protect them as endangered children. Second, US agencies contradictorily treat unaccompanied minors as both 'adults in miniature' and as dependants incapable of agency (Aitken et al, 2014).

As we show, the overlap of these imperatives is an important point of contact between humanitarian borderwork and children's geographies, both within the social work system and within the legal system.

US legislative framework for unaccompanied minor migrant protection

Two major pieces of US legislation have configured the legal framework of unaccompanied minor migrant[4] protection. The first is the 2002 Homeland Security Act. The Act transferred the care for unaccompanied minor migrants out of the hands of the US immigration-enforcement bureaucracy and into the auspices of the federal Department of Health and Human Services (see Figure 8). However, the 'best interest of the child'[5] standard was never formally extended to children in immigration detention, although it is both a mandated 'consideration' and a key principle of the domestic child welfare system. The second piece of legislation is the 2008 William Wilberforce Trafficking Victims Protection Reauthorization Act (TVPRA), directed specifically at unaccompanied migrant minors. TVPRA both clarified and expanded the set of protections for migrant children in the US from non-contiguous countries. Section 1232(a)(3) mandates that personnel of US Customs and Border Protection (CBP), which operates migration controls at US territorial borders, determine four items when detaining an irregular migrant minor for possible

Figure 8: US migration enforcement and unaccompanied minor migrant protection agencies

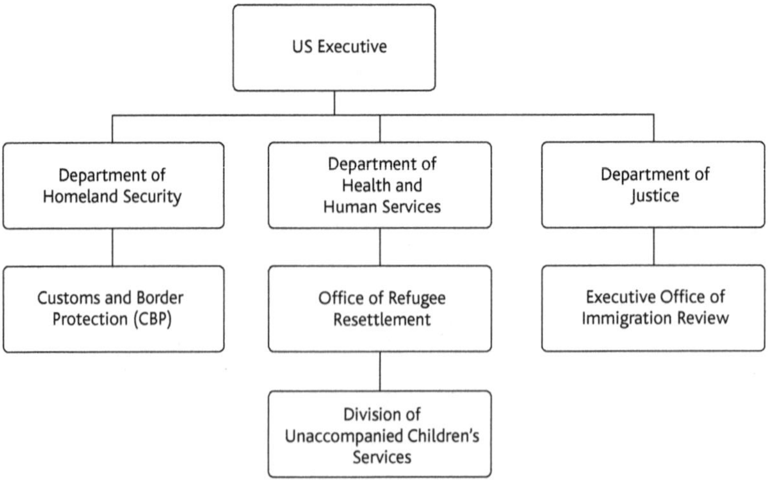

```
                          US Executive
         ┌───────────────────┼───────────────────┐
   Department of       Department of        Department of
   Homeland Security   Health and           Justice
                       Human Services
         │                   │                   │
   Customs and Border   Office of Refugee    Executive Office of
   Protection (CBP)     Resettlement         Immigration Review
                             │
                       Division of
                       Unaccompanied Children's
                       Services
```

repatriation. The CBP can immediately repatriate only minors who (a) can and do accept voluntary return, (b) have no possible claims of asylum, (c) have not been potential victims of trafficking, *and* (d) are Canadian or Mexican nationals. All others are to be transferred to the Office of Refugee Resettlement (ORR), outside the Department of Homeland Security (DHS).

The CBP must decide all four of the above items within the first 48 hours, as a consequence of legal settlement in the case of *Flores vs. Reno* (1996). As a safeguard, even minors for whom the CBP has not decided within the deadline are transferred to ORR custody, specifically the Division of Unaccompanied Children's Services, although the CBP might make an alternative determination after 48 hours has elapsed. A separate bureaucracy, the Department of Justice's Executive Office of Immigration Review, conducts hearings to adjudicate the rights of unaccompanied minor migrants' cases. The ORR often releases unaccompanied minor migrants to 'sponsors', who assume legal guardianship of the minor and who may not have regular migration status. Thus, when unaccompanied migrant minors encounter a CBP agent, whether at a port of entry or between ports of entry, they move across migration-enforcement and social-services bureaucracies, sometimes several times (Byrne and Miller, 2012: 7). Without detailing the multiple legal avenues that migrants have for establishing their continued or permanent residence in the US, it suffices to note that minor migrants' cases can take substantial amounts of time, and that permanent detention is often not practicable for the US government.

Internal tensions in US protection of migrant minors

Unaccompanied minor migrants' initial contact with state agents occurs with the CBP, which is both metaphorically fitting and indicative of a broad state orientation. A deep distrust of migrants pervades the system. CBP agents do not evaluate minor migrants' 'best interests' or protection needs, nor elicit testimony that might be favourable to them as rights claimants. Rather, CBP agents evaluate unaccompanied minor migrants' stories for their perceived truthfulness and their adherence to definitional standards of asylum (Mountz, 2010; Fassin and Kobelinsky, 2012). Yet this sceptical consistency belies an inconsistency: CBP agents are widely regarded as poorly trained in asylum procedures, much less for work with children, which entails inconsistent application of rules for protection (UNHCR, 2014). Indeed, a major complaint of CBP agents' union has been that agents must care for minor migrants without really knowing how (National Border Patrol Council, 2014). Conversely, ORR provides unaccompanied minor migrants with access to education, housing, health care, mental health services and legal assistance services. These social welfare imperatives exist alongside discretionary powers, for example to determine minors' housing placements on a continuum from sponsored release to 'staff-secure' facilities with severely restrained mobility (Terrio, 2015). In practice, ORR and DHS decide individual minors' confinement through both mission and cost, especially social-reproductive costs (Terrio, 2015; see also Williams and Massaro, 2016).

Judicial oversight is characterised by a second set of tensions. On the one hand, CBP and ORR have an affirmative duty of protection after apprehending unaccompanied minor migrants, and – apart from deportation – may only discharge that duty by placing minor migrants with 'sponsor' caregivers, because minors cannot be legal agents. The legal scholar Sarah Rogerson writes that 'rather than existing as persons with individual substantive and procedural rights, children are subjected to the presumption that they lack self-sufficiency and are therefore innately dependent' (2017: 846). On the other hand, in court minor migrants are treated as 'adults in miniature' – subject to identical evidentiary and burden-of-proof criteria, responsible for finding legal counsel, and without age-specific protections from expulsion when contrary to their best interests (Heidbrink, 2013; Terrio, 2015; Rogerson, 2017). Mexican minors are likewise capable of consenting to their removal, as above. Such a system leads to the absurd spectacle of three- and four-year-olds 'representing themselves' in immigration court (Coxon-Smith, 2017).

The Federal Appellate case *Flores v. Sessions* (2017) provides a concrete example of both sets of legal tensions. *Flores v. Sessions* considered and then affirmed minor migrants' right to a bond hearing while under ORR custody – that is, a hearing to determine if they may be granted release on bond[6] in certain circumstances. At first glance a minor procedural issue, the right to a bond hearing also establishes other rights for minor migrant detainees, including rights to be represented by legal counsel, to an assessment of detention by an immigration judge outside the ORR, to present evidence and respond to government evidence, and to build a public record of custody (Prandini and Kamhi, 2017). The exercise of any of these rights, however, comes within an ORR context in which minors have few rights to exercise on their own behalf – because they are not legally competent to exercise rights, nor carry responsibility for potential immigration offences (Martin, 2011; Bosniak, 2013; Heidbrink, 2013;

Rogerson, 2017). The form of legal challenge used, the class action, parallels these tensions. A class action posits that some group has rights but is unable to exercise those rights in a practical way. Thus in the first instance, the court adjudicates that rights exist and are denied – that, for instance, unaccompanied minor migrants have rights to bond hearings. But in the second instance, the legal system removes the negotiations over the specific content of those rights to a level where class members are not present – such as legal proceedings in which minor migrants are not competent to practise and require others in order to have rights.

These bureaucratic tensions offer two points of contact across scholarship on humanitarian borderwork and children's geographies. First, the titular 'Flores' of the above legal cases is a single person: Jenny Lisette Flores, a detained migrant who was a minor in the 1980s. *Flores* lawsuits concern the dual use of confinement for both policing and protecting unaccompanied minor migrants. In the 30-year history of *Flores* lawsuits, the Department for Homeland Security (prior to 2003 the Immigration and Naturalization Service, INS), have continued to defend confinement as the single, combined, appropriate response to both enforcement needs and humanitarian emergencies (Terrio, 2015; in other contexts, see Williams, 2011; Vaughan-Williams, 2015). Detaining children both protects them 'from threats by smugglers, traffickers, and gangs' (DHHS, section 6.2.2) and protects a social body outside of detention from a minor migrant who 'poses a danger to himself or others, or … presents an escape risk' (DHHS, section 1.4.2). 'Protecting' unaccompanied minor migrants does bordering work without a necessary recourse to expulsion or deportation, in part but not exclusively by spatially segregation (Coutin, 2010). The discursive conflation of policing and punishment is a productive instance of confinement practice, even as representation organises practices and procedures of who to confine, where, in what forms of facilities, and to what ends.

A second point of contact appears within the law, which both distinguishes political rights and differentiates individuals. The US legal system lacks a workable conception of children's agency, instead burdening children with contradictory positions of independence/dependency and responsibility/irresponsibility. If immigration judges in courtrooms are to settle competing interpretations of law, they must also arbitrate what a child is, can do and might be responsible for. A context that is external to the law is necessary for the law to function. Legal contradictions arise when the legal petitioners comprise a set of actors who are not 'full' citizens or fully endowed with legal forms of liberal subjectivity (Aitken, 2001; Varsanyi, 2008). Yet the terms on which that context is absorbed into the law – judges have a large leeway to declare 'legal facts' but cannot enact any reality they choose – reveal a broader set of power relations. When judges adjudicate questions of statutory language, as in *Flores v. Sessions*, they arbitrate how a classificatory status of a generalised human condition – childhood – is recognised against an immigration status. Unaccompanied minor migrants thus have two corresponding figures of contrast, at once adult irregular migrants but also citizen minors invested with legal rights. At the level of borderwork, the critical power relation concerns how (non-)agents' claims to security and assistance are made to function in a territory that is refusing them residence, perhaps temporarily and perhaps indefinitely (Gorman 2017).

Discussion: towards a relational account of minor migrant protection

This section draws out four points of convergence between the Mexican and US state protection systems to analyse how protection that is granted or withheld in one jurisdiction affects unaccompanied minor migrants' decisions and experiences in the other. In refusing to stabilise the border as the single site of differentiation between systems, and thereby incorporating longstanding critiques of methodological nationalism (Glick Schiller, 2005), we offer an account of migrant protection as a set of interrelated systems that operate across borders rather than within them. The continuities occur twice over: first, in the meshing of the boundaries of the systems of protection, the 'geolegal space' in which agencies rather than nation states provide the relevant boundaries; and in the continuities and linkages that minor migrants as well as state agencies create across space.

To begin, we suggest that 'best interest of the child' be understood as an international discourse, notwithstanding national difference in its uptake, that includes institutional conceptions of childhood and child dependence. In facilities and for parent institutions, social service provision is directed at children rather than collaboratively working with minors towards their development. Milton's case illustrates this nicely, since the FM4 shelter was both the only organisation concerned with Milton's participation rather than acquiescence but was also forbidden from helping him. Facilities for unaccompanied children in both countries commonly evaluate their success based on services provided rather than outcomes for individuals, especially in terms of psychosocial, educational, or health outcomes. Further, unaccompanied migrant minor 'protection' takes place in the facilities and general processes that are veiled and largely closed off from exterior scrutiny. Protecting the 'vulnerable' and 'dependent' minors within (Terrio, 2015; Doering-White, 2018) is to be judged only on its alignment to the checklists of proper humanitarian responses for the right sorts of victims (Fassin and Kobelinsky, 2012; Galli, 2018). Yet recurring motifs present children as consumptive burdens, and facilities are put under consistent pressure to cut costs or operate with greater economic efficiency. US facilities in particular are oriented to presume that detained children are inherently potential risks to the public, which means that as a class they are burdens to systems of law and order (Heidbrink, 2013), and that burden must be weighed against their claims to services.

Next, both the Mexican and US systems presume and legally produce 'unaccompanied minors' as non-agential children. On the one hand, the repetitious attempts to call the figure of the dependent child into being presume that the child conforms to the figure necessary for the organisation of institutionalised services (Heidbrink, 2017). As Susan Terrio's work (2015) has shown, minors can be severely sanctioned when they fail to do so. On the other hand, the impossibility of creating a non-agential child in an embodied person makes both the institutions, and the care-enforcement tension that they manifest, vulnerable to unruly behaviours. For facilities and their organising institutions, unauthorised behaviours and departures fail the institutional mandate to confine and control children, the bureaucratic need to compete with other agencies for state resources, and the moral imperative to care. When children do not receive adequate care, they strategise for ways to leave and to find what they need – and they do so without especial regard for borders (see also the discussion of the young people dispersed from the Calais camp in Chapter One, and the young people who leave reception centres in Nordic countries in Chapter Nine).

The messy everyday relationships between care and enforcement should further trouble a state-centric approach that takes state borders as the primary boundary. While we implicitly conceptualised care and enforcement (or policing) as two poles on a single continuum above, the lived experiences of both unaccompanied minor migrants and social workers in actual facilities tend towards oscillations between discrete practices of care and enforcement. We see less broad state prerogatives towards care or enforcement taken up by agencies than instances of care or enforcement responding to immediate institutional needs. For example, Mexican state procuradurías, their counterparts in the federal agency DIF and facilities in the US' ORR system are often poor caretakers. At the same time, what qualifies as legally sufficient care for individuals is often morally insufficient. This situation may appear to place social workers and care workers in an unenviable bind between state power, shifting institutional priorities, and their ethical and occupational obligations to minor migrants (see also Chapters Three, Five, Six and Seven). Yet it also multiplies the sites for resisting a dominant state priority of expulsion within agencies and institutions. As the story of Milton demonstrates, agencies can work to undermine one another's projects, rather than multiplying power by subordinating one agency to another as in the US.

Finally, shared categories (such as 'unaccompanied minors') and principles (such as 'the best interest of the child') are key sites for a production and regulation of subject positions, as well as a production and regulation of differential mobilities (Mezzadra and Neilson, 2013; Williams and Massaro, 2016). But when political subject positions are shared both across agencies and across national boundaries, new possibilities for alliances emerge. Agencies such as the Procuraduría, INM and the State Human Rights Commission all claim an authority devolved from the Mexican national state even as they may refuse to share in the priorities of other agencies and/or take up priorities opposed to their missions. The Jalisco Procuraduría might, for instance, work with the INM to enable unaccompanied minor migrants to arrive at the US border, transferring the 'burden' to US asylum and border-enforcement officials. The INM and CBP also have an extensive history of collaborations that exceeds the legal mandates and statutory authority of either agency, and more recently have collaborated to subvert Mexico's Law of Migration (Hernández, 2010; Márquez Covarrubias, 2015). More humanely, 'best interest of the child' is an international standard, which at once proposes an effective abnegation of national difference – the standard of 'best' might be fulfilled in either the US or in Mexico for unaccompanied minor migrants – and positions the Mexican and US systems as allied rather than competing. Shared categories and principles comprise one condition of possibility for strategic alliances across agencies, but these alliances are not automatically constrained by state borders.

Let us conclude by returning to the question of minors' agency. Migrants can and do make choices within this system, even though its workings are continually obscured, sometimes by bureaucratic functioning as in Milton's story and sometimes by deliberate acts to undermine migrants' claims to stay (Terrio, 2015). Doering-White (2018) briefly discusses several minors who chose not to undertake the Mexican asylum process or who abandon it to continue their US-bound journeys. Minor migrants leave the Mexican process not because it is 'bad' for them, but because it takes too long, subjects them to humiliations, and denies them access to everyday and developmental needs. Glibly, we might recognise these non-agential minors as making decisions regarding their 'best interests,' revealing a final interrelation between the Mexican and the US systems of protection: that migrants themselves employ a calculus of their best option. Yet a necessary reciprocity also exists. The reality of minor migrant agency enables a bureaucratic 'game', similar to that between FM4 and the Jalisco Procuraduría, in which the latter gambled that FM4 would assume the costs of Milton's survival. The logic of the 'game' crosses borders, enabled by shared conceptual forms and discourses of protection. Mexican agencies including, but not limited to the state procuradurías, can engage in a certain strategic withholding of services. On the one hand, an absence of provision can mean that other agencies will take up the slack, whether in Mexico or in the US, without denying minors their 'best interest'. On the other hand, agencies in Mexico know they are effectively backstopped by US protections because, for the vast majority of Central American unaccompanied minor migrants, Mexico is not their final, desired or best choice to make a life.

Conclusion

This discussion of the Mexican and US systems of protection recognises that both systems share tensions between care and enforcement, specific orientations to what the 'best interest of the child' means, and in their attempts to declare minor migrants as non-agential children. We suggest that unaccompanied minor migrants' agency and their strategies reveal how the social limits of a common 'humanity' (Butler 2015: 35–44) are continually produced and enacted, that is, the terms on which unaccompanied minor migrants are normatively valued and the outcomes of the social processes of valuation. These valuations are not, however, ever finalised; they are contested both by migrants and through the struggles that bureaucratic institutions' internecine struggles, within states and across borders. Further, both the care-enforcement tension and the problem of child agency are fundamental to the present organisation of systems of minor migrant protection. These problems arise from a political orientation towards migration and asylum, as well as a judicial system that must adjudicate questions outside of its purview in order to adjudicate the problems inside its domain.

The regimes to protect minor migrant children, in both Mexico and the US, establish a subject position of the unaccompanied minor migrant. This subject position gives both a criterion for prescribing individual minor migrants' behaviours and a reference point to establish how far deviations will be tolerated by institutions and their workers. This account tracks closely with recent work in feminist geopolitics to account for how geopolitical initiatives can be lived through individuals' bodies when individuals are made to present as political subjects (Massaro and Williams, 2013; Williams and Massaro, 2016; Brickell and Cuomo, forthcoming). In the law – and the categories and principles that the law codifies – socio-spatial experiences are co-constituted with identities and perhaps with subjectivities. Shared categories and principles become key sites for a production and regulation of subject positions and a production and regulation of material mobilities for the different subjects marked out through these processes.

Epilogue

We complete this chapter in a moment (July 2018) in which the US government has been punitively separating minors from their parents, including for asylum claimants. Framed as 'zero tolerance', it manages to be both extrajudicial punishment and in contradiction to settled understandings of immigration law and *Flores* lawsuits. The US bureaucracy can be observed moving towards migration enforcement and away from migrant care, in part by exploiting children's status as migrants (such as no right to counsel). Future judges may very well decide that the practices are legal – obviating much of this analysis – among a set of much-worse consequences. Yet we caution that such an event would corroborate our orientation here: that the law is a field of struggle. From a sociolegal perspective, we should not assume that the law is inherently stable, but rather that any apparent stillness results from the relations of power that configure it.

Notes

[1] At time of writing there is no generally accepted English translation for the current Mexican constitution. Because international legal terminology can be extremely nuanced, this and all subsequent translations should be treated as paraphrases.

[2] For further information about FM4 Paso Libre see www.fm4pasolibre.org/

[3] *Procuradurías* are government agencies charged with helping individuals access their legal rights. One translation would be 'ombudsman', but for Latin American legal contexts, 'ombudsman' lacks the obligation to help that is crucial to *procuraduría*.

4   The US legal system uses the term 'unaccompanied alien minors', or UAMs. Our references to unaccompanied minor migrants encompass UAMs when referring to legal contexts.

5   US legal discourse uses both 'best interest of the child' and 'best interests of the child'. We use the singular 'best interest of the child' to underscore parallels between the Mexican and US conceptions.

6   The ORR guidance as of February 2018 states that 'Although these hearings are known as 'bond hearings,' ORR does not require payment of any money in the event a court grants bond' (2.9).

References

Aitken, S.C. (2001) 'Global crises of childhood: Rights, justice and the unchildlike child', *Area*, 33(2): 119–27.

Aitken, S.C., Swanson, K. and Kennedy, E.G. (2014) 'Unaccompanied migrant children and youth: Navigating relational borderlands', in S. Spyrou and M. Christou (eds) *Children and Borders, Studies in Childhood and Youth*, London: Palgrave Macmillan, pp 214–39.

Bosniak, L. (2013) 'Arguing for amnesty', *Law, Culture and the Humanities*, 9(3): 432–42.

Brickell, K. and Cuomo, D. (forthcoming) 'Feminist geolegality', *Progress in Human Geography*, http://journals.sagepub.com/doi/10.1177/0309132517735706.

Butler, J. (2015) *Notes toward a performative theory of assembly*, Cambridge, MA: Harvard University Press.

Byrne, O. and Miller, E. (2012) *The flow of unaccompanied children through the immigration system: A resource for practitioners, policy makers, and researchers*, New York: Vera Institute of Justice.

Carens, J.H. (2015) *The ethics of immigration*, Oxford: Oxford University Press.

Coutin, S.B. (2010) 'Confined within: National territories as zones of confinement', *Political Geography*, 29(4): 200–8.

Coxon-Smith, M. (2017) 'The fate of thousands of unaccompanied children is decided in immigration court', *Tucson Sentinel*, 5 November, www.tucsonsentinel.com/local/report/110417_unaccompanied_kids/

Doering-White, J. (2018) 'The shifting boundaries of "best interest": Sheltering unaccompanied Central American minors in transit through Mexico', *Children and Youth Services Review*, 92: 39–47.

Fassin, D. (2007) 'Humanitarianism as a politics of life', *Public Culture*, 19(3): 499–520.

Fassin, D., and Kobelinsky, C. (2012) 'How asylum claims are adjudicated: The institution as a moral agent', *Revue française de sociologie (English Edition)*, 53(4): 444–72.

Galli, C. (2018) 'A rite of reverse passage: the construction of youth migration in the US asylum process', *Ethnic and Racial Studies*, 41(9): 1651–71.

Glick Schiller, N. (2005) 'Transnational social fields and imperialism: Bringing a theory of power to Transnational Studies', *Anthropological Theory*, 5(4): 439–61.

Gorman, C.S. (2017) 'Redefining refugees: Interpretive control and the bordering work of legal categorization in U.S. asylum law', *Political Geography*, 58: 36–45.

Harcourt, B.E. (2005) *Illusion of order: The false promise of broken windows policing*, Cambridge, MA: Harvard University Press.

Heidbrink, L. (2013) 'Criminal alien or humanitarian refugee?: The social agency of migrant youth', *Children's Legal Rights Journal*, 33(1): 133–90.

Heidbrink, L. (2017) 'Assessing parental fitness and care for unaccompanied children', *RSF: The Russell Sage Foundation Journal of the Social Sciences*, 3(4): 37.

Hernández, K.L. (2010) *Migra!: A history of the U.S. border patrol*, Berkeley: University of California Press.

Hiemstra, N., and Conlon, D. (eds) (2016) *Intimate economies of immigration detention: Critical perspectives*, London: Routledge.

Márquez Covarrubias, H. (2015) 'No vale nada la vida: Éxodo y criminalización de migrantes centroamericanos en México' ['Life is worthless: Exodus and criminalisation of Central American migrants in Mexico'], *Migración y Desarrollo*, 13(25): 151–73.

Martin, L. (2011) 'The geopolitics of vulnerability: Children's legal subjectivity, immigrant family detention and US immigration law and enforcement policy', *Gender, Place & Culture*, 18(4): 477–98.

Massaro, V.A. and Williams, J. (2013) 'Feminist Geopolitics', *Geography Compass*, 7(8): 567–77.

Mezzadra, S. and Neilson, B. (2013) *Border as method, or, the multiplication of labor*, Durham: Duke University Press.

Mountz, A. (2010) *Seeking asylum: Human smuggling and bureaucracy at the border*, Minneapolis: University of Minnesota Press.

National Border Patrol Council (2014) 'NBPC Statement on Influx of Juveniles in RGV Sector', 16 June, https://bpunion.org/press-releases/nbpc-statement-on-influx-of-juveniles-in-rgv-sector/

Pallister-Wilkins, P. (2017) 'Humanitarian borderwork', in C. Günay and N. Witjes (eds) *Border politics: Defining spaces of governance and forms of transgressions*, Cham, Switzerland: Springer, pp 85–103.

Pasqualucci, J. (2008) 'The right to a dignified life (*vida digna*): The integration of Social and economic rights with civil and political rights in the Inter-American human rights system', *Hastings International and Comparative Law Review*, 31(1): 1–32.

Philo, C. (2017) 'Less-than-human geographies', *Political Geography*, 60: 256–8.

Prandini, R. and Kamhi, A. (2017) *Practice Alert on* Flores v. Sessions. *Ninth Circuit holds that all detained children have the right to a bond hearing*, San Francisco and Washington DC: Immigrant Legal Resource Center, www.ilrc.org/sites/default/files/resources/flores_v._sessions_practice_alert_final.pdf

Puga, A.E. (2016) 'Migrant melodrama and the political economy of suffering', *Women & Performance: a journal of feminist theory*, 26(1): 72–93.

Rogerson, S. (2017) 'The politics of fear: Unaccompanied immigrant children and the case of the southern border', *Villanova Law Review*, 61(5): 843–906.

Seelke, C.R. and Finklea, K. (2017) *U.S.-Mexican security cooperation: The Mérida Initiative and beyond*, Washington DC: Congressional Research Service.

Swanson, K., and Torres, R.M. (2016) 'Child migration and transnationalized violence in Central and North America', *Journal of Latin American Geography*, 15(3): 23–48.

Terrio, S.J. (2015) *Whose child am I?: Unaccompanied, undocumented children in U.S. immigration custody*, Berkeley and Los Angeles: University of California Press.

Thompson, A., Torres, R.M., Swanson, K., Blue, S.A. and Hernández Hernández, Ó.M. (2017) 'Re-conceptualising agency in migrant children from Central America and Mexico', *Journal of Ethnic and Migration Studies*, https://doi.org/10.1080/1369183X.2017.1404258

United Nations High Commissioner for Refugees (UNHCR) (2014) *Finding and recommendations relating to the 2012–2013 missions to monitor the protection screening of Mexican unaccompanied children along the US-Mexico border*, www.immigrantjustice.org/sites/immigrantjustice.org/files/UNHCR_UAC_Monitoring_Report_Final_June_2014.pdf

Varsanyi, M.W. (2008) 'Rescaling the "Alien", rescaling personhood: Neoliberalism, immigration, and the state', *Annals of the Association of American Geographers*, 98(4): 877–96.

Vaughan-Williams, N. (2015) '"We are not animals!" Humanitarian border security and zoopolitical spaces in Europe', *Political Geography*, 45: 1–10.

Villafuerte Solís, D. and García Aguilar, M. del C. (2015) 'Crisis del sistema migratorio y seguridad en las fronteras norte y sur del México' (Crises of the migration system and security at Mexico's northern and southern borders), *Revista Interdisciplinar da Mobilidade Humana*, 23(44): 83–98.

Vogt, W.A. (2017) 'The arterial border: Negotiating economies of risk and violence in Mexico's security regime', *International Journal of Migration and Border Studies*, 3(2/3): 192–207.

van Wichelen, S. (2015) 'Scales of grievability: on moving children and the geopolitics of precariousness', *Social & Cultural Geography*, 16 (5): 552–66.

Williams, J.M. (2011) 'Protection as subjection', *City*, 15(3–4): 414–28.

Williams, J.M. (2015) 'From humanitarian exceptionalism to contingent care: Care and enforcement at the humanitarian border', *Political Geography*, 47: 11–20.

Williams, J.M. and Massaro, V.A. (2016) 'Managing capacity, shifting burdens: Social reproduction and the intimate economies of immigrant family detention' in N. Hiemstra and D. Conlon (eds) *Intimate economies of immigration detention: Critical perspectives*, London: Routledge, pp 87–104.

Woodward, K. and Bruzzone, M. (2015) 'Touching like a state', *Antipode*, 47(2): 539–56.

Court cases

Flores v. Sessions. No. 17-55208, 2017 U.S. App. LEXIS 11949 (9th Cir. July 5, 2017).

Flores v. Reno, Stipulated Settlement Agreement. Case No. CV85-4544-RJK (C.D. Cal. 1996).

NINE

Unaccompanied migrant youth in the Nordic countries

Hilde Lidén

Introduction

Policies across the Nordic countries to ensure unaccompanied asylum-seeking minors' (UAMs) care and protection display some common features but also interesting diversities. These similarities and differences are related to the ambiguities raised by the young people's dual status as migrants and as children. In 2015, the number of unaccompanied minors seeking asylum in Denmark, Norway and Sweden increased from about 5,000 per year to over 40,000, with most UAMs being male and applying for asylum in Sweden. Since then the number of new applications has declined to a few thousand, but the impact of the inflow of asylum seekers (both adults and children) has left a legacy in the region. During 2018, the Nordic countries are redefining their processes to create new narratives about immigration and integration policy, and are all torn by dilemmas and competing policies to handle the challenges of a generous welfare state, national identity policies and an active endorsement of human rights. These are tension-filled processes involving ambiguity and competing discourses each claiming hegemonic positions. The countries share a particular type of welfare state characterised by universal access to generous benefits and comparatively high levels of income redistribution. The Nordic region also faces some common challenges around the integration of refugees.

The balance between control policy and humanitarian obligations has led to the development of ambiguous policy designs that legitimise new hierarchical systems of civic stratification (Jørgensen and Thomsen, 2016). The Nordic countries have taken different stands, and the region can be studied as a test site of control and integration policies. While Sweden is well known for its multiculturalism and relatively liberal stance towards refugees, Denmark is known for one of the more restrictive immigration regimes in Europe, and Norway and Finland are positioned somewhere between the others (Brockman and Hagelund,

2011). Additionally, the countries have different formal affiliations with the EU; Norway is outside the organisation, while the other countries are EU members. However, within the field of asylum and immigration, EU policy is also significant for Norwegian regulations, as the country is a member of Schengen[1] and included in the EU's Dublin Regulations policy[2] (Brekke and Vevstad, 2007). In contrast, Denmark has made reservations to the EU's judicial cooperation and its common asylum policy, and has restrictive practices in cases under the Dublin Regulation.

Nordic political discourses have been embedded in the language of humanitarianism, justice, solidarity, equality and decency (Hagelund, 2003; Gullestad, 2006). In particular, this has been the case when it comes to asylum-seeking children (see Schiratzki, 2000; Nilsson, 2007; Vitus and Lidén, 2010; Lundberg, 2011; Wernesjö, 2014; Lidén et al, 2017). The political identity of 'asylum seeker' activates discourses of border control based on institutionalised suspicion, welfare restrictions and the expansion of an asylum system (Giner, 2007). By contrast, the political identity of 'children' refers to an inclusive childhood discourse and policy framework based on children's indiscriminate rights. The UN Convention on the Rights of the Child (UNCRC) is implemented in national legislation in Norway and Sweden, ensuring child-sensitive policies and assessments of the best interests of the child in administrative decisions. Denmark, however, makes no reference to the UNCRC in its legislation and administrative practices. Although the asylum policy, procedures and practices in the four countries differ, there are more similarities in their new regulations in the aftermath of the significant increase in the flow of refugees from 2015. The new and more restrictive immigration policies have vital consequences for child migrants, making the conditions they face more common.

This chapter aims to explore the ambiguities and changes in regulations concerning UAMs within, as well as across, the Nordic countries, with regard to the gap between restrictions, new policies and practices on one hand, and the human rights standards set out in the UNCRC and in immigrant-related legislation on the other. The chapter will focus on Sweden, Denmark and Norway as cases (the regulations and organisations of the asylum procedure in Finland have some key similarities with Norway). In terms of numbers, more UAMs have travelled to Sweden than to the other Nordic countries; however, Norway has also received a high proportion of the unaccompanied minors arriving in Europe. Fewer UAMs have applied for asylum in Denmark, although most minors pass through the country on their way further north.

The chapter is based on my own research projects in Norway and reviews of research and policy reports on asylum systems and practices in Sweden and Denmark. The research combines studies on documents and legal analyses (human rights conventions, national laws, regulations and court cases); an analysis of quantitative data from immigration authorities to identify particular areas of concern; and qualitative research, including fieldwork and interviews with unaccompanied minors, staff in reception centres, legal guardians and immigration authorities.

Overview of research on UAMs in the Nordic countries

The research on migrant children in the Nordic countries can be divided between sociology-based applied research with a focus on vulnerability, health-related research and legal studies with a human rights focus. The different approaches to immigration policy among the countries also reflect some of the main differences in research approaches: for instance, Denmark has conducted several studies on refugees' health. Research in Norway has mainly been applied to studies of the asylum system, while research in Sweden has often investigated the consequences of asylum policy for refugees. In Sweden and Norway, research typically includes a human rights perspective; however, this is less common in Denmark.

Sociology-based applied studies are expected to provide answers for policy makers and are often less theory driven. These studies explore topics such as living conditions and access to welfare services (Vitus and Nielsen, 2011; Lidén et al, 2013; Stretmo, 2014; Berg and Tronstad, 2015; Celikaksoy and Wadensjö, 2017). Further, the research explores access to education and the processes of resettlement and reintegration (Vitus, 2010; Eastmond, 2011; Oppedal and Idsoe, 2012; Seglem, 2012; Nilsson and Bunar, 2016; Pastoor, 2015, 2017; Söderqvist et al, 2016), including the consequences of polarised discourses about resettlement for young refugees (Wernesjö, 2012, 2014; Eide et al, 2014; Stretmo, 2014). Another group of studies covers children's experiences of the resettlement journey, including human trafficking (Øien, 2010; Tyldum et al, 2015; Lidén and Salvesen, 2016). Less research has been done on family reunifications (Brekke and Grønningsæter, 2017) or forced or assisted returns (Bendixsen and Lidén, 2017).

The second perspective that dominates the research field is studies with a health perspective. This research is extensively international and identifies post-traumatic stress disorder (PTSD) among refugees (see, for example, Jakobsen et al, 2014). The research finds that PTSD can be triggered after minors apply for asylum or have been resettled in a new country (Montgomery, 2011; Jensen et al, 2013; Vervliet et al, 2014).

Research with a legal and human rights perspective includes the assessment of how basic principles of the UNCRC have been implemented in legislation and policy development (see, for example, Schiratzki, 2000; Vitus and Lidén, 2010; Eastmond and Ascher, 2011; Lundberg, 2011; Hedlund and Cederborg, 2014). The research also covers the asylum procedure (Lundberg, 2011; Hedlund, 2016; Celikaksoy and Wadensjö, 2017; Lidén, 2017), including children's participation rights (Lidén and Rusten, 2007; Stang and Lidén, 2014; Kjelaas, 2016; Kaukko, 2017) and age assessments (Hjern et al, 2012; Hedlund, 2016; Munir, 2017). Still, there are important knowledge gaps; for example, little has been written to date about the systems and practices related to minors' legal representatives or the use of interpreters during asylum interviews (see, for example, Keselman, 2009).

Vitus and Lidén (2010), discussing the ambivalent position of asylum-seeking children in Norway and Denmark, draw on theories about the creation of hegemonic discourses (Laclau and Mouffe, 1985; Laclau, 1996). The argument is that separate values or identities that claim distinctiveness cannot be asserted without implicit references to what is claimed to be distinct. Separate values and identities of each discourse, then, implicitly refer to each other to claim their distinctiveness. This interdependence creates an ambiguous relationship between often antagonistic identities. The authors argue that, rather than superseding the ambiguity between political identities, what is possible, and often the result, is a series of continuous negotiations (Vitus and Lidén, 2010). The theory, referring to how hegemony is created within discursive fields, is highly relevant to understanding the ambiguity of the status of an asylum-seeking child, either as an asylum seeker or as a child, and how children's rights have been used differently as a legal instrument among the Nordic countries. This approach is elaborated in the following analysis.

Legal frameworks

Sweden and Norway have promoted the high profile of human rights in general, and especially as they relate to children's rights. In 2003, Norway incorporated the UNCRC into its national legislation through the *Menneskerettsloven*[3] (Human Rights Act) of 1999, which gives the UNCRC, as one of five UN Conventions, a semi-constitutional legal status, positioned between the Constitution and ordinary formal parliamentary legislation, in Norway's legal hierarchy. The Immigration Act has specific regulations addressing children as asylum seekers, and the Norwegian Directorate of Immigration has developed guidelines on hearing procedures, child-specific forms of prosecution and on the assessment of the best interest of the child in immigration cases. The regulations also state that the standard of proof is lower for children than adults, and that different rules may apply to the application of the burden of proof.

Sweden, although a signatory member of the UNCRC, has not implemented child-specific paragraphs in its legislation on asylum procedures. Nevertheless, the Immigration Act includes a passage in its introduction that emphasises that all matters that include a child must take into consideration the child's health, development and the best interests of that child (Immigration Act, Kap. 1, paragraph 10). Then, the Migration Agency, according to Swedish law, must specifically consider the best interest of the child in the asylum procedure (Schiratzki, 2000). However, researchers who have assessed the legal practices stress that the guidelines are rather vague and noted that there are no national regulations regarding how to apply the guidelines, hence they are open to interpretation (Lundberg, 2013; Stretmo, 2014). In her research, Lundberg (2013) demonstrates how the Migration Agency officers may use the UNCRC principles to legitimise rejections of UAMs' asylum applications, thus revealing the often-ambiguous relationships and interpretations of asylum-seeking children, vulnerability and responsibilities.

Although Denmark has ratified the UNCRC and its protocols, it is seldom referred to in public debates and legislation on child and family policy, in contrast to the situation in Sweden and Norway (Vitus and Lidén, 2010). This is also the case for Danish immigration policy. In Norway and Sweden, despite the implied ambiguities, the status of children has been given a hegemonic definition that supersedes their status as asylum seekers and migrants. In Denmark, however, the UNCRC has seldom been used in practice when considering children's asylum cases. Their status as an asylum seeker is the most significant, and similar requirements are set for children and adults. Hence, the position as an asylum seeker and migrant, with connotation and discourses referring to the collective of people and objectified juridical cases, are given a hegemonic definition over migrants as children.

The asylum procedure

According to UNCRC Article 22, member states are obligated to provide special protection to refugee children, including access to basic rights under the Convention, appropriate asylum procedures and humanitarian assistance. What do the differences in immigration policies and the implementation of children's rights discussed above imply for these countries' asylum procedures?

Here, similarities and differences can be discerned. Norway and Denmark segregate minors in reception centres and have a more centralised asylum procedure. Anyone wishing to lodge an application for asylum in Denmark or Norway is directed to the office of the Immigration Service, which is situated in or near the countries' capital cities. The initial registration procedure includes the submission of a formal asylum application and inquiries about the claimant's identity and travel route, followed by an asylum interview. By contrast, Sweden has a more decentralised system where the main tasks, such as accommodation, care and hearings procedures for children are distributed to regional immigration offices and social services are addressed at the municipality level.

The implication of being a child applicant during a hearing procedure is interpreted rather differently. In Denmark, with no reference to being a child featured in the legislation, applications are still processed according to the child's maturity. If the child is assessed to be less capable of assisting with the asylum proceeding and the child cannot be returned to his or her family, a residence permit is granted until the child's 18th birthday, without processing. Norway and Sweden, however, stress the child's position as a legal subject without discrimination, including the right for all asylum children to be heard; they do this by referring explicitly to UNCRC Article 12 (on participation) and Article 2, 1-2 (both on non-discrimination) in national legislation and practice. The UAM undergoes the same asylum procedures as an adult.

One challenge when it comes to UAMs with trauma experiences, or experiences resulting from repressive political regimes where there is no reason to trust public authorities, is that a single asylum interview does not always create the safe and positive atmosphere that is needed for a child to communicate his or her real fear of persecution or other human rights violations (see Chapter Two for discussion of the situation in the UK). Their experiences from, for example, sexual abuse, torture or forced participation in armed conflict, may still be unvoiced (Stang and Lidén, 2014; Tyldum et al, 2015).

In all the three countries, the representatives who guide children through the process are voluntary lay persons, helping the UAMs to access their legal rights and welfare services. The systems of recruiting representatives face various challenges and considerations, such as independence, commitment, expertise and availability. In Denmark, the representatives are recruited from NGOs, often the Red Cross, the organisation that is also the main body responsible for the accommodation of asylum seekers. In Norway, an on-call legal guardian service is offered so that UAMs can register asylum claims with a legal guardian, called a 'representative', present at any time. A new representative is offered when the minor moves to a new reception centre, which may disturb the continuity and representatives' awareness of the case. Delays in the appointment of representatives have been reported as a problem in Sweden, as these have impact on UAMs' access to, for example, hearings procedures and education (Celikaksoy and Wadensjö, 2017). Child applicants also enjoy the support of legal experts; in Norway, a lawyer is provided to give UAMs three hours' free service, while in Sweden, a custodian, often a lawyer, assists the minor during the asylum procedure.

In each of the countries, an applicant can appeal a rejected application to a refugee appeal court. In Sweden, the Migration Agency organises a meeting with the rejected minor to explain the implications of the decision. This is also the case after a rejection at the appeals court level. In Norway, however, a lawyer is responsible for explaining the implications of any rejection to the minor.

Age assessments

The age assessment procedures vary between Norway, Denmark and Sweden. Few unaccompanied minors, like other refugees and migrants who are dependent on human smugglers, bring any kind of identification documents to the immigrant authorities, such as proof of their age. Procedures for age assessment aim to determine the status of a minor where there is doubt about his or her age. Although age assessment methods have been heavily criticised, they may be used extensively (NOAS, 2016; see also Crawley, 2007; Hjern et al, 2012; Munir, 2017). For the minors, distrust about their age may result in both identity and psychological distress, in addition to the risk of an overage assessment, which can have significant consequences due to the special care and protection rights given to unaccompanied minors (see also discussion in Chapter Three about the age assessment process in England).

In Norway, immigration authorities usually register minors' stated ages and assess whether the age seems to be reasonable. If the minor is clearly underage, they may decide to exempt him or her from an age assessment. However, those who are declared to be of age 16 to 18 are frequently referred for an age assessment. In some cases, immigration authorities may also initiate procedures to assess whether a child is younger than 15 years old, as children younger than 15 are placed in special childcare facilities (see below). There, age assessments involve a dental examination and hand x-ray, in addition to observations and a medical statement organised by the Public Health Department. The age assessment determines the likelihood (by percentage) that the person is of the claimed age. It is on this basis that an assessment is made regarding whether the person is likely to be above the age of 18. The same medical examinations are used in Denmark.

In accordance with these regulations, additional information should be taken into consideration before a final decision is made. However, if the minor or his or her representative, supported by other documents, comes to another conclusion about the age than that declared by the immigration authorities, the authorities have the final say.

In Sweden, age assessments may be disputed. Because of the uncertain content of the standards for medical age assessment, the tests have been used less often there than in Norway. Under the Swedish asylum process, further investigation is conducted regarding the minor's age. If it is obvious that he or she is not a child, the Migration Agency can register the person as above 18 years. The Migration Agency is also obliged to inform the unaccompanied minor about the *option* to undergo a medical age assessment and hand it in to the Migration Agency, as evidence to support a stated age.

Care arrangements under the asylum procedure

Due to its decentralised nature, the Swedish Migration Agency either arranges accommodation for UAMs in municipalities, in shared apartments operated by private firms or the asylum seeker can find their own accommodation with financial support. The social services in the municipality where the minor is settled are responsible for his or her care and access to education and health services. These expenditures are financed by the Migration Agency.

In Denmark, young applicants stay first in a transit centre for UAMs, until their initial registrations and interviews are complete; they then move to a more permanent reception centre for UAM. Financial support for living is only given if they stay in a reception centre. This is also the case in Norway for UAMs who have turned 15. Norway splits UAMs between those over and those below 15 years of age. Since 2008, UAMs younger than 15 have been entitled to live in special care centres administered by the Directorate for Children, Youth and Family Affairs. The intention was to ensure that all UAMs, without discrimination, have access to the same standards of care and support as other children in child protection institutions. Despite the political approval of the care reform, the Norwegian government later decided to postpone indefinitely expanded reforms for those between the ages of 15 and 18. UAMs below 15 are immediately placed in care centres after registration and enrolled in introduction classes at the local school. In accordance with the Child Welfare Act, they receive better provisions and standards, and the help of better-qualified staff members, than those minors over the age of 15 who are housed in ordinary reception centres for UAM. The regulations governing UAM reception centres stipulate the clear obligations for centre staff to investigate the children's special needs for care and protection and accordingly make individual follow-up plans, and to enforce regulations on children's right to privacy and protection against unlawful or arbitrary use of forced measures. However, the qualifications and number of staff members are limited.

The living standards of UAM in Sweden have changed in recent years. After 2015, many municipalities experienced a large increase in the number of arriving UAMs; this was a serious challenge. By amending the Swedish Social Services Act, the Swedish Parliament introduced a new type of accommodation for UAMs, 'supported accommodation'. This type of accommodation is intended for those UAMs who require a somewhat lower level of care than others.

Residency

Until 2015, the rate of successful UAM applications for residence in Norway was around 70%, and in Sweden it was nearly the same. Those UAMs who are granted a residence permit in Norway and Denmark are placed either in group homes, a flat share, or, for the youngest, foster care, in the municipality that has agreed to care for the child. In Sweden, a child with a residence permit preferably continues to stay in the same municipality and in the accommodation administered by the social services as he or she did during the asylum procedure. Some, but not all, municipalities support the young refugees until they turn 21. Although the same rights are given to UAMs as to vulnerable children born in Sweden, the care arrangements for these minors may have lower standards. This is due to the ambiguity of treating them as children or a group of refugees, who are expected to be more robust in preparation for an independent life.

The young refugees get financial support while participating in introduction programmes, which for the minors mainly entail finishing secondary school or further education. After the introduction period, they have the same rights to support and loans for studies as other young people.

In all Nordic countries, *permanent* residence permits are given after a specified number of years of legal residency; in Sweden and Norway, this is three years of legal residency, while in Denmark this is an option after six years. New legislation in Sweden and Norway gives the states a new option to withdraw a UAM's legal residency before granting *permanent* residency if the conditions in his or her home country have changed significantly.

Citizenship can be granted after four years of permanent residency in Sweden, after seven years in Norway and after eight years in Denmark. All countries identify specific requirements related to identity, language skills and good conduct/criminality. Denmark and Norway's processes include a citizenship test.

Access to education and welfare services

The Nordic welfare system is based on the universal provision of education and the public delivery of services for those who are citizens. The welfare model also implies certain standards, values and expectations, such as gender equality, acquiring sufficient skills for labour participation, integration and broad social engagement (Esping-Andersen, 1996). All education is free of charge, and most pupils in Norway attend public schools in their local community; private schools are more common in Sweden and Denmark.

In Denmark, school introduction classes are most often organised within the reception centre. In Sweden, the UAMs have the same rights to an education as Swedish residents from the day they arrive. In Norway, asylum-seeking children younger than 16 years old have the same rights to primary and lower secondary school education as other children and are most often enrolled in local schools. Since 2014, 16–18 year olds have also been granted access to education. Minors who have completed lower secondary school before arriving in Norway are enrolled in upper secondary school after taking an introduction class. However, most UAMs do not have an education equivalent to lower secondary school when they arrive in Norway so they must attend classes to complete this level as part of their local schools' introduction classes. Those who receive residency permits have the same rights to education as Norwegian citizens.

Asylum-seeking children in all three countries are entitled to regular benefits from the local healthcare system and child welfare services, if needed. However, while children's asylum proceedings are underway, health institutions may be reluctant to start treatment for mental problems or chronic health problems, due to the uncertain timeframe. In Sweden, social services are the key agencies for providing care and integration, which may strengthen these agencies' sense of accountability. In contrast, researchers have found that the local child welfare offices in Norway only follow up on grave problems involving UAMs (Lidén et al, 2013; Paulsen et al, 2014; Tyldum et al, 2015). When UAMs are not granted a residence permit, they only have access to emergency health services.

New amendments, rejections and returns

In 2015, Sweden and Norway were among the countries that received the highest numbers of UAMs in the EU. Furthermore, there were more applicants younger than 15 years old than in previous years. Almost 35,400 UAMs applied for asylum in Sweden in 2015, accounting for almost 40% of all UAMs applying for asylum in one of the EU member states that year, and more than five times as many as in 2014. UAMs comprised about one fifth of all applicants in Sweden. In Norway, almost 5,400 UAMs applied for asylum in 2015, a figure five times greater than the year before. In Denmark, 2,100 UAMs applied, which was seven times more than the years before (see Table 4). Most applicants were boys (between 80% and 90%), and minors from Afghanistan continued to be the most common country of origin for UAMs arriving in the Nordic countries, followed by Syria (who mainly went to Sweden and Denmark) and Eritrea (who mainly went to Norway).

The increase in applicants led to new discourses on control regimes, national values and public debates about welfare states under threat. What implications did this new discourse and amendments have for the UAMs, the support for children's rights discourse and the intentions of child-sensitive regulations and procedures?

In all the Nordic countries, UAMs are granted residence permits as refugees on the grounds of non-refoulement and the fear of persecution. Young unaccompanied asylum applicants may also be granted residence permits on humanitarian grounds, if they do not qualify for refugee

Table 4: Applications from unaccompanied minors and outcome of applications, Sweden, Norway and Denmark, 2013–17

	2013	2014	2015	2016	2017
Sweden					
Applications	3,852	7,042	35,369	2,199	1,336
Accepted	1,955	3,269	3,076	6,853*	5,429*
Rejected	435	509	426	1,121	1,428
Norway					
Applications	1,070	1,204	5,480	320	191
Accepted	456	695	1,071	1,612	397
Rejected	23	34	27	316	98
Temporary permit until 18	17	21	150	150	361
Denmark					
Applications	354	818	2,144	1,184	No data
Accepted	40	154	497**	446**	No data
Rejected	33	40	46***	162***	No data

Notes: * Since July 2016, 'accepted' means a temporary permit for two years, or until the UAM turns 18; ** Temporary until turning 18 but, in some cases, a new application can be assessed and accepted; *** May be given a temporary stay until 18, if they do not have family members to return to.

status. However, this option has mainly been exercised in cases where the immigrant authorities could not identify caregivers to whom the child would otherwise be returned. In all three countries, there is also an option for the minor to be granted a residence permit until he or she turns 18. Temporary stays until turning 18 are the rule in Denmark. In Norway, the use of this paragraph came into force in 2009, and it has been used more extensively since 2015. Today, this is the main option for applicants coming from Afghanistan. In November 2015, the Swedish government announced a temporary law restricting the possibility of being granted a residence permit for protection purposes. This also included the right to family reunification. According to the proposal, refugees and persons eligible for subsidiary protection in Sweden will be granted temporary residence permits. The Swedish Migration Agency also strengthened its age assessments, and forced returns to Afghanistan became a real option.

In Sweden and Denmark, minor applicants may be given an opportunity for a new assessment that can lead to a permanent residence permit after the first permit expires. In Norway, a temporary permit until turning 18 allows no such second option.

Table 4 shows the divergent levels of applicants in the three countries. Further, it reveals the increase in applicants in 2015, followed by a decline in 2016 and 2017. After 2015, most UAM applicants in Norway from Syria and Eritrea were granted residence permits, unlike those coming from Afghanistan, who were increasingly granted temporary permits after a new regulation came into force in the autumn of 2016. In Sweden, most minor applicants from all countries were granted limited stay status, due to the new regulations in 2016 discussed earlier.

The rate of the UAMs who were assessed as over age is not identified. Although a delay in the assessment process is obviously part of the picture, Table 4 shows that the number of minors whose applications were assessed was significantly lower than the number of applications. This discrepancy also includes those who returned to another European country under the Dublin Regulation, those who turned 18 before their application was assessed and those who disappeared from the application process. In Norway, more than 500 minors disappeared from the reception centres in 2017, including those granted a limited permit and those assessed as overage. For example, Washim, who turned 18 before his application was assessed, left the reception centre on a small island in northern Norway, where he had lived for 18 months after migrating from Afghanistan. He illegally crossed the border into Sweden and then travelled with the help of a smuggler and asylum activists via car, train and bus before arriving in Paris in December 2017. He now lives on the street, sleeping in a tent under a bridge along with other young Afghans, or he stays overnight with helpers he meets. He lost confidence in the Nordic countries' asylum systems, which, in his opinion, did not assess applicants thoroughly or understand the difficult and unsecured conditions he fled in Afghanistan. However, remigration exposes him to vulnerable settings and gives him little hope for an improved and safer future.[4]

Claims of childhood overruled by new control regimes

Some major steps have been taken to implement children's rights in the Nordic countries' immigration legislation, and in other measures such as health, education and child welfare services. The countries formally meet the criteria of the UNCRC's Article 22 on refugee children; they 'take appropriate measures to ensure that a child who is seeking refugee status […] receive[s] appropriate protection and humanitarian assistance' (UNCRC, 1990, art. 22). At least, is this the case in terms of basic shelter and legal guardians, when their applicants are assessed, and until the minors turn 18. Still, the ambiguities of their status, as either children or asylum seekers, are revealed in several areas. Furthermore, the 2015 rise in asylum applications has reversed regulations and measures that have diminished the status of the UNCRC.

Although there are some common trends in the Nordic countries, there are also some important differences, as evidenced in the cases including legislation, asylum processes, age assessments, accommodation and residency. In Norway, the implementation of the UNCRC in the Immigration Act has led to some important and explicit child-sensitive paragraphs in the regulations, such as hearings procedures for all asylum-seeking children (accompanied children in families are also heard), recognising child-specific forms of persecution, a lower threshold for granting residency for children and that the best interest assessments have to be included in all decisions concerning children. In Sweden, this is not specified in the Immigration Act, but these concerns are still attended to in the regulation of practices. In Denmark, the minors' maturity is eventually a focus; however, their need for protection is assessed as if they were adults.

We also find variations in the countries' accommodation practices. Sweden resettles applicants in group homes in the local communities from the beginning; these provide better standards for care arrangements and support from social services than in Norway and Denmark. In Norway, the care arrangements for those under 15 are more in line with the standards for child welfare services guaranteed for children living permanently in Norway. For those who have turned 15 in Norway, and unaccompanied minors in Denmark, the minimum standards of care and living conditions in reception centres make this type of accommodation only acceptable for short stays. However, for many minors, the stay in the reception centres has been prolonged due to long asylum assessment procedures and the new practice of granting only limited stays until the UAM turns 18. This not only increases the UAMs' uncertainty about the future, it also exacerbates the living conditions and health problems of these minors.

Until recently, the residency rates for UAMs in Norway and Sweden were generously high. Those who have been granted residency have been granted access to education and welfare benefits that are equivalent to other residents. Research in Norway has found that the likelihood of young refugees being either in education and work after the first five years is high; this is especially the case for young refugee women and for young refugees from Afghanistan (Pastoor, 2015; 2017; Dalgard et al, 2018). In Sweden, studies have documented UAMs' capacity and resilience in terms of employment (Celikaksoy and Wadensjö, 2017). Given the empowering effect of employment, this also has positive effects for UAMs' language and social skills development, given that they get opportunities to advance their careers, rather than be stuck in certain types of jobs. Still, the resettlement process may be challenging. Research on mental health demonstrates that young refugees are more prone to psychological problems after resettlement than other groups of young people (Seglem, 2012).

The situation for those not granted residency is even more challenging. The countries' new legislation on temporary limits adds to the conditions that lead to health problems (see Chapter Five on how this uncertainty affects the health of UASC in the UK). Living with limited permission to stay also seems to influence the relationship between the minors and public welfare services. Educators, health personnel and child protection services can be uncertain about what rights should be granted and what exceptions should be made due to temporary stays (Aasen et al, 2016). The minors face few options in the long run, other than returning to their home country by force or with assistance from the International Organization for Migration (IOM) or re-migrating (Bendixsen and Lidén, 2017). Many minors choose re-migration to a new European country.

Both the similar and divergent practices of the three countries reflect the status and ambivalence of the discourse on children and children's rights. The comparisons show that the UNCRC is irrelevant to the way in which Danish asylum politics is talked about and practically implemented. Norway and Sweden, by contrast, have shown their political intention to take responsibility for treating asylum-seeking children as 'children', in the terms defined in the UNCRC. However, both practical difficulties and political priorities make living up to these intentions difficult. Since 2015, the immigration policies in each of these countries have become more similar, with an increased emphasis on immigration control in all three. Thus, the discourse about the threat posed by asylum seekers has overruled claims of childhood for asylum-seeking children as a universal political position from which to speak. UNCRC principles have even been used to legitimise restrictive asylum policies and the rejection of UAMs' asylum applications; for example, policies implemented to prevent children from taking the risk of travelling to Europe have been used as a main argument for using limited permission to stay until they turn 18.

Although the regulations and asylum systems in the Nordic countries reflect how the discourse of immigration regulation versus children's rights is negotiated, immigration regulations appear to have taken precedence over children's rights once more in the support for new restrictive measures in the aftermath of 2015. The 'negotiators' who contribute to giving voice to children and to children's rights in the democratic struggles for hegemony have been weakening (Laclau and Mouffe, 1985). Control measures have led to additional ambiguities, in both discourse and practices, with regard to whether asylum-seeking children are defined primarily as children or as asylum seekers. Thus, in all the countries, despite the different positions each country has taken on this issue, the act of asylum seeking creates 'another kind of children'. Young refugees are first treated as equal when they have gained citizenship, although they legally have the same rights when obtaining a permanent residence permit.

Conclusions

In concluding I will emphasise three key challenges for protecting the rights of UAMs and providing the equal opportunities in line with international conventions including the UNCRC. The first challenge is the weaknesses of the asylum procedures; it is vital to address the practices of age assessment, insufficient access to legal guardians and (child) competent interpreters, and credibility given to asylum applications due to the experience of child-specific forms of persecution, inhuman treatment and human trafficking. Although many minors are granted asylum or residence permits on subsidiary refugee status, there remain significant numbers of minors whose reasons for asylum are not given credibility (Staver and Lidén, 2014; UNHCR, 2014; Tyldum et al, 2015).

Another issue is the increase in granting limited residency permits for UAMs, which is contrary to the state authorities' responsibility according to UNCRC to find a sustainable or durable solution for minors. The practice gives hegemony to the discourse and policy of stricter immigration regulations over the best interests of the child. Limited permits might lead to situations where more minors spend a significant period of time living with uncertainty about their future, which might reduce their aspirations for education and inclusion. The high number of minors disappearing from reception centres and increases in illegal young migrants in European countries supports this hypothesis (Aasen et al, 2016). The practice of granting time-limited residency permits and the rising numbers of missing UAMs are problematic for both minors and wider society.

The final challenge relates to practices of resettlement and integration. More knowledge is needed about best practices and the kinds of support that minors need to integrate into their new society and to ensure their access to education and work. Young refugees report discrimination, difficulties in the education system and problems gaining access to the labour market (Eide et al, 2014; Pastoor, 2015, 2017; Celikaksoy and Wadensjö, 2017). In spite of these challenges, research from the Nordic countries also reveals success stories of resettlement and integration.

Notes

[1] The Schengen Area comprises 26 European states that have officially abolished passport and all other types of border control at their mutual borders. The area mostly functions as a single jurisdiction for international travel purposes, with a common visa policy.

[2] The Dublin Regulation (Regulation No. 604/2013) is an EU law that determines the EU Member State responsible for examining an application for asylum seekers seeking international protection under the Geneva Convention and the EU Qualification Directive, within EU.

[3] Lov om menneskerettighetenes stilling i norsk rett, LOV-1999-05-21-30. [Act on the Status of Human Rights in Norwegian Legislation]

[4] Article 22 states in part: '1. States Parties shall take appropriate measures to ensure that a child who is seeking refugee status or who is considered a refugee in accordance with applicable international or domestic law and procedures shall, whether unaccompanied or accompanied by his or her parents or by any other person, receive appropriate protection and humanitarian assistance in the enjoyment of applicable rights set forth in the present Convention and in other international human rights or humanitarian instruments to which the said States are Parties'.

References

Aasen, B., Dyb, E. and Lid, S. (2016) 'Forebygging og oppfølging av enslige mindreårige asylsøkere som forsvinner fra mottak og omsorgssentre' ['UAM disappearing from care/reception centres'], NIBR Report, 17, Oslo: NIBR Oslo University College.

Bendixsen, S. and Lidén, H. (2017) 'The forced-voluntary continuum in return migration Return to wellbeing? Irregular migrants and assisted return in Norway', in Z. Vathi and R. King (eds) *Return migration and psychosocial wellbeing discourses, policy-making and outcomes for migrants and their families*, London: Routledge.

Berg, B. and Tronstad, K.R. (2015) *Levekår for barn i asylsøkerfasen* [*The living conditions for asylum seeking children*], Trondheim: NTNU Samfunnsforskning AS.

Brekke, J.P. and Grønningsæter, A.G. (2017) *Family reunification regulation in Norway and the EU*, Report 06:2017. Oslo: Institute for Social Research.

Brekke, J.P. and Vevstad, V. (2007) 'Asylum conditions for asylum-seekers in Norway and the EU', ISF Report, Oslo: Institutt for samfunnsforskning.

Brockman, G. and Hagelund, A. (2011) 'Migrants in the Scandinavian welfare state. The emergence of a social policy problem', *Nordic Journal of Migration Research*, 1(1): 13–24. DOI: 10.2478/v10202-011-0003-3

Celikaksoy, A. and Wadensjö, E. (2017) 'Policies, practices and prospects: The unaccompanied minors in Sweden', *Social Work and Society*, 15(1), www.socwork.net/sws/article/view/499

Crawley, H. (2007) *When is a child not a child? Asylum, age disputes and the process of age assessment*, London: ILPA.

Dalgard, A.B., Wiggen, K.S. and Dyrhaug, T. (2018) 'Enslige mindreårige flyktninger 2015–2016. Demografi, barnevern, arbeid, utdanning og inntekt' ['Unaccompanied minors in Norway 2015–2016'], *SSB Report 2018/3*, Oslo: Statistic Norway.

Eastmond, M. (2011) 'Egalitarian ambitions, construction of difference: The paradoxes of refugee integration in Sweden', *Journal of Ethnic and Migration Studies*, 37(2): 277–95.

Eastmond, M. and Ascher, H. (2011) 'In the best interest of the child? The politics of vulnerability and negotiations for asylum in Sweden', *Journal of Ethnic and Migration Studies*, 37(8): 1185–200.

Eide, K., Guribye, E. and Lidén, O.H. (2014) 'Refugee children: Ambiguity in care and education', in G. Overland, E. Guribye and B. Lie (eds) *Do we really care? Nordic work with traumatised refugees*, Cambridge: Cambridge Scholars Publishing, pp 119–131.

Esping-Andersen, G. (1996) *Welfare states in transition: National adaptations in global economies*, London: Sage.

Giner, C. (2007) 'The politics of childhood and asylum in the UK', *Children & Society*, 21(4): 249–60.

Gullestad, M. (2006) *Plausible Prejudice. Everyday experiences and social images of nation, culture and race*, Oslo: Universitetsforlaget.

Hagelund, A. (2003) 'The importance of being decent: Policy discourses on immigration in Norway 1970–2002', Master's dissertation, University of Oslo.

Hedlund, D. (2016) 'Drawing the limits: Unaccompanied minors in Swedish asylum policy and procedure', PhD dissertation, University of Stockholm.

Hedlund, D. and Cederborg, A.-C. (2014) 'Legislators' perceptions of unaccompanied children seeking asylum', *International Journal of Migration, Health and Social Care*, 11(4): 239–52.

Hjern, A., Brendler-Lindqvist, M. and Norredam, M. (2012) 'Age assessment of young asylum seekers', *Acta Paediatrica*, 101(1): 4–7.

Jakobsen, M., deMott, M. and Heir, T. (2014) 'Prevalence of psychiatric disorders among unaccompanied asylum seeking adolescents in Norway', *Clinical Practice and Epidemiology in Mental Health*, 10(1): 53–8.

Jensen, T.K., Fjermestad, K.W., Granly, L. and Wilhelmsen, N.H. (2013) 'Stressful life experiences and mental health problems among unaccompanied asylum-seeking children', *Clinical Child Psychology and Psychiatry*, 20(1): 106–16.

Jørgensen, M. B. and Thomsen, T.L. (2016) 'Deservingness in the Danish context: Welfare chauvinism in times of crisis', *Critical Social Policy*, 36(3): 330–51.

Kaukko, M. (2017) 'The CRC of unaccompanied asylum seekers in Finland', *International Journal of Children's Rights*, 25(4): 140–64.

Keselman, O. (2009) 'Restricting participation: Unaccompanied children in interpreter-mediated asylum hearings in Sweden', PhD dissertation, Linköping University.

Kjelaas, I. (2016) 'Barns deltakelse i institusjonelle samtaler: En studie av samtaler mellom enslige asylbarn og miljøarbeidere på omsorgssenter', PhD dissertation, NTNU, Trondheim.

Laclau, E. (1996) *Emancipation(s)*, London: Verso.

Laclau, E. and Mouffe, C. (1985) *Hegemony and socialist strategy: Towards a radical democratic politics*, London: Verso.

Lidén, H. (2017) *Barn og migrasjon. Mobilitet og tilhørighet* [*Children and migration. Mobility and belonging*], Oslo: Universitetsforlaget.

Lidén, H. and Rusten, H. (2007) 'Asylum, participation and the best interests of the child: New lessons from Norway', *Children & Society*, 21(4): 273–83.

Lidén, H. and Salvesen, C.H. (2016) 'De sa du må. Mindreåriges erfaringer med menneskehandel' ['Minors' experiences of human trafficking'], ISF Report 2016:09, Oslo: Institutt for samfunnsforskning.

Lidén, H., Stang, E.G. and Eide, K. (2017) 'The gap between legal protection, good intentions and political restrictions. Unaccompanied minors in Norway', *Social Work & Society*, 15(1), www.socwork.net/sws/article/view/497

Lidén, H., Eide, K., Hidle, K., Nilsen, A.K. and Wærdahl, R. (2013) 'Levekår på mottak for enslige mindreårige asylsøkere' ['Living conditions for UAM in reception centres'], ISF Report 2013:02, Oslo: Institutt for samfunnsforskning.

Lundberg, A. (2011) 'The best interests of the child principle in Swedish asylum cases: The marginalization of children's rights', *Journal of Human Rights Practice*, 3(1): 49–70.

Lundberg, A. (2013) 'Barn i den Svenska Asylprocessen', in M. Bak K. and von Brömsse (eds) *Barndom och migration*, Stockholm: Borea Bokförlag, pp 47–76.

Montgomery, E. (2011) 'Trauma, exile and mental health in young refugees', *Acta Psychiatrica Scandinavia*, 124(s440): 1–46.

Munir, A. (2017) 'Aldersundersøkelse av enslig mindreårige asylsøkere. 'Jeg kom ikke hit for å finne ut hvor gammel jeg er" ['Age assessment of unaccompanied minors. I didn't travel to find out about my age'], Master's thesis, Institute of Social Anthropology, Oslo.

Nilsson, E. (2007) *Barn I rättens gränsland. Om barnperspektivet vid prövning om uppehållstilstånd*, Stockholm: IUSTUS Forlag.

Nilsson, J. and Bunar, N. (2016) 'Educational responses to newly arrived students in Sweden: Understanding the structure and influence of post-migration ecology', *Scandinavian Journal of Educational Research*, 60(4): 399–416.

Norwegian Organisation for Asylum Seekers (NOAS) (2016) *Over eller under 18. Aldersvurdering av enslige mindreårige asylsøkere* [*The age assessment of unaccompanied minors*], Oslo: NOAS.

Oppedal, B. and Idsoe T. (2012) 'Conduct problems and depression among unaccompanied refugees: The association with pre-migration trauma and acculturation', *Anales de Psicologi*, 28(3): 683–94.

Pastoor, L. de W. (2015) 'The mediational role of school in the lives of unaccompanied refugee minors in Norway', *International Journal of Educational Development*, 41: 245–54.

Pastoor, L. de W. (2017) 'Reconceptualising refugee education: exploring the diverse learning contexts of unaccompanied young refugees upon resettlement', *Intercultural Education*, 28(440): 1–22.

Paulsen, V., Thorshaug, K. and Berg, B. (2014) *Møter mellom innvandrere og barnevernet: Kunnskapsstatus* [*Immigrants and the child welfare service: research review*], Trondheim: NTNU.

Schiratzki, J. (2000) 'The best interests of the child in the Swedish Aliens Act', *International Journal of Law, Policy and the Family*, 14(1): 206–25.

Seglem, K.B. (2012) 'Predictors of psychological adjustment among young unaccompanied refugees after resettlement: A population-based study', PhD dissertation, University of Oslo.

Söderqvist, Å., Sjoblom, Y. and Bulow, P. (2016) 'Home sweet home? Professionals' understanding of "home" within residential care for unaccompanied youths in Sweden', *Child & Family Social Work*, 21(4): 591–9.

Stang, E.G. and Lidén, H. (2014) *Barn i asylsaker. Evaluering og kartlegging av hvordan barns situasjon blir belyst i Utlendingsnemndas saksbehandling, herunder høring av barn.* [Children as asylum seekers. Evaluation of children's participation rights in the Norwegian Asylum Appeal Court] NOVA Report 14/2014. Oslo: NOVA.

Staver, A. and Lidén, H. (2014) *Unaccompanied minors in Norway: Policies, practices and data in 2014*, Rapport 2014:14, Oslo: Institutt for samfunnsforskning and EMN, www.udi.no/globalassets/global/european-migration-network_i/studies-reports/emn-final-report-unaccompanied-minors-2014.pdf

Stretmo, L. (2014) 'Governing the unaccompanied child: Media, policy and practice', PhD dissertation, University of Gothenburg.

Tyldum, G., Lidén, H., Skilbrei, M.L., Dalseng, C.F. and Kindt, K.T. (2015) *Ikke våre barn. Identifisering og oppfølging av mindreårige ofre for menneskehandel i Norge* [*Those children are not our responsibility. Identifying and following up children exposed for human trafficking*], FAFO Report 2015:45, Oslo: FAFO.

UNHCR (2014) *The heart of the matter. Assessing credibility when children apply for asylum in the European Union*, Brussels: United Nations High Commissioner for Refugees, www.refworld.org/docid/55014f434.html

Vervliet, M., Meyer Demott, M.A., Jakobsen, M., Broekaert, E., Heir, T. and Derluyn, I. (2014) 'The mental health of unaccompanied refugee minors on arrival in the host country', *Scandinavian Journal of Psychology*, 55(1): 33–7.

Vitus, K. (2010) 'Waiting time: The de-subjectification of children in Danish asylum centers', *Childhood*, (17): 26–42.

Vitus, K. and Lidén, H. (2010) 'The status of the asylum-seeking child in Norway and Denmark: Comparing discourses, politics and practices', *Journal of Refugee Studies*, 23(1): 62–81.

Vitus, K. and Nielsen, S.S. (eds) (2011) *Asylbørn i Danmark – en barndom i undtagelsestilstand* [*Asylum seeking Children in Denmark – a childhood in a State of emergency*] (1. udg.) Copenhagen: Hans Reitzel.

Wernesjö, U. (2012) 'Unaccompanied asylum-seeking children: Whose perspective?' *Childhood*, 19(4): 495–507.

Wernesjö, U. (2014) 'Conditional belonging: Listening to unaccompanied young refugees' voices', PhD dissertation, Uppsala University.

Øien, C. (2010) *Underveis. En studie av enslig mindreårige asylsøkere* [*Causes and motives which underpin unaccompanied minors migration*], Oslo: FAFO.

TEN

Life (forever) on hold: unaccompanied asylum-seeking minors in Australia

Kim Robinson and Sandra M. Gifford

Introduction

Australia's policies towards asylum seekers arriving unauthorised by boat have had a particularly harmful impact on unaccompanied children. An estimated 1,832 unaccompanied asylum seeking minors (UAMs) arrived in Australia between 2008 and 2012 (Houston et al, 2012). The majority of UAMs are male and from Afghanistan, Iran and Sri Lanka, and many identify as stateless.

In 2012–2013 there were 1,900 UAMs in immigration detention in Australia (Phillips, 2017a). This is of course in contravention of the UNCRC (United Nations Convention on the Rights of the Child, 1989). However, as is discussed later, although Australia is a signatory to the UNCRC, there is nothing enshrined in Australian law that requires it to honour such an obligation. Since the reintroduction in 2013 of the boat 'turnbacks' policy – the practice of removing unauthorised maritime arrivals in Australian waters – (Phillips, 2017b), the number of asylum seekers including UAMs arriving in Australia by boat has fallen dramatically.

It is difficult to obtain accurate statistics of how many UAMs currently reside in Australia as most would have arrived as teenagers prior to 2014 and many will now be 'aged out' – that is over the age of 18 years and thus no longer considered to be a minor. These young people are part of what is referred to as the 'asylum legacy' and as of February 2016, there were an estimated 32,000 persons in this category with approximately 23,000 released into the community on bridging visas (Phillips, 2017c). Many of these bridging visas are now being transferred to being Temporary Protection Visas (TPVs) or Safe Haven Enterprise Visas (SHEVs).[1] Approximately 5,739 of the 'asylum legacy' caseload are between the ages of 12 to 25 years of age; however, not all of these young people arrived unaccompanied (Multicultural Youth Advocacy Network, 2017).

Under current policy, UAMs who arrived by boat, including those who are now over the age of 18, are likely never be issued permanent protection visas. Instead, they are issued temporary visas (TPV or SHEV). While they can reapply for these visas (after three and five years respectively), they are not permitted to apply for a permanent protection visa. This situation effectively puts their lives on hold. They have little hope of ever being settled in Australia; are not able to participate in higher education beyond secondary schooling unless they pay overseas student fees; are denied the right to be reunited with their family; and have limited work rights (RCOA, 2017). Importantly, Australian policy towards unauthorised asylum seekers arriving by boat remains one of deterrence (Phillips, 2017c) and, while receiving much criticism both within Australia and internationally (Jureidini and Burnside, 2011; Mares, 2016; UNHCR, 2017), currently (July 2018) has support from the two major political parties, the Liberal Party and the Labor Party, and is thus unlikely to change in the near future.

A further factor impacting on UAMs in Australia is that they receive different entitlements and kinds of care depending on when and how they arrived (by boat or plane), the 'stream' through which they are 'processed', the type and quality of the detention they are kept in while awaiting their status determination (community, closed or offshore), and the 'lottery' of fragmented service provision they receive should they be allowed to live in the community.

This chapter describes the situation of unaccompanied children who have sought asylum and are living in Australia. It critiques their treatment within a human rights and rights of the child framework and discuss the challenges and dilemmas faced by service providers charged with the care and supervision of these children. It concludes with some reflections on models of care that address young people's needs, promote their rights and challenge the broader political and policy context that impacts so determinately on these children and young adults' current wellbeing and on their futures.

Setting the scene: the Australian context

Consider the situation of four young men, Malek, Ahmad, Maamat, and Zohib, all Hazara by ethnicity, all from Afghanistan, all living in Australia and all having arrived alone when they were under the age of 18 years and with no family in Australia. These four young men have similar claims for asylum; however, the year and manner in which they arrived has resulted in vastly different circumstances in regard to their entitlements to protection and care and prospects for their futures.

Malek arrived in Australia in 2009 as an unaccompanied humanitarian minor (UHM) on the offshore special humanitarian programme (DIBP, 2018). Although unaccompanied, he was not an asylum seeker, instead arriving as part of Australia's offshore humanitarian programme. He was granted a permanent protection humanitarian visa in advance of his arrival and travelled to Australia by plane. On arrival, Malek was eligible for a range of settlement services (DIBP, 2017) and, although settlement has not been easy, he has gained Australian citizenship, completed secondary school, is attending university, has a part-time job and is able to sponsor his family members to migrate to Australia through the split family stream of the special humanitarian programme.

The other three young men all travelled to Australia by boat as unaccompanied asylum-seeking minors (UAMs). For these young men, the year of their arrival determines the differences in their entitlements and claims for protection. All three left for Australia after spending time in a transit country, Indonesia. All three were subject to mandatory closed detention but Ahmad, having arrived prior to August 2012, was able to secure the assistance of a lawyer to help him get his permanent protection visa. He has completed high school and is studying at university, and he can sponsor family members under the split family stream of the humanitarian programme.

Maamat arrived in Australia shortly after August 2012. Although he could have applied for permanent protection, changes in the Migration Act mean that he will never be eligible to sponsor his family members under the humanitarian migration stream. He initially believed he could apply though other migration streams but retrospective legislation introduced in December 2014 has denied permanent settlement to *anyone* arriving by boat. Zohib travelled to Australia after December 2014 where a further change to the Migration Act prohibits any asylum seeker travelling to Australia by boat from *ever* being granted resettlement in Australia.

Although these last three young men are now living in the community on Temporary Protection Visas (TPV) (DIBP, 2017), and while they can attend high school, they cannot attend university unless they pay extremely high overseas student fees. Finally, for Zohib, the last young man to arrive in Australia, unless another country is willing to accept him for resettlement, he is 'stuck' – his future is indefinitely on hold.

A major factor impacting on the wellbeing of the three young men who arrived by boat is that they all have been held in immigration detention either in Australia or offshore. As we will discuss below, the impact of mandatory detention has had a serious negative influence on their physical and mental health.

The current social and political context framing the situation of UAM must be understood within a volatile policy environment focused on deterrence. This has entailed ongoing changes in migration policy and legislation, uncertainties in the care of UAMs awaiting status determination and (re)settlement, variations in care arrangements across state and territories, and restrictions on access to higher education, employment, family reunion and, importantly, permanent protection through being granted settlement in Australia.

Key issues facing young people

There are four key factors unique to the Australian context that impact especially negatively on all UAMs: firstly, as we explained above, all UAMs have spent some time in immigration detention. Australia was the first country to have a policy of mandatory detention for all asylum seekers arriving unauthorised by boat, including children. Mandatory detention takes three forms: closed detention in Australia; offshore detention on Nauru or Manus Island, Papua New Guinea; and community detention (Phillips, 2017a). Because of current policy prohibiting permanent settlement in Australia, if another resettlement country cannot be arranged or if return is not viable, all forms of detention are effectively indefinite. This prolonged and indefinite detention has had (and continues to have) a strong negative impact on both physical and mental health and wellbeing. There is now a large body of research evidence including the findings from two national inquiries into children in immigration detention (Human Rights and Equal Opportunity Commission, HREOC, 2004, Australian Human Rights Commission, AHRC, 2014) documenting the negative impacts on children and young people. The short-term and long-lasting harms of this policy are indisputable with a senior psychiatrist noting: 'It is hard to conceive of an environment more potentially toxic to child development' (HREOC, 2004: 397).

The prolific body of research documenting the detrimental effect of detention on children in Australia and elsewhere (HREOC, 2004; Crock, 2006; AHRC, 2014; Corbett et al, 2015; Zwi and Mares, 2015; Bosworth, 2016; Essex, 2015), along with activism and protest nationally and internationally, has finally, as of September 2017, shifted policy to discontinue detaining asylum-seeker children including those who have no family with them in closed and offshore facilities.

However, although UAMs are now living in community settings, their possibilities remain limited due to restricted access to education, employment and family reunion and, importantly, because of the ongoing insecurity about if, when and where they might settle in the future.

Second, although Australia is a party to the United Nations Convention on the Rights of the Child (UNCRC) (1989), there is nothing enshrined in Australian law that requires it to honour its obligation. Unlike other common law countries, Australia has no constitutional or legislative Bill of Rights that protects the rights of children (AHRC, 2014: 10). While Australia's policy of mandatory detention of all persons including children who arrive by boat breaches children's rights under international law (Kaldor Centre for Refugee International Law, 2015), there is no mechanism in the domestic Australian context that requires the Australian government to enact its international obligations. This adds an additional layer of vulnerability for unaccompanied asylum-seeking children who have arrived in Australia by boat.

Third, there is an inherent conflict of interest in the guardianship arrangements for unaccompanied children. The Australian Immigration Guardianship of Children Act introduced in 1946 names the Minister of Immigration and Border Protection as the legal guardian of every non-citizen child (defined as a person under 18 years of age who enters Australia without a custodian and who intends to become a permanent resident) (DIBP, 2017). The Minister can then delegate his or her powers to any of the Commonwealth, State or Territories. However, the Minister retains the power to revoke his or her delegation and can exercise power to intervene on any matter. States and Territories have different procedures governing the care of these children (Federal Register of Legislation, 2014). While the Minister can and does delegate guardianship to other government authorities, these legal arrangements create a conflict of interest because while the Minister is required to act in the child's best interest he or she is also required to carry out the duties of the immigration portfolio, including border control. Thus, it is the Minister of Immigration who as the legal guardian must act in the best interest of the child and who has the final say in their visa status determination process (Crock and Martin, 2015).

A key issue in guardianship is related to the determination of the age of the unaccompanied youth (Kenny and Loughry, 2018). In Australia the process for determining the age of young asylum seekers is by the Department of Immigration and Border Protection (DIBP) officers. There is limited research on this issue in Australia. Two reports by Amnesty International (2013, 2014) describe age assessments conducted by the DIBP as unlawful, in violation of meeting the obligations of the UNCRC and as 'plainly inadequate' (2013: 76). This is supported by Evenhuis (2013) in his analysis of the legal positions taken by the Department that dismiss international obligations.

Hurley and Beaumont (2016) identify discrepancies and inequities in the age determination process and question the proficiency of DIBP officers conducting age assessments. They note: 'It is unclear the extent to which the two-day training programme offers specific child-focused, cross-cultural training, but is likely to be inadequate given that age determination officers need not have any prior experience or qualifications in working with children' (Hurley and Beaumont, 2016: 32). Age determination processes impact on the young person's access to services and supports, and in addition have been implicated in the assessment of credibility, which ultimately impacts on refugee determination (Opray, 2014; Kenny and Loughry, 2018). (See Chapters Three and Nine for discussion on age-assessment processes in England and the Nordic countries.)

Fourth, and finally, the legislative context in Australia in relation to asylum seekers provides some flexibility, but in some elements it is becoming increasingly rigid. This is highlighted by two legislative changes that impact directly on these young people. The current visa context for UAMs is they can be granted a bridging visa that allows them to reside in the community while their immigration status is being determined. Then they may apply for one of two kinds of visa: a Temporary Protection Visa, which is good for three years; or a Safe Haven Enterprise Visa, which requires the holder to move to a regional or rural area in Australia and is good for five years (DIBP, 2017). These visas have many restrictions and, most crucially, legislation passed in June 2014 prevents these visa holders from *ever* being eligible to apply for Permanent Protection Visas (Refugee Council of Australia (RCOA) 2017).

Additionally, in August 2012, the federal government passed legislation such that all asylum seekers who arrive by boat, regardless of visa status, are ineligible to sponsor their family under the Special Humanitarian Program. This directive applies to all asylum seekers who travelled to Australia after August 2012. Those who arrived before August 2012 and have been granted a permanent protection visa must apply to sponsor family members under other migration streams. These applications are more costly and are given the lowest priority (RCOA, 2017). Thus, most UAMs in Australia face long-term or permanent separation from family members and those who arrived after June 2014 are left in limbo being unable to apply for settlement in Australia.

These four factors – mandatory detention, lack of children's rights inscribed in Australia's constitution, guardianship under the Minister of Immigration, and a fluid and restrictive policy context – create a context in which UAMs living in Australia have little or no control over their futures and little opportunity to develop their skills, hopes and aspirations. These children are living in a range of community arrangements and on temporary visa arrangements that are unlikely to lead to permanent residency in Australia. Everyday life remains precarious and with few opportunities for building confident and viable futures.

Care and support arrangements for UAMs in Australia

This section briefly describes the care and support arrangements that have been in place for UAMs and their access to education, employment, health and family reunion. Although the Minister for Immigration is the legal guardian, practical guardianship is delegated and custodial and care arrangements for UAMs are not uniform across Australia. Financial and other assistance is funded by the federal government and is provided to UAMs who are living in the community through two schemes – the Asylum Seekers Assistance Scheme and Community Assistance Support Program (Phillips, 2015). Support services are delivered primarily through the NGO sector where organisations must engage in a tender-based process to win government contracts. The system through which the government has procured contracts for the provision of services sets up a climate of competition and is focused very much on performance indicators aligned with federal funding rather than the best interests of asylum-seeking minors. So, for example, funding agreements have clauses that stipulate the extent to which contracted organisations can advocate on behalf of their clients or be critical of governmental policy and practice (Westoby and Ingamells, 2009; Masocha and Robinson, 2016; Sampson, 2016). This is discussed in more detail in the section on advocacy and the international context later in this chapter.

The care and custodial arrangements for UAMs vary across Australia (MYAN, 2012). For those young people who are in community detention or on bridging visas they face a number of challenges and problems related to being cared for by approved carers. This process requires police clearance, and often the assessment results in not being approved. Programmes have been piloted to assist with transition for young people; for example, the Refugee Youth Support Pilot (MYAN, 2012) and the Youth Transition Support Project (Australian Government Department of Social Services, 2017) prepare them, when they turn 18, to move into the adult system, as their needs as children are no longer recognised. Young people may be moved from state to state and have limited access to financial support, housing, recreation and advocates who lobby on their behalf. Increasingly, NGOs and other volunteers, including families and community groups (both refugee communities as well as, for example, churches) provide supportive services and have been advocates for these young people.

UAMs living in the community have been entitled to a minimal weekly living allowance funded by the Department of Immigration and administered by the Red Cross. It was approximately A$227.00, which is 89% of the youth welfare allowance available to other same-aged economically-disadvantaged Australian youth and significantly below the poverty line (estimated a A$415.00 per week) (ASRC, 2017: 27). From this allowance, these youths are expected to cover their costs of food, clothing, transport, phone, rent and utilities. Their financial precariousness exposes them to poor quality and crowded housing and exploitation in the workforce.

As noted above, unaccompanied asylum-seeking children face particular stresses in being in Australia, facing separation from their family as a result of having left, or been sent from, their country for their own safety. Nardone and Correa-Velez (2015) highlight the many issues facing young people as they negotiate the complex journey to Australia, and how they navigate both looking back to family by sending remittances, and forward to their own settlement needs. Many struggle with the guilt of not being able to send money back to family still living in dangerous and poverty ridden conditions (Correa-Velez et al, 2017).

In general, UAMs who have been granted a Temporary Protection Visa or a Safe Haven Enterprise Visa move into the Unaccompanied Humanitarian Programme and are eligible for a range of support services including trauma counselling, healthcare, English language classes and work rights (depending on their age) (DIBP, 2017)

Key to young people establishing their identity, social development and future wellbeing is education provision (Wells, 2011; RCOA, 2015; Correa-Velez et al, 2017) and this includes attending a formal structured educational setting such as school or college. Research in the UK with children with disrupted or minimal school education highlights the challenges of being suddenly immersed in a new education system (Fazel et al, 2012). Racial discrimination and bullying, exacerbated by policies to accommodate asylum seekers in already impoverished and disadvantaged areas, are widespread. There is evidence to suggest similar experiences in Australia of this type of experience.

Although UAMs are able to continue their education, they are only able to go as far as secondary school. The charging of fees for students who are not permanent residents of Australia is set by individual states and territories and most have formally waived fees. Informally, however, as of September 2017, we understand that no primary or secondary schools have barred access to UAMs because of their inability to pay. Higher education in technical colleges and universities is another matter. Although the federal government does not prohibit UAMs from enrolling in higher education, they are treated as overseas students and must pay full international student fees. However, a number of universities have established special scholarships to assist this cohort of youth continue with their education (RCOA, 2017). Those who had been living in closed detention facilities should, in theory, have had access to education; in practice, their education is severely limited.

Work entitlements for UAMs are restricted and are linked to the type of temporary visa they have been issued. In particular, UAMs on bridging visas are not allowed to work unless they are able to demonstrate a 'compelling case to work'; for those on TPVs or SHEVs, while work is allowed it is very difficult to access. The upshot is that these youth are at risk of exploitation in the employment sector and are also at risk of making an income in the informal sector.

Australia's universal healthcare (called Medicare) covers UAMs who are able to access public hospitals and general practitioners and community health centres in the same way as other Australians. However, there are specific barriers for these youth in relation to their physical and mental health and wellbeing, and these include cultural differences regarding sexual and reproductive health, mental health and physical symptoms.

Australian research has highlighted the benefits for young people of a safe place for health and wellbeing (Sampson and Gifford, 2010; Denov and Akesson, 2013) and a study, based on different scales of belonging, identifies predictors of wellbeing after three years of settlement for young people (Correa-Velez et al, 2015). There is a large body of literature that explores the mental health and wellbeing of young people seeking asylum and settlement (Gifford et al, 2009; Coffey et al, 2010; Newman 2013; McFarlane et al, 2011; see also Chapter Five). Much of this has focused on trauma that young people have experienced due to systematic oppression, loss, displacement and exposure to violence. Many different factors affect the mental health of forcibly-displaced children and, increasingly, evidence shows that pre-migration exposure to violence is strongly predictive of psychological disturbance. While exposure to violence has been shown to be a key risk factor, stable settlement and social support in the host country have a positive effect on the child's psychological functioning. This also means taking a trauma-informed approach to practice when working with young people which balances an understanding of the complexity of trauma with the exposure to disadvantage and structural inequality present for many with refugee backgrounds (Allan and Hess, 2010; Quiros and Berger, 2015). The literature review by Bosworth (2016) examines the impact of immigration detention on mental health and highlights children as a specifically vulnerable group.

Data from the submissions to the Australian Human Rights Commission (2014) show children's descriptions of detention as crazy-making, depressing, boring, hopeless, awful, frightening and painful (2014: 152). Their reasons for leaving their country were described as fearing for their life, war, persecution by government, death of family members, torture, family violence, and for a better life in Australia (2014: 153). When children were asked whether their emotional and mental health had been affected since being in detention, every one of the 42 respondents answered yes (2014: 153). The emotional and mental health of unaccompanied children was described as always worrying, not sleeping well, agitation, going crazy, sadness, anxiety, nightmare and attempted suicide (2014: 154).

The leak of the 'Nauru files' to the *Guardian* newspaper (2016) highlighted the conditions inside Australia's immigration detention system experienced by those working with children in the years 2013–2015. The files comprise more than 2,000 incident reports from the Nauru detention centre, written by guards, caseworkers and teachers on the remote Pacific island. They record attempts at self-harm, sexual assaults, child abuse, hunger strikes, assaults and injuries. Some of these cases have been reported by the *Guardian* and other news organisations, and are also included in the AHRC report (2014); they highlight the extent of harm caused by prolonged detention in Australia's offshore detention centres.

The challenges for services working with UAMs

In Australia, advocacy on behalf of UAMs is both robust and dispersed in the community sector. Having effectively stopped new arrivals with offshore processing, and introducing a raft of policy changes, the current asylum-seeker service network is effectively being defunded and services withdrawn due to a reduced client load, and its role is increasingly under doubt. Despite this, unaccompanied children still need help and guidance if they are to navigate immigration and asylum processes. Deterrent measures should not be allowed to deny the vulnerability or to override the needs of the child. This is most particularly so where the child has been sent out alone in search of safe haven (Crock and Bensen, 2018: 7).

There are specific issues pertinent to Australia that differ from other parts of the world. The role of those working with asylum seekers has been significantly curtailed with the introduction of specific legislation introduced in the Australian Border Force Act (2015). This affects all those staff including healthcare professionals and in child support working offshore in detention centres. The Australian Border Force Act (2015) states in Part 6 (Secrecy and disclosure provisions) that a person commits an offence if the person makes a record of, or discloses, Immigration and Border Protection information (2015: 37). Health professionals and social workers have argued that working in Australia's immigration detention centres risks condoning torture (Briskman et al, 2012; Isaacs, 2017). While the recent reports and leaks highlighted throughout this chapter illustrate the damage done to children in detention, there has been a reluctance by the Australian government to act on it.

Australia's treatment of UAMs within the international context of human rights and the rights of the child

Australia's reception and treatment of asylum seekers who arrive by boat, including unaccompanied minors, is in violation of a range of international human rights laws and treaties to which it is a signatory. Australia continues to be criticised for failing to uphold both its formal and informal obligations in relation to the rights and care of UAMs. The detention of children is in direct violation of international human rights law and contravention of the UN Convention of the Rights of the Child, to which Australia is a signatory. In particular the Convention prioritises the care, development, wellbeing of children and states, 'recognition of the inherent dignity and of the equal and inalienable rights of all members of the human family is the foundation of freedom, justice and peace in the world' (UNCRC, 1989: 1).

One could argue that this is consistent with the international research on unaccompanied minors, particularly in Europe, which has focused on the context of their care in countries of the Global North (Crawley, 2007, 2010; Watters, 2008; Chase, 2013; Bloch et al, 2014; Crock and Danisi, 2018) and on discussion of best practice in policy and care provision (Hayes, 2004; Kohli and Mitchell, 2007; Bianchini, 2011; Wright, 2012; Robinson and Williams, 2015). Much of this work is from the UK and EU where significant arrivals of refugees and asylum seekers have dominated political and social policy, as this book illustrates.

The international research evidence shows how young people are often represented in ways that highlight a stigmatised identity rather than as bearers of rights as people (Crawley, 2007; Chase, 2013; Schuster and Majidi, 2015; Mikola and Mansouri, 2015). In addition, the threat of detention, homelessness and destitution is imminent and real (Kohli, 2011; Gladwell and Elwyn, 2012; Bloch et al, 2014; Flatau et al, 2014). Internationally, children often fall between two conflicting areas of law of child protection and migration: 'In general, migration law is adult-centred, and child welfare law privileges citizens, with the result that unaccompanied and separated children tend to fall through a series of significant cracks' (Bhabha and Crock, 2007: 61).

Australia has created conditions where there is little hope for UAMs who are living on temporary protection visas. In this sense their situation echoes the conclusions of Hilde Lidén in Chapter Nine, that these young people are living in conditions described by Hannah Arendt as 'not the loss of specific rights, then, but the loss of a community willing and able to guarantee any rights whatsoever', which is the most damaging outcome of statelessness (Arendt, 1968: 297).

Furthermore, these young people are under strict surveillance and because Australia is an island continent, unlike other UAMs in Europe, they have no way of disappearing into the informal economy or of moving on. This is fundamentally different to young people in the UK and elsewhere in Europe who can leave via clandestine methods and re-enter the country, go underground and draw on networks across the region. Despite the fact that Australia is a signatory to a range of human rights declarations protecting the rights of the children, UAMs continue to live without this overarching protection for planning their futures.

The UNCRC defines children as all human beings under the age of 18, unless countries have legislation that specifies otherwise. There has been considerable concern identified by academics and advocates working with young people about the care of unaccompanied minors seeking asylum in Australia (Miller et al, 2013; Newman, 2013; Crock and Bensen, 2018). As other chapters in this book highlight, significant international work has been conducted in this area of refugee children migrating alone (Bhabha and Crock, 2007; Kohli and Mitchell, 2007; Chase and Allsopp, 2013; Crea et al, 2018). While there have been policy changes to move children out of closed detention and into the community we would argue this still has long-term negative ramifications.

Unaccompanied minors who have arrived by boat in Australia as asylum seekers continue to have limited opportunity to work or participate in education beyond secondary school, and most will likely never be granted permanent residency. Thus, these young people are, in every sense of the word, stuck – in time and in place. It is this situation that has made Australia different to all other western countries when it comes to the care and treatment of UAMs.

Conclusions and reflections on the future for UAMs in Australia

Despite these constraints and challenges, we see opportunities for resistance and a positive future. An emerging field of research in the UK and EU recommends a cultural approach in line with Elaine Chase's (2013) findings and the 'Life projects' approach, discussed by Matthews (2014), which promotes the stability and future contribution of young people. This approach, connected to Article 3 of the UNCRC and developed by the Council of Europe, aims to promote the best interest of the child and the future prospects of all concerned with their welfare and protection. In Australia the recommendations made by Mansouri and Skrbis (2013; and Nelson et al, 2017) can contribute to the broadening out of reforms to all young people who stand to gain from intercultural practices (UNESCO, 2013).

As researchers, we have found accessing specific data and information about these young unaccompanied minors difficult, and this is compounded by rapidly-changing circumstances in politics and policy. Surprisingly little research has investigated the experiences of UAMs in Australia. A recent qualitative study conducted with unaccompanied minors revealed that many of these youth, especially those from Afghanistan, had a very clear goal of Australia as their destination country (Correa-Velez et al, 2017). Most did not have family currently living in Australia, but rather chose Australia because they deemed it to be a safe place where they would be able to get a job and sponsor their families to join them (Nardone and Correa-Velez, 2015). These youth have been resourceful in making the long and challenging journey to Australia and they bring with them a deep sense of responsibility to be able to provide financially for family left behind. Research carried out with young refugees settled in Australia through the (offshore) Humanitarian Resettlement Program highlights the importance young people place on the opportunities afforded by Australia especially in relation to education and employment, making something of themselves by working towards a positive future (Centre for Multicultural Youth, 2013; Nunn et al, 2014). However, many of these opportunities are denied to UAMs within the current policy context of deterrence.

Returning to the beginning of this chapter, policies of deterrence continue to dominate politics and to impact negatively on asylum seekers who have arrived by boat in Australia. Despite the local, national and international condemnation of Australia's policies, these policies are not likely to change in the near future (Phillips, 2017c; Issacs, 2017). In an ideal world, the best interest of the child would guide policy and practice. The Australian government has consistently evaded international human rights laws and conventions in spite of numerous academic studies and national and international inquiries. Within this context, we conclude by arguing for four key areas of change impacting on the current situation of unaccompanied asylum seeker youth living in Australia .

First, all people in the asylum legacy should be granted an amnesty and offered permanent settlement in Australia. In arguing for an amnesty we recognise that these young people have done nothing wrong – but they require permanent protection and the right to settle in Australia. Second, these young people should be supported in their education and treated as domestic students in pursuing higher education. Third, they should have full work rights and entitlements. Finally, they should be granted the right to sponsor family members for reunion in Australia under the humanitarian migration scheme. These four changes would go a long way to improving the life chances of young people who sought asylum in Australian and now find themselves stuck in a limbo with no end in sight.

We consider that Australia has a moral, ethical and practical responsibility to these young people who have their futures ahead of them. It is time for Australia to open opportunities for these resourceful youth so that they can harness their talents and reach their full human potential.

Acknowledgements

We would like to thank our colleagues for providing a close read of a draft of this chapter. In writing this chapter we note the political sensitivity around these issues. Several of our colleagues who provided input asked not to be named in the acknowledgements.

Notes

1. Visa categories (adapted from RCOA, 2018, and MYAN Guidance on UAMs):
   - Bridging Visa (subclass E): These visas allow people to live in the community pending resolution of their protection claims. Most asylum seekers living in the community on Bridging Visas have access to Australia's universal healthcare system, Medicare, and receive a basic living allowance equivalent to the 89% of Centrelink Special Benefit.
   - Temporary Protection Visas (TPVs): These were reintroduced on 5 December 2014 for all people found to be owed protection but who arrived in Australia without a prior valid visa (by sea or by air). TPVs allow a refugee to stay in Australia for a maximum of three years, after which time their protection claims are reassessed.
   - Safe Haven Enterprise Visas (SHEVs): This temporary visa is similar to the TPV but is issued for a period of five years. A refugee living on a SHEV will need to indicate an intention to work and/or study in a designated regional or rural area. If SHEV holders undertake study or work without accessing income support for at least three and a half years, they will be able to apply for another type of temporary or permanent visa (such as a skilled or family visa but not a permanent protection visa).

References

Allan, J. and Hess, L. (2010) 'The nexus between material circumstances, cultural context and experiences of loss, grief and trauma: complexities in working with refugees in the early phases of settlement', *Grief Matters: The Australian Journal of Grief and Bereavement*, 13(3): 76–80.

Amnesty International (2013) *Australia: This is breaking people: Human rights violations at Australia's asylum seeker processing centre on Manus Island, Papua New Guinea*, London: Amnesty International, www.amnesty.org/en/library/info/ASA12/002/2013/en

Amnesty International (2014) *Australia: This is still breaking people: Update on human rights violations at Australia's asylum seeker processing centre on Manus Island, Papua New Guinea*, www.amnesty.org/en/documents/asa12/002/2014/en/

Arendt, H. (1968) *The origins of totalitarianism*, San Diego, CA: Harcourt, Inc.

Asylum Seeker Resource Centre (ASRC) (2017) *Myths facts and solutions*, www.asrc.org.au/wp-content/uploads/2013/07/MythBusterJuly2013FINAL.pdf

Australian Border Force Act (2015) www.legislation.gov.au/Details/C2017C00354

Australian Government Department of Social Services (2017) 'Youth Transition Support Services', www.dss.gov.au/settlement-services/programs-policy/settlement-services/youth-transition-support-services

Australian Human Rights Commission (AHRC) (2014) *The forgotten children: National inquiry into children in immigration detention*, www.humanrights.gov.au/our-work/asylum-seekers-and-refugees/national-inquiry-children-immigration-detention-2014

Bhabha, J. and Crock, M. (2007) *Seeking asylum alone: Unaccompanied and separated children and refugee protection in Australia, the UK and the US*, Sydney: Themis Press.

Bianchini, K., (2011) 'Legal aid for asylum seekers: progress and challenges in Italy', *Journal of Refugee Studies*, 24(2): 390–410.

Bloch, A. Sigona, N. and Zetter, R. (2014) *Sans papiers: The social and economic lives of young undocumented migrants*, London: Pluto.

Bosworth, M. (2016) *Mental health in immigration detention: A literature review. Review into the welfare in detention of vulnerable persons*, Cm 9186. London: HMSO; Criminal Justice, Borders and Citizenship Research Paper No. 2732892, https://ssrn.com/abstract=2732892

Briskman, L., Zion, D. and Loff, B. (2012) 'Collusion or care in asylum seeker detention', *Ethics and Social Welfare*, 6(1): 37–55.

Centre for Multicultural Youth (2013) *Settling or Surviving? Unaccompanied young adults aged 18–25. A CMY policy paper*, Melbourne: Centre for Multicultural Youth, www.cmy.net.au/sites/default/files/publication-documents/Settling%20or%20Surviving%202013.pdf

Chase, E. (2013) 'Security and subjective wellbeing: The experiences of unaccompanied young people seeking asylum in the UK', *Sociology of Health & Illness*, 35(6): 858–72.

Chase, E. and Allsopp, J. (2013) *Future citizens of the world? The contested futures of independent young migrants in Europe*, Oxford: Refugee Studies Centre, Oxford Department of International Development.

Coffey, G.J., Kaplan, I., Sampson, R.C. and Tucci, M.M. (2010) 'The meaning and mental health consequences of long-term immigration detention for people seeking asylum', *Social Science and Medicine*, 70(12): 2070–9.

Corbett, E.J., Gunasekera, H., Maycock, A. and Isaacs, D. (2015) 'Australia's treatment of refugee and asylum seeker children: The views of Australian paediatricians', *Journal of Paediatrics and Child Health*, 51: 5.

Correa-Velez, I., Gifford, S.M. and McMichael, C. (2015) 'The persistence of predictors of wellbeing among refugee youth eight years after resettlement in Melbourne, Australia', *Social Science & Medicine*, 142: 163–8.

Correa-Velez, I., Nardone, M. and Knoetze, K. (2017) 'Leaving family behind: Understanding the irregular migration of unaccompanied asylum-seeking minors', in M. McAuliffe and K. Koser (eds) *A long way to go: Irregular migration patterns, processes, drivers and decision-making*, ANU Press, pp 141–65.

Correa-Velez, I., Gifford, S.M., McMichael, C. and Sampson, R. (2017) 'Predictors of secondary school completion among refugee youth 8 to 9 years after resettlement in Melbourne, Australia', *Journal of International Migration and Integration*, 18(3): 791–805.

Crawley, H. (2007) *When Is a Child Not a Child?* London: Immigration Law Practitioners Association.

Crawley, H. (2010) *Chance or Choice. Understanding why asylum seekers come to the UK*, London: Swansea University and Refugee Council, www.refugeecouncil.org.uk/assets/0001/5702/rcchance.pdf

Crea, T.M., Roth, B.J., Jani, J. and Grace, B. (2018) 'Unaccompanied immigrant children: Interdisciplinary perspectives on needs and responses: Introduction to special issue of *Children & Youth Services Review*', *Children & Youth Services Review*, https://doi.org/10.1016/j.childyouth.2018.05.018

Crock, M. (2006) *Seeking asylum alone: A study of Australian law, policy and practice regarding unaccompanied and separated children*, Sydney: Themis Press, http://idcoalition.org/wp-content/uploads/2009/06/ssa-australia.pdf

Crock, M. and Martin, H. (2015) 'Finding refuge in Australia: How law and policies affect the entitlements of children entering as refugees and humanitarian migrants', in M. Crock (ed) *Creating New Futures: Settling children and youth from refugee backgrounds*, Sydney: Federation Press, pp. 49–69.

Crock, M. and Benson, L.B. (2018) 'Central issues in the protection of child migrants', in M. Crock and L.B. Benson (eds) *Protecting Migrant Children*, Cheltenham: Edward Elgar Publishing, https://doi.org/10.4337/9781786430267

Crock, M. and Danisi, C. (2018) 'Immigration control and the best interests of the child in Europe', in M. Crock and L.B. Benson (eds) *Protecting Migrant Children*, Cheltenham: Edward Elgar Publishing, https://doi.org/10.4337/9781786430267

Denov, M. and Akesson, B. (2013) 'Neither here nor there? Place and placemaking in the lives of separated children', *International Journal of Migration, Health and Social Care*, 9(2): 56–70.

Department of Immigration and Border Protection (DIBP) (2017) *Immigration Detention and Community Statistics Summary*, www.homeaffairs.gov.au/ReportsandPublications/Documents/statistics/Immigration-detention-statistics-30-september-2017.pdf

DIBP (2018) 'Unaccompanied Humanitarian Minors programme', www.homeaffairs.gov.au/about/corporate/information/fact-sheets/uhm-programme

Essex, R. (2015) 'Ethics, foreseeability, and tragedy in Australian immigration detention', *Journal of Bioethical Inquiry*, 12: 537–9

Evenhuis, M. (2013) 'Child-proofing asylum: Separated children and refugee decision making in Australia', *International Journal of Refugee Law*, 25(3): 538.

Fazel, M., Reed, R.V., Panter-Brick, C. and Stein A. (2012) 'Mental health of displaced and refugee children resettled in high-income countries: risk and protective factors', *Lancet*, 79(9812): 266–82.

Federal Register of Legislation (2014) Immigration (Guardianship of Children) Act 1946 No 45 (1946), www.legislation.gov.au/Details/C2015C00008

Flatau, P., Colic-Peisker, V., Bauskis, A., Maginn, P. and Buergelt, P. (2014) *Refugees, housing, and neighbourhoods in Australia*, AHURI Final Report No.224, Melbourne: Australian Housing and Urban Research Institute, www.ahuri.edu.au/__data/assets/pdf_file/0015/2058/AHURI_Final_Report_No224_Refugees,-housing,-and-neighbourhoods-in-Australia.pdf

Gifford, S., Correa-Velez, I. and Sampson, R. (2009) *Good Starts for recently arrived youth with refugee backgrounds. Promoting wellbeing in the first three years of settlement in Melbourne, Australia*, Melbourne: La Trobe Refugee Research Centre.

Gladwell, C. and Elwyn, H. (2012) *Broken futures: Young Afghan asylum seekers in the UK and in their country of origin*, Research Paper No. 246 Geneva: UNHCR Policy Development and Evaluation Service, www.unhcr.org/5098d2679.html

Guardian (2016) 'The Nauru Files', 10 August, www.theguardian.com/australia-news/ng-interactive/2016/aug/10/the-nauru-files-the-lives-of-asylum-seekers-in-detention-detailed-in-a-unique-database-interactive

Hayes, D. (2004) 'History and context: The impact of immigration control on welfare delivery', in D. Hayes and B. Humphries (eds) *Social work, immigration and asylum: Debates, dilemmas and ethical issues for social work and social care practice*, London: Jessica Kingsley

Houston, A., Aristotle, P. and L'Estrange, M. (2012) *Report of the Expert Panel on Asylum Seekers*, http://artsonline.monash.edu.au/thebordercrossingobservatory/files/2015/03/expert_panel_on_asylum_seekers_full_report.pdf

Human Rights and Equal Opportunity Commission (HREOC) (2004) *A last resort? National inquiry into children in immigration detention*, www.humanrights.gov.au/sites/default/files/document/publication/alr_complete.pdf

Hurley, M. and Beaumont, E. (2016) 'Reforming Australia's age determination procedures: Giving asylum seekers the benefit of the doubt', *Alternative Law Journal*, 41(1): 30–3.

Isaacs, M. (2017) *The Undesirables: Inside Nauru*, Hardie Grant Publishing.

Jureidini, J. and Burnside, J. (2011) 'Children in immigration detention: a case of reckless mistreatment', *Australian and New Zealand Journal of Public Health*, 35(4): 304–6.

Kaldor Centre for Refugee International Law (2015) *Factsheet: Immigration Detention*. 21 October, www.kaldorcentre.unsw.edu.au/publication/immigration-detention

Kenny, M.A. and Loughry, M. (2018) 'Addressing the limitations of age determination for unaccompanied minors: A way forward', *Children and Youth Services Review*, DOI: 10.1016/j.childyouth.2018.05.002

Kohli, R.K. and Mitchell, F. (eds) (2007) *Working with unaccompanied asylum seeking children: Issues for policy and practice*, Basingstoke: Palgrave Macmillan.

Kohli, R.K.S. (2011) 'Working to ensure safety, belonging and success for unaccompanied asylum-seeking children', *Child Abuse Review*, 20: 311–23.

McFarlane, C.A., Kaplan, I. and Lawrence, J.A. (2011) 'Psychosocial indicators of wellbeing for resettled refugee children and youth: Conceptual and developmental directions', *Child Indicators Research*, 4(4): 647–77.

Mansouri, F. and Skrbis, Z. (2013) *Active citizenship among migrant youth in Australia*, An Australian Research Council Linkage Project, Centre for Multicultural Youth.

Mares, S. (2016) 'Fifteen years of detaining children who seek asylum in Australia – evidence and consequences', *Australasian Psychiatry*, 24(1): 11–14.

Masocha, S. and Robinson, K. (2016) 'Divergent practices in statutory and voluntary sector settings? Social work with asylum seekers', *British Journal of Social Work*, 47(5): 1–17.

Matthews, A. (2014) *"What's going to happen tomorrow?" Unaccompanied children refused asylum*, London: Office of the Children's Commissioner.

Mikola, M. and Mansouri, F. (2015) 'Race lines and spaces of political action among migrant youth', *Journal of Youth Studies*, 18(4): 500–14.

Miller, K., Irizarry, C. and Bowden, M. (2013) 'Providing culturally safe care in the best interests of unaccompanied humanitarian minors', *Journal of Family Studies*, 19(3): 276–84.

Multicultural Youth Advocacy Network (MYAN) (Australia) (2012) *Unaccompanied Humanitarian Minors in Australia: an overview of national support arrangements and emerging issues*, www.myan.org.au/file/file/MYAN%20UHM%20Policy%20Paper%20Sept%202012.pdf

MYAN (2017) *Information Sheet: Humanitarian and Migrant Youth Arrivals to Australia July 2015–2016.*

Nardone, M. and Correa-Velez, I. (2015) 'Unpredictability, invisibility and vulnerability: Unaccompanied asylum-seeking minors' journeys to Australia', *Journal of Refugee Studies*, 29(3): 295–314.

Nelson, D., Price, E. and Zubrzycki, J. (2017) 'Critical social work with unaccompanied asylum-seeking young people: Restoring hope, agency and meaning for the client and worker', *International Social Work*, 60(3): 601–13.

Newman, L. (2013) 'Seeking asylum – Trauma, mental health and human rights: An Australian perspective', *Journal of Trauma & Dissociation*, 14(2): 218.

Nunn, C., McMichael, C., Gifford, S.M. and Correa-Velez, I. (2014) '"I came to this country for a better life": factors mediating employment trajectories among young people who migrated to Australia as refugees during adolescence', *Journal of Youth Studies*, 17(9): 1205–20.

Opray, M. (2014) 'How Immigration decides asylum seekers' age', *The Saturday Paper*, 6 September, www.thesaturdaypaper.com.au/news/politics/2014/09/06/how-immigration-decides-asylum-seekers-age/1409925600

Phillips, J. (2015) 'Asylum seekers and refugees: what are the facts?' Parliament of Australia, 2 March, www.aph.gov.au/About_Parliament/Parliamentary_Departments/Parliamentary_Library/pubs/rp/rp1415/AsylumFacts

Phillips, J. (2017a) 'Immigration detention in Australia: a quick guide to the statistics', Parliament of Australia, 21 March, www.aph.gov.au/About_Parliament/Parliamentary_Departments/Parliamentary_Library/pubs/rp/rp1617/Quick_Guides/ImmigrationDetention

Phillips, J. (2017b) 'Boat turnbacks in Australia: A guide to the statistics since 1976', Parliament of Australia, 17 January, www.aph.gov.au/About_Parliament/Parliamentary_Departments/Parliamentary_Library/pubs/rp/rp1617/Quick_Guides/BoatTurnbacks

Phillips, J. (2017c) 'A comparison of Coalition and Labor government asylum policies in Australia since 2001', 2 February, www.aph.gov.au/About_Parliament/Parliamentary_Departments/Parliamentary_Library/pubs/rp/rp1617/AsylumPolicies

Quiros, L. and Berger, R. (2015) 'Responding to the sociopolitical complexity of trauma: an integration of theory and practice', *Journal of Loss and Trauma: International Perspectives on Stress and Coping*, 20(2): 149–59.

Refugee Council of Australia (RCOA) (2015) *Barriers to education for people seeking asylum and refugees on temporary visas*, www.refugeecouncil.org.au/wp-content/uploads/2014/08/1512-Education.pdf

RCOA (2017) 'Recent Changes in Australian Refugee Policy', updated 8 June, www.refugeecouncil.org.au/publications/recent-changes-australian-refugee-policy/

RCOA (2018) 'Get the facts', www.refugeecouncil.org.au/get-facts/

Robinson K. and Williams, L. (2015) 'Leaving care: Unaccompanied asylum seeking young Afghans facing return, *Refuge*, 31(2): 85–94.

Sampson, R. (2016) 'Caring, contributing, capacity building: Navigating contradictory narratives of refugee settlement in Australia', *Journal of Refugee Studies*, 29(1): 98–116.

Sampson, R. and Gifford, S.M. (2010) 'Place-making, settlement and well-being: The therapeutic landscapes of recently arrived youth with refugee backgrounds', *Health and Place*, 16: 116–31.

Schuster, L. and Majidi, N. (2015) 'Deportation stigma and re-migration', *Journal of Ethnic and Migration Studies*, 41(4): 635–52.

United Nations High Commissioner for Refugees (UNHCR) (2017) Global Trends Forced Displacement in 2016, www.unhcr.org/5943e8a34

United Nations Human Rights: Office of the High Commissioner (1989) Convention on the Rights of the Child (CRC), www.ohchr.org/en/professionalinterest/pages/crc.aspx

UNESCO (2013) *Intercultural competences. Conceptual and operational framework*, Paris: UNESCO.

Watters, C. (2008) *Refugee children: Towards the next horizon*, London: Routledge.

Wells, K. (2011) 'The strength of weak ties: the social networks of young separated asylum seekers and refugees in London', *Children's Geographies*, 9(3–4): 319–29.

Westoby, P. and Ingamells, A. (2009) 'A critically informed perspective of working with resettling refugee groups in Australia', *British Journal of Social Work*, 40(6): 1759–76.

Wright, F. (2012) 'Social work practice with unaccompanied asylum-seeking young people facing removal', *British Journal of Social Work*, 44(4): 1027–44.

Zwi, K. and Mares, S. (2015) 'Stories from unaccompanied children in immigration detention: A composite account', *Journal of Paediatrics and Child Health*, 51(7): 658–62.

Conclusion

Sue Clayton, Anna Gupta and Katie Willis

In this collection we have presented research across various themes – the politics of borders; the law; social care; mental health; media and representation – to try and better understand the circumstances of unaccompanied asylum-seeking children as they enter, and progress through, what ought to be a system of care and protection.

The work in this collection has had two key driving factors: first, its interdisciplinary approach; and second, its focus on social justice and human rights. In terms of its interdisciplinarity, this collection builds on the 'Uncertain Journeys: Exploring the challenges facing separated children seeking asylum' seminar series that the co-editors ran in 2013–16. The Uncertain Journeys[1] events allowed for a wealth of interaction between those who, though working on very similar issues (such as legal protection; social care; psychotherapy), had not necessarily encountered the research findings of each other's specialised fields.

Some examples of cross-disciplinary insights have been for instance:

- The problematising in Chapter One of the notion of 'border' as a singular, fixed entity, and exploring its many and often conflicting iterations – border as defined by geographical feature, by nation states, by international treaty – enhances subsequent discussions of legal issues (Chapter Two) and the international case studies (Section 3). A range of actors, including unaccompanied young migrants themselves, are involved in both recreating and challenging borders through their actions. Thus the work of legal professionals, social workers, psychotherapists, media reporters and NGO volunteers is implicated in working with and reinforcing existing borders, or seeking to transform or remove them (see Crawley and Skleparis, 2018, on migrant categorisations).
- Work around identity and belonging, by Sue Clayton (Chapter Four) and Gillian Hughes (Chapter Five) has been helpful to those working in social care.
- Issues discussed by Gillian Hughes, and by Lousie Drammeh (Chapter Six), inflect questions to do with young people's behaviour in the courts and giving evidence.

- Insights about the complexities of age assessments (Anna Gupta, Chapter Three), and the ethical and professional dilemmas that conducting these imposes on social workers, have been brought to the attention of the legal and policy making sector.
- The book creates a better understanding of the UK system within the wider perspective of other state regimes; as described in Chapters Eight, Nine and Ten, and of a rapidly-changing world order, as we discuss in Chapter One.

The different disciplinary and professional perspectives raise many similar themes surrounding the experiences of unaccompanied young migrants; tensions between child welfare and immigration law, and the challenging contexts for practice in the UK and other countries are two salient ones. We hope that the reader will find and make their own connections in this collection, and see that assembled here this is not just an exposition about child refugees but also a wealth of information and views on how we as a civil society respond to such young people, and what that response says about our society and ourselves. We thank not just the chapter contributors but all who took part in the conference and seminars for their commitment to the honest and sometimes very challenging debates that took place, which helped to form these chapters.

We have attempted to do this from a social justice and human rights perspective. Returning to the work of Nancy Fraser (2005), which we discussed in the Introduction, she argues that social justice crucially refers to 'parity of participation', since 'justice requires social arrangements that permit all to participate as peers in social life' (p 73). Fraser's social justice framework explicitly includes three crucially interlinked dimensions of social injustice that can impede this parity: maldistribution (economic injustice); misrecognition (cultural injustice); and misrepresentation (political injustice). As part of this latter dimension, she identifies 'misframing' as arising in situations where 'polity's boundaries are drawn in such a way as to wrongly deny some people the chance to participate at all in its authorized contests over justice' (Fraser, 2008: 408). The experiences of the young unaccompanied people relayed directly to some of the authors and indirectly through the research projects discussed include examples of material inequality, particularly once 18 and support services are severely reduced or on occasions withdrawn completely. Young people's lives are framed by intersecting power relationships and complex, multiple identities. The voices of young migrants, included in this collection, spoke about stigmatisation because of their immigration status, and a 'culture of disbelief' from professionals; some also spoke about racism and discrimination on the basis of their religion. Fraser's third dimension is particularly relevant to this group of young people, some of whom in the words of Arendt (1966, quoted in Chapter Seven) would appear to have no or very limited right to have rights, as Sue Clayton's work in Calais (see Chapter One) so vividly portrays.

While it is important to recognise structural inequalities and the damaging impact these have on individuals and communities, a theme of this collection is also the importance of harnessing the power and agency of young people and workers despite these constraints. Although discussing social work with families living in poverty, Krumer-Nevo's (2009: 318) words ring true for all work with unaccompanied young migrants:

> [We need] research and practise grounded in an equilibrium of structure and agency, that tell the stories of men and women, youth and adults who live in poverty as tales of pain on the one hand and of struggle and power, on the other, as tales of structure – limiting and damaging – on the one hand, and of subjectivity and agency – rich and human – on the other.

Most social workers and other practitioners work with individual young people, and in this book we have discussed the challenging contexts for practice, particularly the predominance of the immigration agenda and implications of budgetary cuts under the 'austerity' agenda in the UK. However, we have also explored possibilities for practice that promote the individual young person's rights and wellbeing. This engagement in affirmative strategies (Fraser, 1995) includes critical reflection on own and others' values, assumptions and 'othering' practices; creating spaces in teams and organisations for ethical dialogue about provision of services within a human rights and social justice framework. The importance of positive relationships, a sense of belonging and being cared about was highlighted throughout the book, and workers have a role in developing these relationships with young people themselves (as discussed in Chapters Three, Five and Six); facilitating the young person's development of these with other professionals and community organisations (for example, good legal representation); and within their peer networks, as described in Chapters Five and Six. Transformative strategies that aim to make private troubles public issues (Mills, 1959), to work alongside young people and other like-minded practitioners to challenge unequal power relationships and the underlying framework of the social order are also important for those working with unaccompanied migrant youth to embrace. We discuss strategies further below.

What emerges from our collective study, is a clear sense of the following.

Overall, it is apparent that since the current 'refugee crisis', with its heavily-increased number of arrivals dating from 2015, the UK is accepting substantially fewer unaccompanied children than many other European countries. As Clayton and Willis discuss in Chapter One, both the Dubs Amendment (Section 67c of the 2016 Immigration Act) and the EU Dublin III regulation, allowed for the provision of some of the almost 90,000 unaccompanied minors who have claimed asylum in Europe to gain legal protection in the UK. As of July 2018, however, funded places made available by local authorities have not been taken up, owing to the government having repeatedly changed, and ultimately obscured, the grounds of what they consider a Dubs eligible child, and the process of application. As we note in Chapter One, two of the three legal challenges brought against the Home Office for their implementation of the amendment have resulted in clear disapprobation by the courts, and all those minors who were refused, now have the opportunity to appeal. However as demonstrated in *Calais Children: A Case to Answer* (2017), lives have been lost and these minors have in the meantime suffered hunger, homelessness, tear-gassing, trafficking, abuse, injury and death as a result of failure to address their claims correctly. However, we need to look beyond these specific pieces of legislation which themselves are circumstantial (Dublin III is subject to the UK's membership of the EU, and the Dubs Amendment was initially framed as an emergency measure). The Home Secretary has in fact a large degree of discretion in asylum cases and this could be more transparently debated and applied. There is also much to debate on country guidance (see Chapters Two and Seven). Immigration staff are required to rely on Home Office commissioned 'country guidance' documents which, it has been argued, are in many cases partial, frequently out of date and, as has been found about Eritrea, simply wrong. For lawmakers, the judiciary, the public and above all the appellants to have confidence in a system based on country conditions, it is vital that information is current and wide-ranging.

National and international conventions are not being applied as they should. There will inevitably be national and regional differences in the treatment of this cohort, but information on such variations needs to be more available, and there needs to be more collaboration between state and NGO actors to ensure consistency of treatment. Otherwise, as our Calais case study in Chapter One illustrates, young people can end up in perpetual limbo, caught between conflicting states and policies.

In the UK the legal framework in which social workers and others must operate continues to demonstrate a fundamental conflict between the demands of immigration law and the requirements of child welfare law, such as the Children Act 1989 in England and Wales. Some ground has been conceded in the Immigration Appeal courts, in terms of recognising the continuing care needs of refugee children after 18. For instance, the judgment in the case *KA (Afghanistan) & Ors v Secretary of State for the Home Department* (Refworld, 2012) states 'there is no temporal bright line across which the risks to and the needs of the child suddenly disappear'. But the care and future options available to UASC and former UASC are very different from those available to UK young people in care, with the situation becoming even harsher following the full implementation of the Immigration Act of 2016. As discussed in Chapter Three, the severe budgetary constraints imposed on local authorities in recent years impacts on social worker responses and services offered to unaccompanied asylum-seeking young people, with them often being regarded as 'less deserving' than other young people in or leaving care. As Lou Drammeh's chapter highlights, good foster care can offer children a sense of belonging, care and advocacy lacking in other options, and needs to be offered to young people on the basis of their needs not arbitrarily on the basis of age (see Chapter Three). However, foster carers also require good quality social work support to understand and respond to young people's needs sensitively. Budgetary restrictions have meant that many social work teams expert in supporting these families either no longer exist or are under threat. It is vital that such services are restored.

One of the main issues in the care sector has been around the contentious issue of age assessment. As Anna Gupta (Chapter Three) explains, the ultimate responsibility for the assessment of a child's age currently rests with social workers whose primary concern is care and support of the child. They know that age is not a matter of simply data recording – an assessment of a young person's age can be the difference between them staying in the UK or leaving; being given foster care or not; getting educational opportunities or going without. Yet social workers are faced with organisational and Home Office pressures to utilise methods of assessment (for instance, medical x-rays as well as DNA testing for proof of kinship) that go against human rights recommendations and medical advice on the impossibility of accurate age testing. A 'culture of disbelief' has been noted to be pervasive in local authority cultures. We argue that the age assessment policy needs to be reviewed to make it a more multi-disciplinary, multi-agency holistic flexible process.

With regard to the issue of durable solutions and longer-term futures, the UK policy operates a policy of opacity with regard to final outcomes for the young people. First, it would be better to address their asylum claim more systematically on arrival and not wait until the age of 18 (Bhabha and Finch, 2006). Second, the state records and releases very little information: it does not keep records of how many former UASC are removed at 18, whether voluntary or forced; has no evidence that those returned at 18 are indeed safe; and does not allow NGOs or others access to information that would allow them to conduct their own monitoring. This means that social workers, educators, mental health professionals and others are kept continually in the dark about what outcomes they may be preparing the young people for.

With regards witnessing, and self-representation, many of the challenges discussed in this collection are aggravated by all parties being forced into interview and assessment systems that are not child-focused. Mario Bruzzone and Luis Enrique González-Araiza highlight this issue in relation to US immigration officials in Chapter Eight. Some European counties have done more to address the need for child-focused processes in their legal frameworks, and their practices of care (see Hilde Lidén's chapter on the Nordic countries, Chapter Nine). It is established by all parties (Bhabha and Finch, 2006) that children have many reasons to report their stories incorrectly on arrival, including being at the behest of traffickers or smugglers, and believing they must protect other family members back home. The children are then in a double-bind, as every statement they make subsequent to arrival is measured by the authorities against their first account, in a way that is arguably more harsh than what should be applied to minors, especially those who have suffered trauma and abuse and lack of care. Also, as Clayton describes in Chapter Four, the notion of 'credibility' is applied to this cohort in a way that goes beyond their immediate circumstances – the courts consider that an unaccompanied child who has lied about one thing cannot be trusted to tell the truth on others. This should prompt us to aim for a more holistic and nuanced view of the child's narrative, one which, as Hughes argues in Chapter Five, should also not individuate the children, but seek to understand their case in the wider context of their family, beliefs, social relations and other circumstances that help us more fully understand their status and identity. In other words, we need to listen to the stories and the needs – and as Chase and Allsopp (2013) argue, the aspirations – of the young people themselves. Work to date in the field of the migrant child has focused very much on origins, journeys and arrival. We have tried here to make signposts to current and ongoing dialogues as well as cooperations and longer-term solutions for the future.

We note with concern that, as described in Chapter Eight, US governmental policies on the border with Mexico have become increasingly harsh for unaccompanied minors as the national security agenda overwhelms that of caring for vulnerable individuals and groups. Additionally, as Bruzzone and González-Araiza highlight at the end of their chapter, these policies are causing children to be separated from their families at the border. It is estimated that many may never be reunited, as they are separated by complex and non-responsive institutional regimes. This situation has at the time of writing (July 2018) attracted wide international media concern. However, as noted by many, the highly-publicised US regime is paralleled, albeit with less fanfare, in Europe, where the UK's 'hostile environment' policies embraced by the UK government since 2013 have resulted in the punishing of those without papers; delaying reunification of UASC with family members; and over-officiously age-disputing children – the latter leading to routine imprisonment of minors. We also note that the French policing of Calais, both before and after the Jungle camp was demolished, has led to three major official investigations of violence used against minors. This policing is part of a 'security' arrangement with France paid for in large part by the UK government (see Chapter One). As Home Correspondent Aditya Chakrabortty writes in the *Guardian* (2018): 'An easy comfort resides in shaking your fist at the foreign monster on your plasma screen, while ignoring the monstrousness done here.'

We would like to end on a self-reflective point – and discuss how we have observed that, since the refugee crisis of 2015 onwards and the hostile climate that has clouded the refugee issue in the UK and elsewhere, many of us in the field have had to, or chosen to, conduct our work differently. We have perhaps been influenced by the vast volunteer mobilisations across Europe, where people have had to respond to unprecedented numbers and situations, and fast-changing crises. Thus in facing state violence, and policies harmful to children and young people, as well as the drastic lack of resources available to remedy severe issues, we have found ourselves working not only as professionals in law, policy, therapy and care, but also as direct advocates. We cite here just a few examples of how practitioners associated with this collection have come up with new practices and with them, enhanced new critical thinking.

Social Workers without Borders[2] was formed to support and mentor professional social workers from across the UK, who in addition to their professional commitments, committed to offer pro-bono Social Work Assessments for unaccompanied children facing removal from the UK, and children with claims to Dublin III family reunification. This includes visiting children in many parts of Europe. Their work has been invaluable in the absence of any state provision of such assessments, particularly in Greece and France. They provided crucial assistance to the ZS High Court legal challenge described in Chapter One of this book, where they worked with Duncan Lewis solicitors. This solicitors' firm has also changed its tack in relation to the recent crisis, and has in four years grown its Public Law team tenfold, from five to 50 staff, so making a series of challenges to public law policy, rather than simply fighting individual cases. The Duncan Lewis team is also working *pro bono* on police violence and other dangers in the Calais Jungle – a radical shift for such a firm.

In a similar vein, Refugee Resilience Collective[3] is a group of therapists mainly working at the Tavistock and Portman Hospital in London (including Gillian Hughes, the author of Chapter Two in this book), who describe themselves as 'developing approaches to enhance resilience at the Jungle Calais Camp'. They work first-hand with young people and with the volunteers who support them, and so have unique insights into a cohort who are actively suffering trauma, who otherwise they would only see in the consulting room in London.

Navigating these new relations, and new boundaries, is challenging, but it does produce new insights and knowledge – arguably essential in times like these.

Notes

[1] For further information, see www.uncertainjourneys.org.uk

[2] For further information, see www.socialworkerswithoutborders.org/

[3] Further information about the Refugee Resilience Collective can be found on its Facebook page: www.facebook.com/CollectiveRC/

References

Arendt, H. (1966) *The Origins of Totalitarianism*, New York: Harcourt and Brace.

Bhabha, J. and Finch, N. (2006) *Seeking Asylum Alone; Unaccompanied and Separated Chldren and Refugee Protection in the UK*, Macarthur Foundation, https://childhub.org/en/child-protection-online-library/bhabha-j-finch-n-2006-seeking-asylum-alone-united-kingdom

Calais Children: A Case to Answer (2017) film, directed by Sue Clayton, UK: Eastwest Pictures, www.calais.gebnet.co.uk and https://vimeo.com/230595898

Chakrabortty, A. (2018) 'How can you condemn Trump but stay silent on British brutality?', *Guardian*, 26 June, www.theguardian.com/commentisfree/2018/jun/26/trump-british-brutality-us-mexico-border

Chase, E. and Allsopp, J. (2013) *Future citizens of the world?: The contested futures of independent young migrants in Europe*, Oxford: Refugee Studies Centre, University of Oxford.

Crawley, H. and Skleparis, D. (2018) Refugees, migrants, neither, both: categorical fetishism and the politics of bounding in Europe's 'migration crisis', *Journal of Ethnic and Migration Studies*, 44(1): 48–64.

Fraser, N. (1995) 'From redistribution to recognition. Dilemmas of justice in a post-socialist age', *New Left Review*, 212: 68–93.

Fraser, N. (2005) 'Reframing justice in a globalizing world', *New Left Review*, (36): 69–88.

Fraser, N. (2008) *Scales of justice: Reimagining political space in a globalizing world*, New York: Columbia University Press and Polity Press.

Krumer-Nevo, M. (2009) 'Four scenes and an epilogue: autoethnography of a critical social work agenda regarding poverty', *Qualitative Social Work*, 8(3): 305–20.

Mills, C.W. (1959) *The sociological imagination*, Oxford: Oxford University Press.

Refworld (2012) *KA (Afghanistan) & Ors v Secretary of State for the Home Department*, [2012] EWCA Civ 1014, United Kingdom: Court of Appeal (England and Wales), 25 July, www.refworld.org/cases,GBR_CA_CIV,500fff2e2.html

Index

A

accommodation 46, 79, 89, 112, 159, 164–71, 177–8, 197, 224, 242–3, 248, 264
activism 8, 127, 147, 247, 286
Adiche, Chimamanda 147
adulthood 6–7, 40, 46, 64, 82, 93–6, 122–3, 129, 137, 159, 173, 187–208, 247, 249, 263, 280, 283, 284
Afghanistan 3, 5, 42, 56–60, 61, 62, 64–5, 80, 92, 96, 106, 109, 112–4, 118, 120–1, 124, 125, 128, 129, 131, 135, 142, 145, 148, 150, 192, 194, 198, 245, 246, 247, 257, 258, 270
age assessment 6, 50, 83–8, 119, 172, 179, 180, 197, 241–2, 250, 261–2, 280, 283–4
agency 41–2, 77, 79, 95, 128–9, 163–4, 174, 176–7, 179, 196–7, 201, 211–2, 221–30, 281
Albania 148, 192
Allan, June 161
Allsopp, Jennifer 95, 129, 199, 202, 285
Amnesty International 15–16, 262
Antonsich, Marco 160
appeal rights exhausted 81–2, 94, 95–6, 161, 180–1, 197
Arendt, Hannah 188, 193, 268, 281
Art Refuge 131
art therapy 120, 131, 149
aspirations 8, 120, 95, 110, 129–30, 195, 197, 202, 250, 263, 270, 285
Asylum and Immigration (Treatment of Claimants) Act 48
asylum process 15, 21, 39–75, 81–2, 111–3, 118–9, 161–2, 193–5, 222–26, 245–50, 258–62
 UASC experiences of 7, 79, 118, 135, 137, 150–1, 162, 164, 167, 168, 177 179–81, 195, 197–8, 201, 217–21, 240
Athens 126
austerity 83, 91, 92, 96, 281, 283
Australia 4, 10, 18, 21, 190, 257–78
Australian Human Rights Commission (AHRC) 266

B

Bangladesh 45–46
Beaumont, Elizabeth 262
Belgium 19, 31, 121, 196
belonging, feelings of 114, 138, 159–86, 193–4, 265, 281, 283
Bergum, Vangie 142
Berry, Mike 115–6
best interests principle 28, 40, 42, 46, 53, 55, 78–9, 96, 191–2, 196–7, 199, 201, 211, 215–6, 222, 223, 226, 228, 236, 239, 248, 250, 261, 269
Bex, Christof 18
Bhabha, Jacqueline 203
blood feuds 168, 179
border policing 1, 15–33, 61, 199, 212, 222–26, 285
borderwork 82, 212, 222, 225–6, 279
Borders, Citizenship and Immigration Act (BICA) 40, 78–9
Bosworth, Mary 266
Brexit 2, 17, 25, 32
Brickell, Katherine 230
Briskman, Linda 97
British Association of Social Workers 85
Burton, Mark 148

C

Calais 9, 18, 19–20, 21–33, 87, 110–1, 117, 121, 124, 128, 145–7, 180, 283, 285, 286
Calais Action 31–2, 126
Calais Refugee Community Kitchen 126
care system 77–101, 159–86, 223–4, 242–5, 248, 263–66
 care leavers 65, 81–3, 93–6, 125, 201, 283
 legal requirements 6, 40, 78–88, 283
Care4Calais 126
Cameron, David 1, 116–7
Canada 223
Catania 124, 125
Catholicism 174
Cemlyn, Sarah 87–8, 179
Central America 10, 211–21, 226–30
Chakrabortty, Aditya 285
Chase, Elaine 6, 90, 93, 95, 129, 161, 163–4, 199, 202, 269, 285

289

child labour 41, 116
Children Act 6, 39, 50, 65, 77–89, 118, 159, 283
Children and Families Act 46
Children (Leaving Care) Act 159, 181
Children's Commissioner for England 79, 92
children's rights 7, 15, 42, 188, 193, 215–6, 219–20, 224, 238–9, 245, 250, 258, 261, 267–9
  see also United Nations Convention on the Rights of the Child (UNCRC)
Christianity 111, 174–6
citizenship 8, 32, 33, 181, 190, 202, 215, 225, 244, 259
Congo 143–4, 148, 152
conscription/forcible recruitment 2, 3, 41, 55, 57, 61–2, 64, 105, 195
Coram Children's Legal Centre 80
Correa-Velez, Ignacio 264
country guidance 60, 282
Crawley, Heaven 93
creative practice 119–21, 149
credibility of asylum claims 5, 7, 47–50, 57, 86–7, 111–2, 118, 194, 223, 250, 262, 284–5
Cronen, Vernon 141, 144
culture of disbelief 5, 7, 83, 87, 194–5, 281, 284
Cuomo, Dana 230

D

De Graeve, Katrien 18
debt bondage 92, 197
Dembour, Marie-Benedicte 192
Denborough, David 144, 149
Denmark 62
deportation 113–4, 200
detention 21, 112, 113, 123, 180, 200, 225, 257, 260–1, 263, 265, 266, 267
Derrida, Jacques 165
detention 129, 227, 259, 260
disability 42
dispersal of asylum-seeking children 49–50, 53, 89, 111
Doering-White, John 228–9
domestic violence 41
Dorling, Kamena 6, 80, 88
Dossetor, John 142
Dublin III Regulation 17–18, 24, 26–28, 31, 40, 191, 236, 247, 282, 286
Dubs Amendment 21, 23–24, 26–32, 121, 282
Duncan Lewis 29, 286
Dunkerque camp 23, 30, 124, 125

durable solution 39, 65, 95, 187–208, 249, 250, 284

E

ECPAT UK 91
education 33, 45, 80, 90, 94, 111, 136, 159, 171–3, 224, 237, 244–5, 248, 250, 258, 259, 264–5, 270
Egypt 189
El Salvador 211
Elwyn, Hannah 96
employment 33, 44, 94, 188, 195, 248–9, 250–1, 258, 259, 264, 265, 270
Epston, David 137
Eritrea 2, 3, 27, 61–4, 105–6, 108, 122–3, 124, 148, 174, 175, 245, 247, 282
Ethiopia 110, 175
European Convention of Human Rights (ECHR) 43, 45–46, 54, 81–2, 96
European Court of Human Rights 181
European Migration Network (EMN) 191
European Return Platform for Unaccompanied Minors (ERPUM) 192
European Union
  asylum policies 17–18, 24, 31, 40–41
  border policing 20–21
Evenhuis, Mark 262

F

family relationships 33, 42, 44–5, 105–6, 108, 112–3, 122–5, 127, 141, 143, 146–7, 165, 197, 269, 285
family reunion 17–18, 40, 188, 189, 191–2, 198, 237, 246, 258, 259, 262, 270
family tracing 57–60, 143, 191
Fassin, Didier 212
female genital mutilation (FGM) 41
filming 105, 120–1, 126–7, 128–30, 132
Finland 235, 236
FM4 Paso Libre 217–21, 226, 229
food 27, 29, 109, 111, 112, 135, 152, 166, 168, 175–6
forced marriage 41, 168
forced removal 57, 92, 96, 112–4, 120, 129, 188, 190, 192, 237, 246, 284
Forensic Oceanography 20
foster care 7, 45–46, 79, 89, 111–2, 122, 124–5, 135, 164–9, 196, 283
Foucault, Michel 160–1
France 19–30, 111, 121, 122, 126, 128, 143, 286

Fraser, Nancy 8, 280–1
Freire, Paolo 140, 149
friendship 107, 109, 125–7, 169, 172, 178
Frontex 1, 20–21

G

gender 2–3, 27, 41, 53, 123–5, 142, 245, 248
Gladwell, Catherine 96
Greece 22, 29, 48, 109, 126, 196, 286
guardianship 7, 80, 92–3, 196, 201, 218, 223, 241, 247, 250, 261, 263
Guatemala 211

H

Hall, Stuart 161–2
Hazara 258
health 6, 90, 237–8, 245, 260, 265
Heidbrink, Lauren 211–2, 217
Heller, Charles 20
Help Refugees 29–30, 126
Hepner, Tricia Redeker 174
Hill, Malcom 93
Hillingdon judgement 80–1
Hollande, François 27
Home Office 7, 22, 28, 29, 32, 40, 43, 46, 47, 52, 54–60, 65–6, 89, 93, 123, 131, 135, 162, 177, 197
   age assessments 50, 84–6, 172, 180
   appeal process 42–3, 55–6, 167, 171
   Calais camp 24, 27, 117, 128
   country guidance 61–2
   credibility 47–8, 65
   interview process 40–1, 49–50, 111, 161, 167
   registration cards 169
   signing in/ reporting 112–3, 127, 128, 195, 197
   social care, links to 164, 179, 196
home-making 138, 160–2, 166, 167
Honduras 211, 217, 219
honour-based violence 168
Hopkins, Peter 93
hospitality 165–9
hostile environment 46, 64, 90, 96, 201, 285
House of Lords European Committee 201
human rights 2, 15, 27, 32, 43, 61–2, 64, 81–2, 115, 192, 214, 219–20, 235, 238, 258, 267–9, 270, 280
human rights assessments 81–2, 96, 181
Hummingbird Project 126

Humphreys, Beth 181
Humphris, Rachel 91
Hurley, Monique 262

I

identity 88, 90, 238, 268, 284–5
   intersectionality 18, 168, 280
   official categorisation 2–5, 6–7, 161–3, 188, 201, 225–6, 228, 236
   reconstruction 121–32, 135–54
   self-representation 6–7, 10, 119–32, 159–86, 194
Idomeni 126
Immigration Act 2016 23–24, 29, 46, 53, 81–2, 95, 282
Immigration Advisory Service 53
Indonesia 259
integration 28, 64, 119, 187, 188, 189, 235, 245, 250
International Organization for Migration 249
Iran 57, 109, 194, 257
Iraq 61, 128
Irish Refugee Council 193, 196
Islam 135, 174–5, 178
Italy 20, 29, 48, 107, 110, 121, 124, 125, 127, 130

J

Jones, Reece 16
Jordan 18–19
Jungle camp 9, 18, 21–33, 87, 110–1, 117, 121, 126, 145–7, 285, 286

K

Kanics, Jyothi 18
keyworkers 170–1
Kohli, Ravi 93, 163, 171
Kotilaine, Jennifer 82
Krumer-Nevo, Michal 281
Kurdi, Alan 116
Kurds 23
Kusturica, Nina 126

L

Lampedusa 20, 22
language 25, 79, 110, 112, 118, 120, 151, 163, 168–9, 174, 175, 238, 264
law
   asylum process 21–31, 39–75, 188, 213–29, 239–42
   court appearances 42–3, 113, 118–9, 137, 197, 224
   High Court challenges 29–30, 121, 282
Le Havre 128
Le Touquet Agreement 19, 22–23, 25, 30

Lebanon 18–19
Legal Action Group 52
legal aid 51–4, 66, 179
legal representation 8, 41, 49, 51–4, 66, 90, 113, 179, 195, 201, 224, 241
Legal Aid, Sentencing and Punishment of Offenders Act (LAPSO) 51–4
Leigh Day 29
Lesvos 126
liberation psychology 120, 139
Libya 15, 20, 22, 106, 107–8, 130, 192
Lidén, Hilde 238
Life Projects Planning Framework 198–200, 269
Lighthouse 126
local authority support 6, 79–86, 89–93, 125, 173, 177, 248
Lundberg, Anna 239

M

Macron, Emmanuel 30
Mai, Nicola 197, 199
Malta 196
Mansouri, Fethi 269
Manus 21, 260
Martín-Baró, Ignacio 120, 139, 141, 151
Massey, Doreen 175
Matthews, Adrian 200, 269
May, Theresa 32, 46, 201
Médecins Sans Frontières 23
media representations 1, 21, 83, 87, 115–7, 127, 136, 137, 150
Mediterranean 20, 21–22, 107–9
Mee, Kathleen 166
Menjívar, Cecilia 188
mental health 48–9, 88, 90, 93–4, 161, 172, 195, 198, 199–200, 203, 237–8, 249, 260, 265–6
  mental health services 135–54, 171, 224, 245, 264
Merton judgement 84–5, 172, 179
Mexico 10, 18, 211–22, 223, 224, 226–30, 285
Missing People 91
Mitchell, Mary 129
mobile phones 107–8, 127, 131, 150
modern slavery 78, 91
Morocco 192
multiculturalism 235

N

Nardone, Mariana 264
Narrative Liberation framework 139–54

Nauru 21, 260, 266
Ni Raghallaigh, Muireann 168, 174
Nigeria 192
non-governmental organisations (NGOs) 7, 15, 25–26, 31, 53, 97, 126, 217–21, 263–6, 283
Nordic countries 10, 198, 235–55, 284
Norway 235–55
Nye, Miriam 87–8, 179

O

offshoring 19–21, 22–23, 260, 267
ontological security 188, 200
orphan 42

P

Pakistan 57, 194
Paris 31, 124, 247
Palermo 124, 125, 127
Papadopoulos, Renos 125
Pathway planning 94–5
Pearce, W. Barnett 141, 144
Pentecostalism 175–6
Pezzani, Lorenzo 20
Phillips, Deborah 178
place-belonging 176–8
Platts-Fowler, Deborah 176
police violence 20, 26, 28, 30, 31, 111, 122, 130, 143, 285
post-traumatic stress disorder (PTSD) 136–8
Project Phakama 120, 124, 149
Protestimony project 131
Protocol Relating to the Status of Refugees 189

R

racism 112, 130, 135, 136, 143, 150, 161, 170
Red Cross 58–60, 241, 264
Refugee Convention 5, 15, 18, 28, 40–2, 161, 189, 190
Refugee Council 116, 120
refugee crisis 1, 21, 22, 115, 235, 245, 282, 285
Refugee Migrant Justice 53
Refugee Resilience Collective 286
Refugee Youth Service 126
religion 5, 18, 41, 79, 97, 111, 125, 128, 135, 141, 146, 147, 159, 168, 173–6, 178, 194
remittances 264
repatriation 189–90, 192, 193, 198, 199, 202, 237, 249
resettlement 187, 189–90, 191, 259–60
resilience 130, 138–54, 188

resistance 145–53, 202, 269
Rigby, Paul 86
Robinson, David 176, 178
Robinson, Kim 199, 200
Rogerson, Sarah 224
Rose, Jacqueline 131
Rudd, Amber 27, 32
Rwanda 93–5

S

Safe Passage 24–25, 30
Sandhurst Treaty 18
Sandri, Elisa 25, 31
Sangatte camp 22, 27
Save the Children 22, 24, 28
Schengen Agreement 17, 236
Schwartz, Caroline 151
Scotland 7, 92–3, 196
Sendor, Meir 151
Senovilla Hernández, Daniel 18
Sennett, Richard 151
sexuality 128, 196
Sicily 107–9, 124, 125, 126, 127
Sigona, Nando 91, 173
Sirriyeh, Ala 165, 167, 168, 170
Skrbis, Zlatko 269
Slovakia 196
social media 127, 149, 150
social networks 45, 90, 91, 113–4, 125–7, 139–53, 159, 169–82, 193, 281, 285
social work 7, 8, 90, 92–3, 97–8, 159–86, 197, 201–2, 281, 283
  age assessments 50, 85–8, 179, 283
  anti racist practice 178–9
  human rights assessments 81–2, 181
  pathway planning 94–5, 180
  potential conflicts of interest 7, 87–8, 97, 178–81, 196, 228, 267, 280, 283
Social Workers Without Borders 286
Somalia 107
South Africa 144
Sri Lanka 257
street children 42
Sudan 28, 106, 145
Sweden 235–55
Syria 3, 18, 23, 28, 61, 110, 116, 245, 247

T

Taliban 58, 60, 106, 142
Terrio, Susan 227
theatre 120, 124
therapy 120, 135–54, 266, 286
trafficking 5, 26, 45, 53, 84, 91, 116, 124, 142, 179, 192, 222, 223, 224, 237, 282
trauma 48–9, 87, 120, 135–57, 171, 194, 240–1, 266, 285, 286

Trump, Donald 1, 2
Turkey 15–16, 22, 109, 116, 130, 189

U

unaccompanied asylum-seeking children (UASC)
  agency 7–8, 41–2, 77, 79, 95, 128–9, 163–4, 174, 176–7, 179, 196–7, 198–200, 202, 211–2, 221–30, 281
  definitions 2–5
  gender 2–3, 27, 142, 245, 248
  journeys 2, 3, 48, 78, 90, 105–11, 121–3, 128, 166, 249, 270
  numbers 2–3, 18, 43, 235, 245, 257
  self-representation 115–33
Ungar, Michael 139
Unicef 20–1, 28
United Nations Convention on the Rights of the Child (UNCRC) 4, 6, 7, 15, 18, 28, 40, 77–9, 88, 96, 188–93, 236, 238, 239–40, 247–50, 257, 261, 262, 267
United Nations High Commission for Refugees (UNHCR) 22, 26, 31, 41–2, 47–8, 57, 187–93, 202
United States 10, 18, 190, 211–13, 221–30, 284
Universal Declaration of Human Rights 15
Utopia 56 126

V

Vervliet, Marianne 197
Vienna Convention on Consular Relations 219
Vietnam 78, 91, 148
violence 2, 27, 42, 105–6, 110, 112, 135, 143, 145–6, 150, 170, 266; see also police violence
Vitus, Kathrine 238
voluntary return 65, 181, 189–90, 192, 200, 202, 223, 284
volunteers 25–26, 31, 53, 111, 120, 124–5, 126, 127, 131, 264
vulnerability 15, 17, 18, 23, 28, 39, 41, 77, 80, 138–54, 163, 165, 167, 179, 198, 202, 212, 237, 261, 266, 267

W

Wade, Allan 145
Wade, Jim 179, 180
Waite, Louise 177
Waldegrave, Charles 137
Warren, Richard 188, 194
Weingarten, Kathy 142–3
welfare system 6, 44, 77–101, 197–8, 224, 237, 242–5, 263–6

wellbeing 6, 7, 10, 120, 135–54, 171, 191, 260–1, 265–6, 281
Welsh Refugee Council 88
Wells, Karen 199
White, Michael 137, 139, 144, 149
Whyte, Bill 86
Wilding, Jo 192
Williams, Charlotte 97
Williams, Lucy 199, 200
Windrush 32–3
Wood, Nichola 177
Wright, Frances 181
Wright, Sarah 160, 166

Y

York, Sheona 188, 194
Yuval-Davis, Nira 160

www.ingramcontent.com/pod-product-compliance
Lightning Source LLC
Chambersburg PA
CBHW070910030426
42336CB00014BA/2360